They Called Us
Exceptional

They Called Us Exceptional

AND OTHER LIES THAT RAISED US

Prachi Gupta

CROWN
NEW YORK

Published in the United States by Crown, an imprint of Random House,
a division of Penguin Random House LLC, New York.

CROWN and the Crown colophon are registered trademarks
of Penguin Random House LLC.

page ii: Self-portrait by Prachi Gupta, copyright © 2000 by Prachi Gupta.

Library of Congress Cataloging-in-Publication Data
Names: Gupta, Prachi (Journalist), author.
Title: They called us exceptional / Prachi Gupta.
Description: First edition. | New York: Crown, [2023] | Includes
bibliographical references.
Identifiers: LCCN 2023011957 (print) | LCCN 2023011958 (ebook) |
ISBN 9780593442982 (hardcover) | ISBN 9780593442999 (ebook)
Subjects: LCSH: Gupta, Prachi (Journalist) | Gupta, Prachi (Journalist)—Family. |
East Indian American women—Biography. | Women journalists—United States—
Biography. | East Indian Americans—Social conditions.
Classification: LCC E184.E2 G87 2023 (print) | LCC E184.E2 (ebook) |
DDC 305.89/1411073092 [B]—dc23/eng/20230419
LC record available at https://lccn.loc.gov/2023011957
LC ebook record available at https://lccn.loc.gov/2023011958

Printed in Canada on acid-free paper

crownpublishing.com

2 4 6 8 9 7 5 3 1

First Edition

Book design by Caroline Cunningham

"A story always starts before it can be told."

—Sara Ahmed, *Living a Feminist Life*

Contents

They Called Us Exceptional

Prologue

Our plan to surprise you was simple. Yush told Papa that he had to work on a project so he couldn't come home over spring break. Papa wouldn't question that, because nothing mattered more than school, and because Papa wouldn't question it, neither would you. Yush drove to my apartment, wearing his tattered Brooks sneakers and my oversize hoodie, the one he'd borrowed with no intention of ever returning. I played DJ, rummaging through a thick black DVD case, picking out CD mixes that we had burned for road trips back home. Alongside Yush, the five-hour drive home from Pittsburgh was serene. We were siblings, but more than that, we were siblings who liked each other, and more than even that: siblings who were friends.

Halfway through, we switched spots. I drove and he DJ'd. When I pulled into the driveway, Yush ran down the slope of our backyard, the grassy hill where, on snow days as teenagers, we dug "bumslides," shallow grooves that we formed with our butts and then slid down on black trash bags. He waited at the basement door, and I entered through the garage. You greeted me with a hug, distracted by the roti you had already begun heating over the stove when you heard the garage door open. I could hear the restrained sadness in your voice.

This was the first time Yush wasn't home from college to meet you. I crept down to the basement and let Yush in, ushering him up the stairs while you were turned away. He crouched at the foot of the leather sofa. I led you to the living room. Yush sprang up. "Hey, Mummy!" he cheered.

"Huh? Yush? What? Yush? How!"

You nearly fell over in excitement. You ran to Yush, gently pushed him, then pinched him several times to see if he was real. Yush laughed at this, and so did I. The idea that in your surprise, in your disarmed state, it was more conceivable to you that your son was an apparition than physically present was so charming and amusing to both of us. It was why we had planned the surprise in the first place, with this adorable reaction in mind.

"Hey, Mummy," Yush said again, grinning. He wrapped his arms around you, pulling your head into his collarbone as if you were his child.

We wanted to surprise Papa, too, but you couldn't contain yourself. When he called from work, you sang, "Yush is here!" As I heard the familiar rustling of the keys behind the garage door, the sound of Papa's arrival, I rushed over to hug him. He opened a bottle of nice wine, and we inhaled your fresh sabzi, roti, and dal, the best food in the world. These moments form my happiest memories: the four of us together, laughing, eating, and talking around the dinner table.

We had so much to celebrate. Papa, a surgeon, had recently opened his own medical practice. Yush was programming robots at college, while I was leading a team of students to victory in a consulting-case competition. You told us about the classes you were taking at a local community college. All of your classmates wanted you to be their mom, you joked. Everything in our lives had fallen into place the way that we'd always dreamed. We had perfected the delicate alchemy of culture, family, and work that resulted in happiness and success in America.

THAT WAS THE STORY about our family that you and Papa likely would have wanted me to tell. I want you to know: I wanted to tell that story, too. I wish that I could have.

But that is not where our story ends. That is where our story begins. In order to tell that story, I have to tell this one, too.

I was thirteen; Yush was eleven. Papa drove us to a fair at what would later become our high school, a private school with a sprawling campus. I was nervous. We had recently moved to a town of corn-fields in the blue hills of Pennsylvania's Lehigh Valley, and today I'd be meeting my new friends outside a classroom setting. It felt like a test. Would they embrace me? Or would they see me as childish if I clung to you and Yush? As I lost myself in my anxiety, Papa asked you for directions. You unfolded a large, unwieldy paper map. I snapped to attention. Bad things happened when that map came out. Papa asked you again. I heard you stumble over the directions. It began.

Papa screamed at you. *Stupid, uneducated, worthless, good-for-nothing, you can't even read a simple map? Read it again! Why are you so stupid! Learn to do it right!* You froze. This made him angrier. His rage, raw and bound-less, could not be quelled once unleashed. He screamed and screamed and screamed and screamed and you fumbled, fumbled, fumbled. I remember si-lently pleading with you to give him the answer he wanted to hear. I was angry that you couldn't just say the right words to make him stop.

It didn't occur to me to be angry at him.

Then Papa jerked the car over to the side of the road at a busy in-tersection and screamed at you to get out. Cars swerved around us.

"Papa!" Yush cried. "No!"

Papa ignored him. He left you stranded and sobbing as he sped off with your children. We watched you become a dot. For a few minutes, I thought I'd never see you again. Yush and I were crying, pleading with Papa to bring you back to us.

Papa reached the school. It was just another mile down the road. He made a U-turn in the parking lot. You stood where he had left you. He pulled up to the curb and you got back in the car without a word.

For a long time, that memory stood alone, without context. I never spoke of it, not even with Yush. But I can still remember the way I froze in the back seat. I can still feel the fear of not knowing if I'd see you again. I can finally locate the anger that rushed through me that day and, with no outlet, fell somewhere deep within me when I realized that Papa wasn't taking us home. He was returning to the school. We had to go to the fair and perform as the exceptional family everyone expected us to be.

TODAY, INDIAN AMERICAN FAMILIES like ours represent an American success story. But it is easy to forget that, long before they called us "the good immigrants," they called us "the bad immigrants."

For much of their history, Canada and America barred Asians from entry. In 1882, America enacted the Chinese Exclusion Act, the first significant race-based immigration ban in the country's history. America later extended the ban to all of Asia. Canada passed a similar set of laws, and both countries curbed citizenship, land, and other rights for Asian laborers already within their borders. While America's racial segregation was more explicit, both countries shared a commitment to building a white nation.

That changed during the Cold War, when America wanted to promote itself as a liberal democracy capable of leading the world. Politicians reversed decades of discriminatory policy, reinventing America as a melting pot. With the Hart–Celler Immigration and Nationality Act of 1965, America established a new system of selection that favored immigrants with professional skills, high educational levels, and strong family ties. Canada followed suit, allowing immigrants like Papa's parents, my Dadaji and Dadiji, into the country.

Growing up, I didn't see myself as Asian or even as Asian American. But I understood that, in America's racial construct, the people whose ancestors came from those distant landmasses in the East were all lumped together. These imperfect labels evolved through movements of solidarity that made the presence of various Asian ethnic communities more visible in America. But I still struggle with what to call myself, rotating between Indian American, South Asian, desi, or, simply, brown. None seem quite right.

White America crafted a tempting story to explain the ascent of Asian Americans—"an important racial minority pulling itself up from hardship and discrimination to become a model of self-respect and achievement," as a 1966 article in *U.S. News & World Report* described Chinese Americans. Those once seen as "Yellow Peril" and "Dusky Peril" became a "model minority," creating a new racial category: Asians were those who could assimilate into whiteness but maintain a distinct cultural identity. In America, riches await, and with a little grit, anyone can reap them. The story tempered the racial progress of the civil-rights era, as if to tell Black people: *If those Asians can be so successful, why can't you?* Racism was a part of America's sordid past. The success of these new Asians proved that.

Indian Americans have since been allotted a specific prominence within the context of this story. In 2009, the year I graduated from college, an article in *Forbes* declared Indian Americans "the new model minority," hailing families like ours as "the latest and greatest 'model.'" Within a little more than a generation, Indian Americans have become one of the wealthiest and most highly educated immigrant groups in the country, earning a median income of more than one hundred thousand dollars. The steep ascent of Indian Americans reified the pernicious model-minority myth. They called us exceptional. We fulfilled their prophecy.

But the story of our subcommunity's rise wasn't one of genetics, nor can it simply be explained by work ethic, as pundits may have one believe. The true story, as described in *The Other One Percent: Indians in America,* is largely due to a rigorous but invisible selection process that often begins in India itself. In India's highly stratified society, middle- and upper-class Indians from dominant castes typically access the best schools and jobs that feed into opportunities in America, which favor immigrants who bring specialized skills in tech and science. The result: an American diasporic community that is roughly nine times more educated than Indians in India. These conditions enabled

Indian families like ours—families that had been thrice-filtered and stratified—to prosper like few other immigrant groups have ever done in America. Even though pockets of Indian Americans still struggle, this insular group has become the poster image for America's post-racial fantasy.

As a girl, I did not know that the story built around the upward mobility of families like ours was used to represent how far immigrants can go in this country if they are determined. I did not know that the way I understood and related to the world was through a myth carefully constructed by those in power to keep Black people locked into low-wage labor to build white wealth. I was, as historian Vijay Prashad observed in *The Karma of Brown Folk*, "unaware of how we are used as a weapon by those whom we ourselves fear and yet emulate." When I was growing up, nothing countered the myth about who we were. Schools did not teach Asian American history. The few characters portrayed as South Asian in American media taught me how little white America cared about the realities of our lives. In the world beyond our network of Indian Americans, our family was a hypothetical. I accepted the only story available to me, which fit with what little I could see.

But if I'm being honest, I liked the story. I *needed* the story.

The story soothed me when, in preschool, a blond girl told me that I could only play house with the white girls if I was their servant. The story shielded us from the pain of realizing that Yush's best friend in first grade wasn't allowed to come over because his mom didn't trust brown people. As a boy who emigrated to Canada at nine, Papa, too, had endured these slights. But now he was a man with authority. The classmates who once bullied him now deferred to him as "Doctor" or "sir." When we had nothing to throw back at the slurs thrown at us, when we had to silently swallow the humiliation of knowing that we were inferior in our own country, Yush and I found solace in the idea that success was part of our destiny. The belief that we were exceptional protected us.

Until it didn't. Because stories designed to uphold hierarchies protect only one group—those at the very top.

Myths imbue the ordinary and mundane with celestial meaning. But this is also what makes them so dangerous: They do not reveal truths. Rather, they obscure any part of our realities that do not conform to the fantastical narrative. The myth creates a strict role to play: Those who project the right image are more likely to be tolerated. Anyone who fails to meet the expectations set forth by white America risks being ignored, overlooked, dismissed, forgotten, abandoned. Asian Americans have the highest income disparity of any ethnic community—a statistic that speaks to both inherent inequity and the category's broad overreach. Dadiji and Dadaji came to the West not to flee war or persecution but to fulfill personal ambition. The racism Yush and I experienced in white suburbia and corporate America, though painful, was nothing like the discrimination, violence, and exploitation experienced by more-vulnerable working-class immigrants, refugees, or undocumented people. But the model-minority myth cares not, recklessly rolling twenty million people into a static image defined by an apparent predisposition to success, stability, and familial unity.

It is not hard to see how the myth reinforces America's existing social and racial order, then, seducing its adherents with the promise of belonging in a country where their position remains tenuous and their acceptance is always in question. Rather than fostering solidarity over the ways in which white America disenfranchises those who look unlike them, the myth sows division among Asian ethnic communities. The myth encourages those at the top of the economic ladder to reinforce it, pushing those at the bottom further down. The privilege of the few sets constraints upon the many.

The myth erases the legacy of racial exclusion from America's collective consciousness while perpetuating racial exclusion. The myth creates cognitive dissonance and then tells us that this dissonance does not exist. The myth splits our psyches, then calls this violence peace.

The myth forces our minds to forget that which our bodies cannot: that belonging is *always* conditional.

I HAD PLANNED TO write my story as a novel. I wanted to mask our identities but preserve the message to challenge the powerful binaries about success, identity, and culture that defined my life, without hurting you and Papa.

But after everything that has happened to us, fictionalizing our lives felt like an act of cowardice. To turn what was true into what could be turned into a parable, erasing real people who struggled with real issues. To portray the truth as hypothetical felt like another way to participate in the lie that had ruined our lives, bending toward the myth of exceptionalism, ever so slightly.

According to the story that I had used to make sense of the world, none of what was happening to you and me was possible. Worse, when I did try to talk about incongruencies at home, my experiences were rewritten to conform to the myth that everyone else used to make sense of us. My problems remained invisible, and the conclusion I drew was that something was deeply, profoundly wrong with me. It has been tiring, and a little humiliating, to always contend with this myth, to again and again compare my real life to a stereotype about who I am supposed to be and to seek to understand who I am by wrestling with the dissonance between this pervasive story and how that story makes me feel. Even I judge myself for invoking it, rolling my eyes for reducing myself to some essentialist, universalizing experience that reflects no one's actual truth.

I think often of Gayatri Chakravorty Spivak's essay "Can the Subaltern Speak?" in which she shows how women's voices in colonial India were appropriated by both the British colonizers and Indian men in power during the struggle for control. Spivak's observations are about oppressed women who have been erased from history entirely, but her insights helped me find a way to articulate my own story and separate it from the myth about who I supposedly am.

The British justified colonizing India by drawing attention to the burning of sati, the esoteric Hindu practice of widow self-immolation. Although Europeans had hunted witches and burned the accused alive at the stake, the British used the ritual to cast brown men as barbarians from whom brown women needed saving. The Hindu male upper-caste elite reacted to British aggression by insisting that the women wanted to die, pushing an "Indian nativist argument, a parody of the nostalgia for lost origins," as Spivak put it. All the while, "One never encounters the testimony of the women's voice-consciousness." Even when women in colonial India spoke or acted, their words and actions were reinterpreted through the stories of those in power: An Indian woman's act of political protest was re-written as hysteria, her sense of duty perceived as desire. In this construct, an Indian woman's feelings and expressions were never her own; she experienced her womanhood as pathology.

I realized: I had struggled to articulate my own story because, when I spoke, my words took on meanings I did not intend. My speech was trapped behind two dueling narratives that claimed to speak for me.

The problems between you and me began when I started trying to create context around things that were meant to be forgotten. Our problems began when I started searching for a way to explain everything that felt so inexplicable. Our problems began when I was expected to shrink myself, as you had been forced to do, but instead I insisted on expanding.

I KNOW THAT BY writing this book, I risk appearing ungrateful for the sacrifices of those who came before me, including your own. I risk turning our pain into a spectacle, further dehumanizing us in this white country.

But the risks of not saying anything are far greater. We abide by their story because we think that is how we gain acceptance in America. But we cannibalize our bodies, our spirits, and our minds to feed a hunger that never abates. We struggle under a weight that the world tells us does not exist. We serve a story that will never serve us, and I fear that the next generation will seek to do the same.

The world we live in, which demands perfection and achievement, teaches us we cannot love ourselves as we are. The myth teaches us to think greatness always resides outside us instead of within us. We must become stronger, taller, richer, thinner, smarter, prettier—and perhaps then, we think, we may be worthy of love. Yet we cannot love ourselves and we cannot love each other well so long as we are preoccupied by the desire to leave ourselves, to abandon ourselves in search of something beyond ourselves. Serving the myth teaches us how to belong but severs our ability to connect.

I used to think that memories followed a straight line, starting at one point and ending at another, held together by the backbone of the strong linear narrative of cause and effect that takes each of us from birth to death. Now I think of memories as haphazard blots of ink in a Rorschach test that we assemble along the spine of the story we are told about who we are. If given enough space, time, and support, we can arrange the memories along a story that we write for ourselves, extracting new meaning from events experienced one way and later understood as another. The memories that stand out to me now, Mummy, and the story I have woven to make sense of them, are likely different from the ones that you hold to support your understanding of our family.

In our family, we learned to love one another for how well we were able to conform to the story they wrote for us—not as who we really are. It was not until I began to articulate my own story that I realized how little I knew about yours. You and I cannot speak because we live on opposite sides of that story. We cannot speak because my truth negates yours, and yours negates mine. My story can never speak for anyone else's, including yours. But maybe by explaining to you why I abandoned the story that I was raised to love, I can make room for others to write their own stories instead.

Chapter 1

Dawn

Kanika has several meanings in Sanskrit, but Papa liked "gold"—an object so striking that people traded it for food and clothing. You preferred the name Prachi. East. Sunrise. Dawn. A nod to the homeland you'd left five years before my birth. A word that, in poetry and literature, represents new beginnings. Papa suggested a creative compromise: Let me decide. If born during daylight, I was to be Prachi. If born at night, I would be Kanika.

I was born just as the sun began its climb into the sky, exercising its full power on a hot day in the middle of July. I had made my choice clear.

I wish I had asked you why you picked the name Prachi. Instead, I remember telling you when I began to hate my name. Jessica and the other white girls in my pre-kindergarten class played a game: One girl had candy in her hands, and she would open and shut her palms quickly. The girl next to her had to pick pieces of candy from her friend's hands before she clamped them shut. I asked Jessica if I could play. She smiled and said, "Give me your hand." Then Jessica grabbed my fingers and yanked them back toward my wrist and looked into my eyes as I yelped in pain. She laughed. The teachers ignored me when I told them that Jessica had hurt me.

I didn't tell you what had happened. Instead, when I came home, the confusing, turbulent feelings inside me distilled to one question: "Why didn't you name me Jessica?" I think you were taken aback, and in your surprise, you apologized. I didn't have the words for racism yet. I only understood that if I was more like Jessica somehow, I wouldn't have been treated that way. "I'm sorry," you said, accepting my feelings as fact, likely unaware of the cruelty children inflict on those who look unlike them. "I liked Prachi."

I wish I could tell you now that I love my name.

We had moved to the Land of Jessicas in New Jersey from Silicon Valley, where we'd lived among one of the biggest Indian communities in the country. In California, Papa owned a townhouse and began a lucrative career as a hardware and software engineer, a rare skill set that positioned him well for the coming tech boom. After your initial years surviving icy Canadian winters, you welcomed the warmth. You looked after me at home, and eighteen months later, to the day, Yush arrived. For most of my childhood, I thought that half birthdays were the day that one's sibling was born.

At first, I envied the attention you gave Yush. You told me that once, while you were changing his diaper in the bathroom, you left him alone for just a moment. I snuck in and locked the door behind me. Like a hostage negotiator, you cajoled and convinced me to open the door. Yush remained unaware of the danger he was in. He was the easy baby: He sat with anyone, content in his own world. He was like you—gentle, mild-mannered, and kind. I was the fussy, possessive, mischievous one, clawing at you for constant attention. My temperament mirrored Papa's—stubborn, opinionated, strong-willed, outspoken, and loud. Traits admired and encouraged in my father but concerning when manifested by a girl. Yet Papa was proud of me. I, in turn, thought that Papa looked the way all papas should: thick curly hair with a nascent bald spot, a strong black mustache, and a slight paunch.

Just as your amorphous future in America acquired a shape, Papa abandoned his promising engineering career and propelled us into the unknown. His decision to pursue medicine came top-down, like a CEO's directive. Dadaji tried to talk Papa out of this doctor business. "Think of what this means for your wife and little kids," Dadaji said. To him, it sounded like another one of his son's impulsive decisions. Papa was angry that his father, who had always felt distant, yet again withheld his emotional support.

Papa said that he made a long list of reasons why it made sense for him to switch careers, as if it were a purely logical decision. But this was not a simple job change; this was accumulating a mountain of debt and earning little income and relocating the family every few years to complete medical school, residency, fellowship, and special-ized surgical training. It was a decision that meant you'd have to raise two young kids in an unfamiliar country with little support as your husband worked long hours. It was a decision that meant you would move too often to build a close circle of friends. You would see your parents only a handful of times again in your life because we could not afford frequent trips to India. When your parents died, we would meet your grief like strangers.

Papa was passionate about medicine and wanted to help people. But somewhere on Papa's list of reasons—the one that stands out to me now above all of the others—is this: He noted that being a doctor would earn him more respect, particularly within the Indian commu-nity. I had underestimated the power and the depth of that desire and how the force of that current swept up the rest of us.

PAPA MOVED TO NEW Jersey for medical school and lived in student housing. He worried that we would distract him from his studies, so he sent the three of us to live with Dadiji and Dadaji in Toronto, where he expected us to stay for the next four years. I remember the ex-tended visit at their apartment building only in flashes: Yush and I running around a 200-meter indoor track on the top floor; entering the narrow mail room with anticipation for packages from Papa; opening a box to find the T-shirts he sent us—a peach shirt with a beach sunset cartoon graphic for me, a tiny blue shirt for Yush. I think it was during that first year that I grabbed ahold of crayons and drew all over the white walls, and then Dadiji and Dadaji had to repaint them, after which I did it again: untamed signs of what would become a lifelong passion for painting and drawing.

I was Dadiji's little Pachu, Yush her Yushie Bushie. Through her broken English, I was never sure how much she understood of what I said, but it didn't matter. She expressed her love by squeezing me so hard with her plump body that for a moment I had to hold my breath. Then she smushed her face into mine, shaking her head so vigorously that her prickly mustache hair scratched my skin and reddened my cheeks, and I closed my eyes to shield them, squealing throughout. Dadiji's apartment housed her entire world: her plants, her original artwork, and photos of family. In the photo that best captures our friendship, Yush and I posed in front of her cascading plants. I am holding him tight, smiling at the camera and squeezing my little brother like he's my doll. He stands warm and protected as he gazes off into the distance.

Dadiji doted on us, but it was Dadaji who animated me. We exchanged love through banter. His voice was thick and knotty, like a banyan tree, later lilted by a slight slur from a stroke. He spoke in concise, pithy sentences and half sentences, weaving between the sardonic and the serious so quickly that either he or I was always on the verge of laughter. The constant pain from sciatica made him stiff, so he hugged not with his arms but with his hands, showing me how much he missed me with each light, excited pitter-patter on my back. Seeing as I was Prachi, the Goddess of the Rising Sun and Destroyer of Darkness, on gray days he'd say, "Prachi, where is the sun? Call the sun!"

"I tried, but the sun didn't answer me!" I'd say.

He'd laugh. "Yes, the darkness is not done yet."

As Papa told it, on his first visit to Toronto that year, I ran to the door and gave him a big hug. As the visit ended, I begged him not to leave. When he left, I cried. When he returned, I was again excited to see him. But as the ritual of Papa's arrival and departure happened again and again, I stopped coming to the phone to take his calls. Then I refused to meet him at the doorway altogether. "When I came back," he said, "you wouldn't even talk to me."

"Why should I?" I apparently said to him on his last visit. "You're just going to leave us again," and I walked off.

He always laughed when retelling that part. "That's when I said, 'Uh-oh, I have to watch out. This girl knows what she wants!'" Papa said that my protest convinced him to move the family to New Jersey, where he completed the next three years of medical school with us in tow.

Please remember: There was a time when my outspokenness brought us together instead of tearing us apart. There was a time when speaking my mind was received not as a threat but as an act of love.

In New Jersey, the four of us settled into a small apartment by a park that hugged a river. We shared a wall with a man who you once saw put a knife to another man's throat in the hallway, around the time that our apartment building began renting to outpatients of a local psychiatric facility. Anytime the neighbor's door stood open, you rushed us through the hallway. Dadaji gave us his bulky brown Toyota Cressida, which you commanded from atop a pillow folded in half. Drivers did double takes as this behemoth car piloted by a phantom driver floated along the road.

Papa told his sister, my Buaji, that he needed some money to make ends meet. Like him, Buaji was raising children on a limited budget, taking on debt to pay for medical school. He then used her money to put me in a private school. After show-and-tell one day, when a girl brought in a photo of her house—a mansion—I came home and asked you if we were poor. We were not poor, but whatever wealth we did have was an illusion. Papa borrowed money to pay for a lifestyle that was beyond his means. He shielded Yush and me from the low-income upbringing he had as an immigrant boy in Canada, teaching us that, though we might not have wealth right now, we were to think of ourselves as rich people and learn their ways.

But it wasn't extravagance that built my happiest moments. I relished our quotidian adventures: walking to the park with you and Yush while licking candy buttons off strips of paper, sitting on the couch as you read out loud to us, drinking your spicy and sweet shikanji lemonade on hot summer days. When you put us to bed, you sang us "Chanda Mama Door Ke." Sometimes Yush and I begged you to sing these Hindi lullabies during the day because we liked to hear your voice in song. When Papa worked overnight, I crawled into bed and cuddled with you until I fell asleep. At the end of the school year, you, Yush, and I held hands and ran around the living room, the three of us screaming, "Happy happy joy joy!" like the cartoon characters Ren and Stimpy did, and then we fell on the floor, giggling. I saw you as one of us but older and wiser. When we asked you questions, you answered and you answered with consideration, never speaking down to us and rarely raising your voice.

One night, as you bent down to hug me good night, I grabbed your face and kissed you on the lips and tried to force my tongue into your mouth. I had never seen Indian people kiss—not you and Papa, and not in a Bollywood movie—but I had seen American adults kiss like this to express their overwhelming love. You jerked your head back and said, "Prachi, what are you doing!" As soon as I did, it felt wrong. But I told you why I tried to kiss you like that, and you laughed, running out of the room to tell Papa.

I am ashamed that, when I look back at my childhood now, I have trouble remembering specific memories and dialogue that we shared. For years I have not had you, Papa, or Yush to help me remember, and now the things unsaid between you and me have calcified and I do not know how to cut through to allow the memories of our joy to flow unobstructed. But I want you to know that when I think of you, I feel your warmth.

IF OUR FAMILY WERE an organism, you were its heart, pumping blood into us all. Papa was the brain, the part that tried to stay in control, well attuned to the fears that threatened our safety. Sometimes the threat to our safety was palpable, particularly in the years after 9/11, when security stopped us at the airport and border crossings for so-called random searches. But most times Papa monitored the existential dangers that American culture posed to our delicate way of life.

You were the only one among us raised in India. In most of the homes we lived, you maintained a tiny altar with unlit agarbatti resting below images of Hindu deities. Rarely did you talk about religion, aside from casual mentions—that as a teen you got high while drinking bhang lassis on Holi, or when you told Yush and me not to leave our books on the floor because it was disrespectful to Goddess Saraswati. I wish now that I had asked you what tradition and culture meant to you.

Instead, it was Papa, not you, who defined and maintained Indian cultural values at home. One day you took me to Supercuts. I returned with a shoulder-length bob. At home, Papa screamed at you. My pride curdled into shame. After yelling at you, he turned to me. "You need my permission to cut your hair," he told me. This is how I learned that Papa had rules about what our hair was supposed to look like.

"Why?" I asked him.

"Because I know what's best for you, and you don't," he said. "You have to have a purpose for cutting your hair. You can't just do it without a reason."

I considered this. Dadiji's hair was shorter than both yours and mine, framing her face with a tight pixie cut. But Papa was a guru who dispensed wisdom that I didn't fully understand. I feared him the way white people feared the wrath of their mercurial Western God, certain that behind his methods was a larger intelligence that I could not yet ascertain. It must have been such a burden for a man to take on so much, I thought, and still have to show us how to behave in the world.

Though it was you who did everything at home for us, it was Papa who we looked up to, as if he personally made the stars and the moon glow bright. Your love was stable, which made it expected and ordinary. Papa's love was mysterious, like the weather patterns during the rainy season in the tropics. Sometimes his affection beamed over me like a hot sun, and other times I was caught in a torrential downpour, unsure if I'd ever see sunlight again. It was a love that felt exciting and curious, a love that we had to jockey and perform for—a love that we could not afford to take for granted, as we did yours. As children, we did not appreciate or understand the effect of love like this. Your love was so synonymous with safety and warmth that I didn't have words to describe its power until I mourned your absence.

Years later, as a teenager, I told Papa that I used to see him as a God. I thought he might find this surprising. I thought he might see that I was transitioning from childhood to adulthood. I thought our relationship may evolve to reflect this change. But in his response, I picked up a feeling of woundedness and a tinge of accusation. He said, "Why did you stop?"

Chapter 2

Color-Blocked

WHEN WE MOVED FROM New Jersey to Pittsburgh for the next part of Papa's medical training, Papa said he didn't want us to be deprived because of his decision to switch careers. He borrowed more money to buy a boxy ranch house with a sloping lawn and a swing set. Papa bought Yush and me bikes and walkie-talkie headsets. We rode them side by side, charting the new territory of our neighborhood like explorers. Papa always said that he wanted Yush and me to be best friends. But neither "sibling" nor "friend" accurately described our bond: Yush was my birthright, the person who anchored me to earth, and the boy who felt like home when no other place did.

I invented most of the games we played, and Yush followed along. One of my favorite games was time travelers. We combined his Legos and my pink and purple Tyco Dreambuilders set and created little rooms, each of which represented a different time period: a medieval room, a robot room, a caveman room. I liked the tiny hearts and curved door trimmings from my set, but I was annoyed that my blocks were not as practical for building large structures, like Yush's blocks were. Our blocks didn't fit together well. I wanted one large set, filled with the best parts of all our blocks, so that we could build better

rooms for our time travelers. It felt like the block-makers were con-
spiring against Yush and me, unnecessarily complicating our game
just because he was a boy and I was a girl. As children, those differences didn't exist between us. But the world was already putting us
into boxes, enforcing rules for each of us based on our biological sex,
slowly teaching us who we could and could not be.

We created a kind of code, a slang that made sense between us but
to no one else. I decided that names were arbitrary, and Yush agreed,
so we made up new names for each other. I called him Blunt Man
Ricky because I thought that was funny when I was ten. He named
me Ingrid. We watched some movie where an American boy said,
"What guy? Oh, *that guy!*" with a strong inflection on "guy," like he
was saying "ghoi," which made no sense to us. Yush and I found this
hysterical. "What ghoi? Oh, that ghoi!" We fell over ourselves laughing the first time we heard it, and then we continued to laugh and we
knew it made no sense, and that just made it funnier. Even when we
were teens, sometimes I'd look at Yush and say, "What ghoi?" and
he'd laugh and say, "Oh, that ghoi!" finishing the line. It meant abso-
lutely nothing and yet, between us, it meant everything.

YUSH AND I WERE short and wispy thin, like blades of cut grass. Although we inherited our stature from you at four foot eleven and Papa
at five four, Papa tried to plump us up to fit in better with American
kids. He often forced us to drink Ensure between meals, treating our
height and thinness as a deficiency to be urgently corrected. The first
time I sipped Ensure, I almost threw up. The thick gloopy liquid
tasted like syrup mixed with the sludge from the bottom of a trash
can. I quieted my gag reflex because I knew that if I didn't drink without complaining or gagging, Papa would make me drink even more.
Behind his back, I asked you to not get the strawberry flavor. If Papa
found out I was being picky about the flavors, he might slap me, or he
might scream at you, and then he'd force me to drink only the bad-
tasting ones until I stopped complaining and pretended to like them.

I didn't want to be so small forever, but I felt ashamed that I couldn't just be bigger like Papa wanted me to be.

Yush and I were different from the other kids at school, not only because they were chalk-white but because Papa studied medicine and their parents worked as office assistants and teachers. Some of the dads in our neighborhood were in jail or were alcoholics, or both. I believed that such hardship could not befall our family because, unlike white families, South Asian families prioritized closeness and success. We stayed so close and performed so well because we followed certain rules—like no divorcing and no dating—that kept us bonded as one impenetrable unit. I thought white people didn't observe these rules because they didn't like one another as much as we liked one another. I thought they were just as mean to others as they were to Yush and me, so it made sense that they didn't care about their families the way we cared about ours. I knew that one day I'd stay at home like you did to raise my kids, and I wanted Papa to arrange my marriage like he and you had done, because I wanted to raise a family that was as exceptional as ours.

ONE DAY I ARRIVED at recess a few minutes late. My friends stood in a line, waiting for me. That made me feel special, like they didn't want to play without me. I rushed over and heard one of them say, "There she is! Run! Don't let her get us!" They squealed and ran away from me as fast and as far as they could. I didn't chase them. I stopped and I watched. I turned back and sat by myself in the empty classroom. Later, one of them told me it was just a game, that they didn't mean anything by it. But it was a game they didn't invite me to play. They had decided among themselves that excluding me was fun. After that, I knew they weren't really my friends, but I didn't understand why or what I'd done. From then on, I spent many recesses in the classroom with Miss Hagerty, who liked me.

Miss Hagerty walked like a runway model, with one foot directly in front of the other so that her hips swayed when she clacked down the linoleum hallway in her high heels. She had a big, blond perm that made her head look like a makeup puff and wore colorful business suits to school that reminded me of an airline stewardess. She taught us how to write in cursive, which felt like art to me. I spent a long time perfecting the slopes of my S's and connecting the letters. I won a John Hancock award for my handwriting. I didn't know awards for handwriting existed, but I knew that adults, particularly Papa, lit up when I got an award. I didn't know how to get the girls in my class to see me as special or good, but I learned that winning over adults was easy. I wanted to feel special, always. During elementary school, I was voted to student council nearly every year, and my art and short stories regularly appeared in the school lobby as a Principal's Pick. Even though my friends were not always nice to me, I felt good about myself because I excelled in school.

I could explain none of my struggles at school to you, and none of what you said could have helped me deal with them. But such explanations were unnecessary with Papa, who understood how to navigate the color-blocked split of our brown home and the white world beyond it. Unlike the other Indian parents we knew, recent immigrants with thick accents, Papa grew up learning the mannerisms and interests of white people. But the lesson of learning how to belong, which deepened our bond to Papa, was the same process that initiated our estrangement from you. Now I wonder who we could have been if we saw our ethnicity not as something to manipulate into belonging in white America but as an opportunity to understand why we were treated differently in the first place.

AT HOME, PAPA OPERATED on tiny green grapes. Grape skin was like human skin, he said. Papa showed me Frank Netter's colorful illustrations in his thick medical textbooks as examples of what I could draw one day. I was in the middle of what Papa fondly called my "shoe period," the year in which I drew nothing but stilettos until I got the curves right. Despite his limited income as a surgical resident, Papa told you to put both of us in art classes, music lessons, and sports, in an effort to make us "well-rounded" and successful, a desire to give us all the things he wished he'd had as a boy.

Papa maintained one rule in the house: We could buy any book we wanted, no questions asked. Every month, Yush and I brought home the Scholastic Book Club's paper catalog and circled all the books we liked. You signed the catalog slip and then, a few weeks later, a large pile of books arrived at school, like magic. Chapter books intimidated me, but Papa told me to think of a big book as a series of the small books that I read. "Just go one page at a time," he said gently. Papa's confidence in me made me feel like I could do anything.

I looked forward to the weekends, when we inhabited our other life: our desi life. Our real life. Every Sunday, we went to Hindi school and met with other North Indian families just like ours, with plenty of parents who worked as doctors or engineers, just like Papa. To them, immigrants who came to America as adults, Papa was an inspiration. He was proof that in the West, it was possible for a desi child to retain his roots and achieve success, giving them hope for their own American-born children. I, in turn, admired the older siblings of my desi friends the way that kids at my school probably looked up to celebrities like Michael Jordan or Mariah Carey. To me, the desi teenagers who went to MIT, Harvard, and Yale were the all-stars. On a trip to Boston, Papa bought me a T-shirt with the Harvard logo. I wore it so often that by the end of elementary school, the image had cracked and faded.

At Sunday school, we practiced writing Hindi and sang "Raghupati Raghava Raja Ram," the devotional bhajan praising Sita and Rama. Later, you drove me to the temple where I learned kathak, the classical dance that connected me to your home city. I practiced in the living room for hours, specifically the fast five-step twirl that made me so dizzy. Every Diwali, you dressed me in a lehenga and helped me put on makeup. Papa turned into the paparazzi, photographing me in different locations in the house like a movie star.

In the evening, we put on plays about Rama, Sita, and Lakshmana's return to Ayodhya and then danced with dandiya sticks all night.

The kids at school had never heard of Diwali. They celebrated Christmas, and I desperately wanted to participate, too. When Miss Hagerty found out, she brought an artificial four-foot-tall tree to school for us to borrow. You and Papa were so embarrassed that this white teacher was taking pity on our family for not exposing their child to Christmas, as if I were deprived. To avoid the embarrassment of anything like that ever happening again, Papa bought a fake tree the following year. I set it up and hung colorful decals from the dollar store on our living room windows. I set out milk and cookies for Santa on Christmas Eve. You found all of this frivolous and told me that it was a waste of food, but Papa shushed you and said, "It's okay, let her do it." Yush asked you if Santa was real and you said no, and then Yush told me and I got mad at him. Yush was giddy for having figured it out before me. You were practical about money and unfamiliar with these strange American customs and traditions, but Papa let us indulge in them because he knew what it was like to feel excluded.

Every now and then, a police officer came to school and he and Miss Hagerty told us that drugs, alcohol, and cigarettes were bad. I rarely saw you or Papa drink, but one day Papa drank beer and I got scared because of what the man had told us about alcohol. I told Papa to be careful and not drink. He laughed, and I got worried because Papa wasn't taking my concerns seriously. But then at the end of the school year, I walked next to Miss Hagerty and I smelled something foul. I realized the stench was cigarette smoke, and the smell came from her. I think I told you about this shocking betrayal when I got home. She and that man had told us how bad smoking was, but here she was, doing it anyway.

Until then, I thought adults always told the truth. I thought that the rules adults enforced existed to keep us safe, and I thought that adults followed all the rules that they made us follow. I saw this as the distinction between childhood and adulthood: Kids didn't know the rules for how to behave, and being an adult meant following the rules well. I wondered, then, if sometimes adults told us things that they thought were good for us because they wanted us to behave one way, but they acted another, because that was more convenient for them. This struck me as the most unfair, wrong, unjust thing in the world. I was angry with Miss Hagerty, and I didn't trust her anymore. I believed this hypocrisy to be one of the worst things that a person could do to another person.

Some adults were like that, perhaps, but I knew that Papa wasn't. In fact, Papa exposed the lies of other adults to us. He told us truths about how the world really worked. When I wanted a Happy Meal, Papa told Yush and me that corporations used us as free advertising for their brands. Neither of us ever asked for a Happy Meal again. We even refused to wear clothes with big designer logos, indignant at the injustice of paying a fashion brand to promote its own label. Papa spoke about magical things, male inventors and scientists who used their brilliance to change the world and get rich, and he asked us questions that left us stumped and dazzled.

One time Papa asked us, "How do you know if you are crazy? If you lose your mind, you can't trust it. So how do you know?"

Yush and I didn't know. The thought that one could lose a sense of reality had never occurred to me before, and the possibility terrified me.

But Papa had a solution. He said that we had to make a list of people we loved and trusted. "And if they tell you you're crazy," he said, "you know you have to listen to them, and they will help you become sane again."

I made a mental note of my list: Papa was at the top, then you, and then Yush.

From these truths, we imbibed Papa's worldview: that therapists were quacks peddling pseudoscience, and that Buaji, his sister, used to be something called a feminazi. I didn't know what feminazis were exactly, but I believed they were mean, angry women who looked down at us because you didn't work outside the home. Buaji had tight coily hair and a voice like honey. She taught me how to plant flowers in her garden and she planned fun activities, like painting pottery, whenever we visited her. But after Papa said that, I didn't fully trust her. We all looked at her husband, my Fufaji, with more suspicion. Papa and Fufaji had been friends as kids, Papa said, but Fufaji lied a lot. According to Papa, my uncle always had some ulterior motive when talking to any of us, so it was best to stay away from him.

Papa dispensed these truths in nightly sermons at the dinner table. He animated Yush and me, but I have trouble remembering your role in these conversations, Mummy. So often, I think you were excluded from them. Either you had to sit and turn into Papa's disciple, as one of us, or you had to withdraw in resignation, unable to contribute—not because you had nothing to say, but because Papa stood at a pulpit for one.

We were not a deeply religious family, because Papa considered himself a man of science and reason. But we were a dogmatic family, fundamentalist in our belief of Papa as an omniscient being who had succeeded in the world because of what he knew. Yush and I would inherit the knowledge of his kingdom.

THE RITUALS OF PASSING on Papa's knowledge accelerated at the end of second grade. Papa took Yush and me to Borders, where, for the next several years, he bought us math and English workbooks two grades above our current level. Papa required us to finish the books during the summer. We had to score perfectly, or as close to perfect as possible, understanding that this was our path to the Ivy League.

One day, Papa asked me how screws worked. I didn't know. Then he asked Yush, who answered the question with ease. Papa wasn't angry at me for not knowing, but he was angry that I had not shown curiosity once made aware of my ignorance. Papa grounded me. He forbade me to read anything that wasn't *The Way Things Work* by David Macaulay, a thick illustrated book with a cheery woolly mammoth that I came to see as an avatar for all that was evil in the world. I knew that if Papa caught me reading a book that wasn't about simple machines, he would scream and maybe break or hit something or slap me, so I had to figure it out.

I didn't stop reading fiction. Instead, I sat in corners of the house where I could hear the garage door, which meant Papa was home, and then I'd stow my book away and take out the book about simple machines. I pretended to go to bed early and then read chapter books under the covers for hours, listening for Papa's footsteps in the hallway, stuffing the book and my penlight under my pillow if I heard any movement. You protected me from Papa's wrath with tiny acts of resistance: You told me when Papa called to say he was on his way home, both of us understanding that it was time to perform in the way that he expected. You were my lookout, warning me when trouble was near.

For the next several weeks, I sat on edge as Papa quizzed me about levers, screws, wedges, and pulleys at random times: at dinner, in the car, before playing outside. Any interaction could flip in a moment. A few times I fumbled, and Papa screamed at me, sending me back to my room to study. Finally, when he was satisfied with my explanations and I could convincingly fake a fascination with wedges, pulleys, and screws, Papa dropped the line of inquiry and lifted the ban on books.

Years later, when I told Papa that I had continued to read fiction behind his back, I thought he might be surprised. Instead, he laughed. "I knew what you were doing," he said. "But it didn't matter. The point is, I got you to learn about simple machines."

YUSH SAID THAT PAPA had a "wartime personality." Yush thought this was a good thing to have, particularly when leading a battle, as someone who needed to make tough decisions for the betterment of the group. I agreed with Yush in theory, but I was also confused. "There's no war," I said to Yush. "What battle is Papa fighting?" The problem with that kind of a personality, I said, was that when everything was peaceful, one had to create wars to feel useful or important.

Papa created little wars all the time but not in front of aunties or uncles or distant relatives. He did it with you mostly but also with Dadiji when she ate sweets like ladoos or gulab jamun. Papa yelled that she needed to lose weight for her health, and he screamed about how hard it was for him to watch his mother stay so fat and how it was wrong that she wouldn't listen to him when he knew what was best for her. She just sat quietly until he was done screaming, and then we all carried on like it never happened. He yelled at Yush because Yush had trouble focusing at school, but he yelled at me least because I was the best student in my class. Back then, I was Papa's little princess.

I asked Papa why he yelled so much, and he said, "Because that's the only way I've found people will listen to me." I didn't know what to say to that. I couldn't think of anyone else who yelled like he did—not my teachers and not you—yet Yush and I still listened to those adults. I reasoned that there must be other ways to get people to listen that Papa hadn't figured out yet, that maybe Papa didn't know how to talk to people nicely because he forgot what it was like to be a kid. I promised myself I wouldn't forget the turbulent feelings of childhood, as I worried Papa had.

Chapter 3

━━━

Mismatched Expectations

THE SCENE I IMAGINED of your first meeting with Papa was cinematic: Papa's family sat with their feet touching the cool marble floor, sipping chai and making small talk with Nanaji and your other relatives in a living room in New Delhi. When you walked into the room, time stopped. A fairy in a lavender organza sari floated in, a face that was all moon-shaped eyes. Your lunar glow lit up the room. You possessed the specific idealized beauty of a Bollywood heroine: hair like strands of diamonds; a figure slim and slight like a hummingbird's; and, most important by India's standards, skin the color of gold-dipped pearls. I have seen the photos of you; I see what Papa must have seen: redemption, power, conquest, validation. A woman so beautiful that she could turn even an outcast into an envied man.

Many of my friends balked at the idea of arranged marriages, but I found their shock misplaced. What I saw in American romance movies seemed absurd. In *The Notebook*, a boy and a girl meet as teenagers, and they fight and make up and fight and make up over a summer. When she leaves town, he writes her letters every day for years and even builds her a house. They called this romantic. In *Sleepless in Seattle*, a woman obsesses over a man she does not know, impressing some idea she has of him upon a voice she hears on the radio, an infatuation that culminates in a meeting. This, too, they called love. At least in the South Asian tradition, we are up front about the spectacle and the arbitrariness of romantic love. At least we mutually agree on the objects of obsession before acting upon our compulsions and fantasies. All of this is to say that, as a girl, I found the story of your marriage romantic.

You met one or two times again after that. Papa asked you if you were willing to move to Canada with him. "I will go wherever my husband goes," you said. Within weeks, you were married.

On your wedding night, you wore a scarlet lehenga and posed on a bed with wooden posts that jutted toward the ceiling like minarets. When I first saw the photo as a teenager, I blushed. Carnal red envelops the entire picture, all fabric. Only your face and bangle-adorned forearms are visible. The photo is modest yet feels too intimate for anyone else—let alone your daughter—to see. It is the only photo I have ever seen of you in which your eyes hunger with desire. I have thought often about the woman in that photo: what she yearned for and what she believed she was about to find. I have long wanted to meet her. I want to understand what happened to her.

I cannot imagine the loneliness and fear you must have felt when you first reached Canada at age twenty-three, and for a long time I did not even try. The stories of your life as a recent immigrant came to Yush and me as jokes, where your isolation or forced assimilation was always the punch line. Papa said that before you came here, you spoke some primitive small-town dialect, a bastardization of Hindi that he pushed you to correct in order to "communicate better," as he put it. You were too embarrassed to speak this dialect in front of us, but one time, as teenagers, we begged you to speak it. Around the dinner table, between mouthfuls of dal chawal you had prepared for us, Papa set up the joke—*listen to how funny this sounds*—gearing up your nasally speech as the gag. You spoke. We laughed.

I never heard you speak that way again.

That language was Awadhi, an ancient tongue that told your people's stories before the British ravaged your lands. A language of rajas and poets that, while still spoken in parts of Northern India, had been pushed aside after the colonizers arrived. In our house, Papa was the colonizer. I wish now I had grown up hearing the ancient song of my ancestors that lives within you.

In India, your male relatives escorted you everywhere in public. I don't think you had ventured beyond your country's borders before your brief honeymoon in Nepal with Papa. Shortly after you arrived in Canada, Papa took you to downtown Toronto and then left you there alone. In an era without cellphones or the Internet, he went off and told you to find your own way back. You were stranded in the middle of a large city full of people who did not look like you or talk like you. You must have been terrified. When he told us this story, Papa emphasized his wit, as if this was a clever way to teach someone "how to be independent." It was his way of saying: *You're in my country now, and I control you.*

Papa said that when you first came to Canada you two "fought all the time," and you chimed in and your eyes widened, embellishing the story with your own line, "Oh, I would get so mad!" and then Papa laughed and so did we. Now I wonder where that anger of yours went. I wonder if the anger I thought I learned from watching Papa instead came from you. Trapped, without an exit, transferred from mother to daughter through the secrets we were both meant to keep.

You RELIED ON LETTERS in blue air-mail envelopes to communicate with your siblings in India. As a girl, I followed you into your bedroom and sat down on the bed next to you while you unfolded paper that smelled of mothballs. You told me what the letters said, explaining to me who was my Mamaji or my Mausiji. I had met my uncles and aunts when I was a baby, but I couldn't remember them. One time a letter came and, when you opened it, your face fell. As you looked at scrawling that I could not yet read, I felt confused. How something that usually made you so happy could now steal all of your joy? Your grandmother had died, you told me as you sobbed. I wanted to console you, but I didn't know the woman you mourned.

Back then, we staged phone calls to India like a theatrical production. We planned them in advance, and whenever someone picked up, the four of us huddled around the phone and talked fast and loudly—partly because of the excitement of getting through, partly because we had to yell to compensate for the poor connection, and partly because we never knew when the line would cut. Aside from a few visits you made to India after marriage, these scattered phone calls and letters were the only contact you had with your home in your first decade here.

I never asked you what hopes and dreams buoyed you amid the all-consuming loneliness and grief of leaving your family and your country behind. I had just assumed that the West, the land of opportunity, was so obviously the best place to live. The idea that the West represents modernity and the East is stuck in some primitive, ancient past rooted in the West's orientalist lie. My own assumptions about who you were and what you wanted, founded upon this lie, made it impossible for me to see you beyond the role you played in our household.

When Papa's sister, my Buaji, asked you why you agreed to marry a stranger who lived in another country, you told her that you wanted to raise a different kind of family—a close, nuclear family unburdened by the drama that came with the joint-family structure you grew up with in India. You once told me that in India, your neighbors were your relatives, but the two families had split the house and cordoned them off with walls. They now rarely spoke to one another. You never explained why. Maybe you thought family unity would be easier to maintain in the West, where women did not live under the control of their husbands' parents and grandparents in the same house. The simpleness of your want for closeness and autonomy, and all that made that dream impossible for you to attain, guts me now.

Papa said that he entered into an arranged marriage out of respect for Dadiji and Dadaji's wishes. This was not uncommon. Many South Asian immigrants brokered marriages for their children from their motherland, particularly in the first immigrant generation. Honoring Indian culture, Papa said, was important to him. While his younger siblings eventually lost fluency in Hindi and grew distant from extended family, Papa strained to relearn the language and deepen bonds with relatives, both here and abroad.

But Papa's siblings had both dated and then married for love. In his family, Papa's arranged marriage was an outlier. As an adult, I began to ask questions about the stories upon which I had been raised, and Dadaji and Buaji told me a very different account of the brokering of your marriage.

Dadaji had long opposed arranged marriages. His own parents had fallen in love. He believed that people should enter into a marriage of their own accord, when and how and with whom they wanted. It was Papa who, while still in college, approached his father with the request to find a bride in India. Dadaji said no. He did not want to be responsible for his son's happiness. "How will I judge whether this girl is good for my son or not? I cannot do that," he told me. "Besides, why are you in such a rush?" he said he asked Papa. "Wait until you have a job and a house to support a new bride."

I do not know what India represented to Papa, but I suspect he carried nostalgia for a place that never existed, a utopia created by the frozen impressions and desires of a nine-year-old boy who moved to a white country that shunned him. "Do you know why I want to go to India and get married?" Buaji recalled Papa asking her. "Because girls raised here are ruined, like you." She shot back, "You're looking for a servant, not a wife." Papa seemingly envisioned Indian-born-and-bred women as pure, like the portrayals of Sita from the *Ramayana* popularized by India's Hindu elite. In the version of the ancient epic that I grew up hearing, Rama repeatedly tests the commitment of his wife, Goddess Sita, daughter of Mother Earth, demanding she prove her purity by walking through fire and later banishing her in a forest over concerns about her chastity. Papa was going to India to find a chaste, obedient, devoted woman. A woman uncorrupted by the West.

In *Speaking the Unspeakable*, sociologist Margaret Abraham explains the tragic consequences of the mismatch of expectations between men like Papa and women like you: Many South Asian women who married South Asian men from the West, as you did, carried expectations that they might have more opportunities here. This is what colonialism advertises. But South Asian men from the West who sought South Asian brides in the East, as Papa did, often played out their orientalist fantasies of a demure, subservient woman who could restore the brown masculinity robbed by white men in the West—also as colonialism advertises. You had been taught that most obstacles in marriage resulted from a woman's failure to please her husband, understanding that divorce was a form of social death. On top of that, you were still a girl in many ways, never having played out the fantasies of intimacy with an actual man. Your family had only a few days to vet this stranger and his family. Then, after marriage, you were removed from your culture, country, and family, entirely dependent upon your husband for your immigration status, income, and access to community. These conditions made you especially vulnerable. Everything was stacked against you, but you had no way of knowing this.

AFTER DADAJI REFUSED TO arrange his son's marriage, Papa apparently threatened Dadaji with an ultimatum: *Find me a bride in India, or I'll marry someone here that you don't like, without your input.* The threat was not idle. He told Dadaji that he knew of an Indo–Guyanese woman who was interested in him. In the upper-caste North Indian community's eyes, this woman would lower the family's status, because South Asians came to the Caribbean as indentured laborers when slavery was supplanted. Papa planned to marry her if his parents refused to comply with his wishes, he said. I was shocked to learn that Papa was willing to gamble with both his future and someone else's in such a profound, devastating, lasting way, and I was astounded that he manipulated bigotry to call my grandparents' bluff.

Dadiji was seemingly unbothered by Papa's disturbing ultimatum, elated that her son sought a traditional arranged Hindu marriage. Dadaji, pressured by his wife's excitement and scared to say no to his brilliant eldest son, relented. He went to India to help Papa find a bride. But on one condition: *Don't bring her to Canada until you have graduated, have a job, and can provide her a real home.* Papa promised.

The family could barely afford the trip to India. Dadaji left his computer-consulting business in the charge of one of Papa's friends. When he came back, he had lost all of his clients. The business dissolved.

Papa never told me about the ultimatum he gave Dadaji. He never uttered a word about the promise that Dadaji said he made. He did once mention dating a woman before meeting you. She wanted to marry him, he said, but he was just having fun. It seemed wrong to string someone along like that, I said, but Papa said that it was fine because he told her from the get-go that he'd never marry her. I remember feeling bad for that woman.

Papa bragged about intentionally rushing your visa—an affair that could easily take a year—with such expediency that you came to Canada within months of marriage. Your family in India was impressed. Given this, I find it hard to believe that he'd ever planned to honor the promise he made to Dadaji.

THE WEST WAS THE land of decadence. I imagine that your family thought this Canadian man and his family bore significant wealth. I don't know what Papa told you about Canada or where you'd be staying, but you must have been shocked when you discovered that your new husband, still in college, had no stable source of income and lived in an apartment with other men. You moved in with his parents in the suburbs while he lived in another city to finish school. But he was a good man. He had been vetted and it had been decided. To question that goodness was to question the entire process, the entire world, and the judgment of everyone that you loved and trusted.

Papa twisted the criticisms of his decision-making into personal attacks against you: When we were kids, he told us that Dadaji didn't want Papa to marry you, and he said that Buaji looked down at you as a servant. It was through this lens that you built relationships with your in-laws, burdened by a disprovable, unshakable suspicion that they did not want you here and saw you as beneath them. You had no choice but to take Papa's words at face value, cementing your loyalty to him as your protector in the face of their harsh judgments.

With the perfect Indian bride by his side, Papa set out to build the perfect Indian American family. Now I wonder if Papa ever thought about what it might mean to raise a daughter in a land of ruined women. Maybe he thought he was powerful enough to keep America from corroding me, that he could galvanize my inherent Indianness, whatever that meant to him, like an alloy coating.

Chapter 4

Origins Obscured

Papa's family became the gravitational center of my cultural identity for one simple reason: They lived here, and your family did not. He told Yush and me that in Hindi, there is no distinct word for "cousin," because cousins are like siblings. Papa made sure that Yush and I would know his sister, my Buaji, and his brother, my Chachaji, and think of their children as our brothers and sisters. Papa's maturity impressed me. Despite his misgivings, he had set aside his personal experiences with Buaji and her husband, our Fufaji, so that Yush and I could form our own distinct relationships with them and our cousins. Most winters, Papa, Buaji, and Chachaji organized family reunions, rotating between our home, Buaji's place in Winnipeg, and Chachaji's house in Ottawa over the Christmas holiday.

The story of Papa's family was one of upward mobility, of ascending the ladder toward security in a country occupied by the British. I was surprised to learn that the metaphor "climbing the ladder," a phrase now ubiquitous within corporate America, had an unusual connection to old board games from South Asia.

Ancient Hindu, Jain, and Muslim versions of the board game called Gyan Chaupar in Hindi guided players to spiritual liberation.

The top of the grid represented spiritual enlightenment and self-acceptance, while the bottom represented a state of earthly egoism, lack of awareness, and illusion. Players moved along squares by rolling die or cowries, advancing or descending levels by landing on squares with a ladder, toward either clarity and knowledge, or a snake, which pushed them deeper into spiritual degradation.

When the British colonized India, they co-opted this ancient game into Snakes and Ladders and stripped it of its spiritual mission, modifying it to teach what *Against Meritocracy* author Jo Littler calls "Christian-capitalist moral instruction." In the British game, ascension no longer meant enlightenment; instead, it signified rising to affluence through punctuality, perseverance, and opportunism. One had to overcome obstacles such as robbery, poverty, and illness, casting one's inability to produce capital as badness. The game later reached America, where the Milton Bradley Company named it Chutes and Ladders to adapt it for children. The board-game characters remained white until 1974, when Black children were told that they, too, now had a chance to climb the ladder to attain wealth and fame. It was around this time that America advertised itself as a place where people like us could advance, unencumbered.

In the forgotten history of this influential board game, I recognize the arc of my own obscured cultural past. I see a deep self-knowledge abandoned and forgotten, replaced with a story that asserts the power of the very people who ensured our history's erasure, then marketed it back to us as our truth.

As a girl, I romanticized Dadaji's life of struggle as a hero's quest to reach his rightful place in the world. Dadaji was born one year after Gandhi marched across India to make his own salt, in defiance of British rule. His own father had grown up poor. As a little boy, my great-grandfather woke up at dawn to walk with a local doctor in his village—the only man he knew who spoke English, knowing even at that age that to improve his situation in life, he must learn the language of the colonizer. He became a doctor of Ayurvedic medicine, a tutor, and a freedom fighter. He fell in love with one of his students, whom he married. On the night that Dadaji was born, my great-grandfather was confined to a British jail cell for inciting protest against colonial rule.

Dadaji spent the earliest years of his life at one of Gandhi's ashrams in Gujarat, a place that lit the inextinguishable flame of curiosity within him. The family later moved to Kota, Rajasthan, where my great-grandfather served as a court physician to one of the few remaining Rajasthani kings. When Dadaji was nine, his father caught an infection from a patient. After battling the illness for a few months, he died. My great-grandmother was no more than thirty. In those days, because she was a woman, she was blocked from inheritance and could not remarry. Tradition dictated that she was now her deceased husband's family's responsibility, but they turned their backs on her.

Upon her brother's insistence, their father reluctantly took her back. In those first few months, as my nine-year-old grandfather rubbed his Nanaji's feet with oil, he overheard the men talking about where to send another relative, who was about Dadaji's age, to school. No one spoke about Dadaji's education. "I realized," Dadaji recalled with a heavy, cracking voice, "they're training me as a servant."

To escape servitude, Dadaji moved to a neighboring city and lived with his mother's cousin, wife, and their dozen or so children. He was able to enroll in school there, but Dadaji cried every night for at least a year because he was not wanted there. He was not wanted anywhere. At school, Dadaji learned Sanskrit, English, and history—but not the history of his people. "History was all what the British viceroys did," he said. "We were taught about that which had no meaning to us." I wonder now how this shaped his psyche and spirit: When, even in his own country, his people's stories did not matter, he was forced to study his oppressor's greatness, and learned to deny his own.

No science or math was offered in what Dadaji now describes as a "backward place." But when he saw a boy in his class apply to a school in another city to pursue science, Dadaji decided to try, too. He was admitted with a partial scholarship; he learned and then aced physics, chemistry, and math. When Dadaji graduated from the twelfth grade, he had far surpassed the expectations of those around him.

Dadaji applied to an engineering college and won a full scholarship. In 1952, he graduated from Birla Engineering College, now called Birla Institute of Technology and Science, as the valedictorian of his class. He could not afford the train ride back to Pilani to attend his graduation ceremony. He received his gold medal by mail.

Shortly after Dadaji graduated, he moved to an industrial city in Bihar to work at a paper mill. Dadaji's mother was dying from intestinal tuberculosis. She had arranged for Dadaji to meet the nineteen-year-old daughter of a man who worked at the paper mill. Her last wish: marry that girl. Dadaji did not want to get married. He wanted to establish his career first and eventually marry for love. But Dadaji could not say no to his mother. He accepted his fate.

Unlike her husband, Dadiji had only an eighth-grade education. She was born to a mother who suffered eleven miscarriages, most of which she witnessed as a girl. Only one of Dadiji's siblings lived to adulthood, a brother she raised because her mother was chronically ill, likely with gestational diabetes. Dadiji was a talented seamstress and painter who dreamed of going to art school, but her duties as a caretaker tied her to a domestic life. I don't know much else about her early life. Once, when I asked her to tell me more, she said, "Kya kahoon? Pata nahi." *What is there to say? I don't know.*

The union between my grandparents was unromantic, forged from obligation and carried out by the hardened dedication of two untethered people who longed for a family they never had. Both of their mothers died before their first wedding anniversary. Dadaji took his resentments out on Dadiji, dismissing her as "an uneducated girl from the village," treating her as an extension of the place he had tried so hard to leave behind. I am not sure if it ever turned into love—at least not love as I understand it—as much as a dependency on each other.

Together, they had three children. Papa was the oldest, then came Buaji and Chachaji, all born in the second decade of a free India.

Prime Minister Jawaharlal Nehru had launched a tech-and-science initiative to revitalize and rebuild the newly independent nation. Dadaji's skills, now highly sought after, earned him top engineering jobs at major tech companies. But in the fragile decades after colonialism, Dadaji discovered a new constraint upon him: Indians did not get promoted to leadership; white men from abroad came to India to manage workers. He realized that his success in his own country was still limited.

Dadaji wished he could forget his shattering loneliness, an alienation that shaped his "lopsided personality," as he later put it. Dadaji and Dadiji had few close relatives to keep them rooted in India. They were not sentimental about a past filled with hardship. The decision was mutual. Following the same ambition that had carried him through his childhood, Dadaji again walked away from the constraints of what he knew and plunged into the expanse of the unknown. They had heard that in the West, opportunity was limitless.

Dadaji did not know where Indians stood in America's racial hierarchy. On his first solo trip to North America, he devised an imperfect litmus test: He visited three diners in America and three in Canada and waited to see how long it took for him to get served at each. He waited longer at American diners. He decided that Canada would be more suitable for his family. Foreign-exchange laws in India at the time barred immigrants from taking much money out of the country. Though the family lived comfortably in India, Dadaji ceded his wealth to move to Canada.

Ultimately, Dadaji's personal ambitions in Canada never materialized. He took a government job that would have offered a good pension, but Dadaji felt stifled and soon quit. He started a computer-consulting firm with some friends but didn't like working in a team. He launched a solo consulting firm that later foundered. After a few years he opened an electronics store in a strip mall. That business, too, failed. The risk-taking impulse that had propelled Dadaji out of Haldaur stunted his ability to provide consistently for his family, and his obstinacy stood in the way of good business sense. In his later years, when he realized that Dadiji had cared for him despite not receiving the comfortable life they'd both assumed he would provide, Dadaji became gentler with her, preparing her tea and warming her dinner as she lost her mobility. Now Dadaji, the child of a freedom fighter who, as a man, pledged his allegiance to the queen of England, asks, "I still am not sure—did I do the right thing by coming here, or not?"

In Dadaji's story, I see how Papa's ancestors grasped for security by seeking educational attainment, specifically through math and science, and by learning the ways of the white man. In Papa's lineage, I see people who strove to ascend to feel secure. It is under these auspices that Dadaji rose from poverty and that Papa rose from a lower-class upbringing in Canada to the upper-middle class as an adult. Papa followed this common immigrant road map and imprinted the map upon Yush and me. But along the way, we forgot that this is not necessarily who we are—it is who we felt pressured to become.

For a long time, Mummy, I saw the history of Papa's family as my own and your past as a separate trail that branched off somewhere else, far away from me. It was easier for me to trace the lines through Papa's lineage, if only because I could relate to some small aspect of the challenges he faced as a brown boy raised in whiteness. As a girl disconnected from my ancestors with no sense of a homeland, little oral history, and few traditions, I adopted the culture of constantly achieving, of doing, of accomplishing, of ascending, as my own, without considering that there were other ways for me to be in the world. Now I wonder how the culture of Papa's family, which consumed you, shaped who you became and how you mothered me.

Your father, my Nanaji, was a moneylender, as was his father before him. In stories I heard as a child—which I remember being narrated by Papa, strangely, and not you—you watched men weigh bars of gold on large scales in your kitchen. When you described a home with marble floors, I imagined a floor of little glass beads crammed together: literal marbles. I was disappointed when we visited and the floor was ordinary and drab. But the parlor, an elegant two-story hall with a balcony, was fit for a nawab. You attended a convent school and later studied English at an all-girls college, molded by Victorian ideals of femininity that must have primed you to admire the West.

You grew up in a large open-air home among three generations of family. As the baby in a house with four older siblings, you were doted on by your father. I met my Nanaji only a few times, and we could barely communicate, my Hindi as broken as his English, but he seemed to laugh more than he spoke. His husky voice and smoky quartz eyes radiated the same warmth I felt from you. It was Mamaji, though, one of your brothers, who enchanted me the most. He laughed so heartily that for years, when I knew him only as a voice over the phone, I imagined a bald, fat, and jolly man, like a Happy Buddha. I was shocked when I was twelve and met him in person: thin with a thick mop of black hair, like Yush.

I barely knew the men who raised you, but I could see the effects of their kindness on you and how that kindness shaped Yush and me. I wondered what it might be like to be raised by men like them, men who did not appear to yell to get what they wanted. I wonder now how their affection shaped your understanding of the world. Maybe you thought all men in the world were that caring, because in your world, they were.

You understood that you were a guest in your home and that you belonged with your future husband's family. If you had been arranged with a kind man, a man like those you knew, would this dream have been enough? I think it could have been.

I understood why Dadiji and Dadaji left India: They had no roots to tend. But your family lived in the same city for centuries, deeply entwined with the land and the local traditions of its people. You had close bonds among generations of relatives, a sprawling network that expanded through the city. In this light, your decision to leave India for a stranger is even more notable and curious to me. When you married someone in Canada, you broke from your family's tradition, seeking something unlike anyone else in your world, for reasons I do not know, pining for something that I do not understand.

Your family was not, at least as I understand it, searching for something more or something beyond. They were content, more or less. Or, to put it another way: They were wary of change, happy enough with what was. Then you married into a family that was fearful of stasis, never happy with what was, always focused on what could be. I cannot shake the feeling that so much of the dissonance between who you are and who Papa expected you to be—and who I am versus who you expected me to be—hangs on your decision to leave home, as if it is the doorway into your soul. I exist on one side of that door, and you have kept it shut. As a girl, I never tried to open that door, and now it is too late to try.

TODAY, TORONTO AND ITS surrounding suburbs form a diverse, majority non-white metropolis, populated by about one million people of South Asian origin. But in the late 1960s, when Dadiji and Dadaji first settled in a working-class neighborhood there, seeing another South Asian face was basis enough to stop and chat. At work, Dadaji befriended an Indian co-worker, Fufaji's dad, and together they formed a group of friends whose families met every Sunday to speak in Hindi and teach their children about Hindu holidays. The women prepared all the food from scratch because grocery stores did not carry South Asian ethnic foods. Dadiji could not find unripened green mangoes at her local grocery store, so she improvised with Granny Smith apples to make chutney, and crumbled unsweetened corn flakes with spiced fried lentils to make the salted lentil snack dal moth namkeen.

Immigration likely molded Papa and his two younger siblings in different ways, by some unknowable interplay between their natural disposition, the age at which they emigrated, and how a new country wary of brown foreigners perceived each of them. The kids spoke English but struggled to understand the rushed cadence of a Canadian accent. They faced a harsh choice: assimilate completely, stripping as many Indian cultural markers as possible to avoid mockery by their white classmates, or hang on to native culture and identity at their own peril.

I think the transition was hardest for Papa. India revered talent in science and tech. But in the West, where Hollywood idolized bad boys and mavericks, mathematically inclined, bookish boys were subject to mockery. A smart, sensitive, nine-year-old Indian boy was taken from a country where his intellect was admired and his short stature was commonplace to one where he became a series of pejoratives: brown, gangly, hairy, awkward, weird, poor, unathletic, accented, short. In Canada, Papa no longer existed as a person but as a symbol of ridicule.

To navigate the jagged terrain of a culture defined by sports and dating, Papa remained defiant, desperately hanging on to a cultural identity that had been irreparably ruptured. He wore a pocket protector and carried a briefcase to school, tempting the bullies and sneering back at them. But beneath the façade of toughness, he must have been profoundly lonely and sad. A deeply sensitive, wounded brown boy grew into a deeply sensitive, wounded brown man who sought to gain respect, status, and security by embracing the only role that embraced him: that of the high-achieving Indian kid.

He found solace in computers. Papa tinkered with robot-making kits as a boy, and by the time he was a teenager, he coded in COBOL and FORTRAN on IBM computers. He even completed little projects that Dadaji brought home from work, where Dadaji had access to a large mainframe computer. Unlike the confusing world of people, computers behaved in predictable ways. I think the binary logic comforted Papa. It was a solitary hobby, one that was special both because

of its exclusivity—few adults, let alone children, had access to computers back then—and because bringing a machine to life was magical, challenging, and creative in its own right.

Dadiji doted on her eldest son like he was Rama himself. Papa, by
virtue of the auspicious combination of his male sex and the order of
his birth, was invincible and incapable of wrongdoing. Dadiji, the
child of a woman who spent her life sick and suffering and an over-
whelmed father who functioned as both provider and caretaker, believed so deeply in the provenance of men that she interpreted it as a
personal moral failing if Papa ever did any housework. If a woman
forgot her duty to serve, a man was within his right to remind a
woman of it by nearly any means—yelling, berating, or threatening—
aside from actual physical violence.

As Buaji recalls, when Dadaji was not at home, Papa took charge.
He disciplined his younger siblings as he saw fit, barking orders and
punishing them when they didn't behave as he wanted them to. Only
Buaji pushed back, intervening or absorbing Papa's anger when he
bullied their younger brother. Papa enforced his own boyish ideas of
Indian girlhood upon his sister. After a girl in second grade made fun
of her for calling her parents "Mummy" and "Papa," Buaji started
calling them Mom and Dad. Dadiji and Dadaji didn't object, but
Papa scolded her for "not being Indian enough" and letting the white
people win. In high school, Buaji got picked on for wearing bulky
homemade clothes, so she asked Dadiji to sew a tapered knee-length
pencil skirt in line with the current fashion. When Papa saw his sister
in form-fitting clothing, he was offended. He chastised Dadiji for allowing Buaji out of the house in the skirt, not realizing Dadiji had
sewn it for her. Papa justified his actions as a moral obligation: *Nobody
seems to care as much as I do. How else will they learn?* Dadiji allowed it.

Papa never suggested that Dadiji treated him with any sort of fa-
voritism. I do not think he saw the treatment as special. He slipped
into authority like a tailored suit. But Papa lived between two ex-
tremes: the home world, where he sat high upon a throne, and the
outside world, where classmates trampled over him like boots on mud.

I wonder how this shaped his understanding of love—whether to be loved was to be made to feel powerful, and to love another was to dominate them. I wonder who that boy would have become, and how that man would have treated you and me, if he had been seen as neither God nor pariah but as an imperfect child capable of making mistakes and seeking help, ordinary and human.

Papa complained that Buaji was Dadaji's favorite child, and Buaji confirmed that Dadaji openly favored her with gifts over her two brothers. But, she says, Dadaji showed Papa the deference reserved for eldest sons. "Your father is the most brilliant man I know," Dadaji still says to me. "He always knew the answer, even before the question is asked."

Dadaji largely stayed out of home affairs, except on matters concerning his daughter. During meals, Dadiji served the family—Dadaji first, then Papa, then Chachaji and Buaji. Buaji was expected to serve Papa and Dadaji refills and then to clean up after the family. She was not allowed to go to sleepovers, and she was required to take a male chaperone—the son of their family friend, my Fufaji, whom she would later date and marry—to parties. At sixteen, she asked Dadaji, "When will I be allowed to make my own decisions?"

"Never," Dadaji told her. "You will listen to me as long as you live in my house, and then you will listen to your husband."

Eventually, Dadaji softened his views. "I brought you to this country without asking you, so it would be unfair to be angry for following the customs of a new place," he said.

The difference in treatment between son and daughter would ripple through generations, one learning entitlement, the other learning injustice. One sibling would lean into nostalgia for lost culture to justify his behavior, while the other would struggle to reclaim her lost culture, observing how tradition was so often invoked to evade accountability and prevent change.

Chapter 5

Me, Me Who Me

AT THE BEGINNING OF first grade, Ms. Barrett asked us to write poems. "Now, this is very important," she said. "You can't copy a poem written by someone else."

I ignored her. I tried to remember a Shel Silverstein poem that I liked and then wrote down whatever came to me. How else was one supposed to write a poem? Ms. Barrett handed out thin newsprint paper with blue lines spaced out by two inches across a wide, horizontal page. This is what I wrote:

Me, Me Who Me
Me who Me hello
Bye Bye

I didn't title mine, because I thought judges titled poems for us. I thought my poem was bad and I forgot about it.

From this exercise, however, I realized that the stories Ms. Barrett read to us were things I could write, too. I wrote short stories about little white girls tending to farm animals. I wondered if what I had written was true of someone, somewhere, and that made me think of writing as a form of time travel, like the game Yush and I played with Legos.

I saw that on the page, my words mattered as much as those of someone like Shel Silverstein. The page could not ignore me or treat me differently just because I was small or dark-skinned or a girl. On the page, I could show people things that I had trouble showing them any other way.

I asked Ms. Barrett for more paper, and I took the pages home and wrote more stories. I gripped the pencil so tightly—as if it might run away from me otherwise—that a tiny callus formed on my middle finger. You told me to loosen my grip, to not write with so much pressure, but my thoughts ran faster than I could record them, so I had to write as fast as I could, as hard as I could, in bursts. My hand cramped up and the callus hurt, but I continued to write.

At the end of the year, Ms. Barrett told me that my poem was to be published in a book: *Anthology of Poetry by Young Americans.* When I saw that every other poem in the book had a title, I was embarrassed. I still thought my poem was dumb, and I thought the judges were dumb, too, for including it. But seeing what I had written on flimsy newsprint in binding, like the books you read to me at home, showed me that what I wrote could also appear in a book for others to read. That meant that someone who didn't know me could know what I was thinking, and they could time-travel with me. A year later, when the school librarian pointed to a wall of books and said to our class, "Maybe one day your book will be up there," I felt as if she was talking directly to me. *Yes,* I said to myself, *it will.*

Creativity poured out of me as a natural expression, touching everything that I did. At home, I maintained multiple art projects. You bought me felt, and I sewed little dolls and made clothes for them and lined them up on the windowsill and named them. At school, after we learned how to make papier-mâché, I wrapped newspaper into balls and made a doll at home. She was ugly, with a head like a cracked egg, but I sewed clothes for her and used wire hangers to attach her head and limbs to her body so that she could move. I painted Monet replicas on wine bottles and used them as vases. You took us to the library often, and there, I bought old *National Geographic* magazines for a dollar and reproduced the covers I liked with colored pencils.

You were so busy at home that I rarely saw you engage in any hobbies, Mummy, and as a girl I assumed that you simply had no interests. It is embarrassing now to admit that I could have ever believed that. But in our house, everyone fulfilled a duty: Papa provided, you nurtured, Yush and I achieved. These jobs defined our identities, so I never thought about what you might want for yourself beyond meeting the expectations of the role you played.

As creative as I was, my imagination was limited. I never thought about what was possible for people like us. In fourth grade, I wrote a short story about a girl named Annie and Hansel, an alien android who crash-landed in her backyard. Hansel didn't remember where he came from or how he had arrived. Annie introduced him to her world, and Hansel shared his reactions to this foreign place. It was so weird how humans cut trees from the earth, decorated them with gaudy baubles, and hung lights on them in their home. Why did humans do this? Annie found him endearing, and he found her strange world exciting. At the end of the story, Hansel stopped searching for his home. In fact, he had never really been searching for it. He had been waiting for Annie to welcome him into her land.

Papa marveled at my unique perspective and commentary, showing my story to aunties and uncles who came to visit us. But, while I had set the story in our Pittsburgh backyard, I had not made Annie an Indian American girl like me. The decision to cut myself out of my own story was automatic and subconscious.

Two decades later I realized that I was, in fact, in my story—but I hadn't recognized myself. I was Hansel, the alien android who wanted desperately to belong in Annie's world, and let Annie define him by settling into the negative space around her. He made sense of himself by pointing out what was foreign about her world. I had seen Annie as human but myself as a malleable hunk of metal, a sidekick to support a white girl on her journey of self-actualization. The story that I grew up telling myself was someone else's—but, like my story about Annie and the android, I didn't know that at the time.

It's not that I wanted to be white, Mummy. I loved my bronze skin. There was no food better than your jeera-and-haldi-spiced aloo gobi. I felt glamorous in the deep-blush silver-lined lehenga that Naniji and Nanaji sent me from India. But I yearned for the freedom that I associated with whiteness. I felt like a simile, my personhood contextualized by whatever popular image I conjured in the minds of others—usually, Apu from *The Simpsons*. "Thank you, come again!" kids joked, asking if my parents owned a Kwik-E-Mart. They wondered out loud why my hands were brown on one side and white on the other and wanted to know where I was *really* from. I was envious that white people didn't have to liken themselves to something else in order to be understood. They could appear as they wanted to appear, without question or comparison.

AFTER PAPA FINISHED HIS residency, we moved to the suburbs outside Philly. We lived in an apartment again, like we had in New Jersey, but this time there was no park nearby, just a busy street and lots of boutiques in one direction and buildings and the highway in the other direction. Yush and I had to share a room again. I got cold at night and he got hot, and we fought over the temperature. I didn't want him around so much, all the time, anymore. I missed our backyard and our house. I missed having a temple nearby and I missed my desi friends. In this new town, there were only a few kids like us. A white woman on the elevator in our building asked you, "Do they speak English?" pointing at Yush and me. Yush glowered at her and blurted out, "No," and the lady looked offended. You and I shushed Yush and couldn't believe he had been so bold in front of a white woman. You smiled at her, putting on that veneer of respectability we all instinctively displayed around white people, and said, "Yes, they do."

On the first day at my new middle school, a girl with red hair approached me and looked at my sneakers, from Payless. She told me that I should buy Doc Martens. "That's what everybody wears," she said. When I looked up the price at a local shoe store, I couldn't believe anyone would spend so much on shoes for a child. I never bothered asking you for a pair. A few days later, the girl approached me again. "You didn't get Doc Martens," she said disapprovingly. She never spoke to me again. In that moment, I knew that my social life here would not be any better than at my last school.

By then, the goal of getting into the Ivy League consumed nearly everything Yush and I did. Nearly every decision I faced, every moment of free time I had, Papa redirected to whether or not this would aid me in the quest for acceptance to Harvard. When Papa couldn't determine the direct impact, he'd make the decision based on what he believed to be most useful or impressive. When I wanted to learn French at school, Papa said no, I had to study Latin. Most words had Latin roots and therefore Latin was the best language to take in order to excel on the SATs, he said. "But no one speaks it," I said. Papa could not be persuaded. Later, I'd learn that my high school didn't offer Latin because Latin was a dead language, as I had said. Again, I wanted to take French. Again, Papa said no. "You have to take Spanish, because more people speak it and that's more useful," he said. Eventually I learned that it was easier to want what Papa expected us to do. Yush, through both his easygoing temperament and his natural ability in science and math, was better at meeting these expectations than I was.

PAPA HAD DISCOVERED SOMETHING even more onerous than the summer workbooks: a program run by Johns Hopkins University called the Center for Talented Youth. Admission into the program depended on SAT scores. The studying never ended in middle school, because once I finished my homework, it was time to work on the SAT prep. Once I finished the SAT-prep workbook, it was time to work on the next SAT-prep workbook.

For the next several years, I spent countless weekend and summer hours stuck in front of a computer screen, completing SAT math sets until I received perfect scores on the hardest questions, which Papa often reviewed during dinner. He made me recount the math problems I'd solved and the thought process I'd used. I kept a deck of index cards and a dictionary on my nightstand, and every time I came across a word I did not know in a book, I wrote the word and the definition on the card. I quizzed myself with the cards every night, just before bed. "Quixotic." "Nefarious." "Uxorious." At dinner, I told Papa what words I'd learned and what they meant. When aunties and uncles came over to stay with us, he made me recite words I'd learned, and they'd be very impressed by such a smart, hardworking, and obedient daughter.

At school, I slipped the words I learned into class assignments to commit them to memory. I used the word "satiated" in an essay. When I turned it in, my English teacher called me to her desk. She was an adult version of the girl who had stopped talking to me because of my Payless shoes. "Prachi, do you know what this word means?" Of course I did. What was the chance that I wrote out this exact combination of letters, used it in an essay correctly, but had made it all up? But I froze. I looked down and shook my head and said no, because I thought that's what she wanted me to say.

I could not explain to her that I was using those words to practice my SAT vocab, that I had flash cards on my nightstand at home, which Papa made me memorize. She thought I was being a show-off, but I wasn't. But even if I was, what kind of English teacher gets mad at a kid for trying to learn more words?

Kids in class turned to look at us. I felt their glares.

"From now on, I want you to use Prachi-size words. Not big words like this. Words that you know."

After her warning, I stopped using the word "satiated." Then one day she asked us to describe a character in a short story we'd read. I raised my hand and said, "He sounds like a chauvinist." My teacher stopped the class.

"Where does it say that, Prachi?"

"What?"

"Where does it use that word—'chauvinist.' Where does that word appear?" she said.

I panicked. My mind went blank, just as it did when Papa yelled at me. I had done something wrong, but I didn't understand what. Everyone watched as I flipped through the book and tried to find a passage that supported my use of "chauvinist." The words blurred together. I couldn't focus. She stared at me, repeating herself. "We'll wait. Show me where you found that word," she said disapprovingly. The class fell silent. I fumbled through the book for what felt like ten minutes.

"Have you found it yet?"

I heard kids whispering and giggling. I didn't want the whole class to see me cry, so I focused my energy on not crying. After an agonizing several minutes, I said meekly, "I can't find it." The character was a chauvinist, I was sure of it. He had a macho, negative attitude toward women. But I didn't know how to speak up in the face of an adult's disapproval.

"That's because it's not there. I told you this already—don't use big words like that. Don't use words that you don't know."

When class ended, a popular boy knocked my binder out of my hands in the hallway. "Stop showing off," he said. "Use normal words, freak." He hovered above me as I bent down to pick up my books. A pretty girl looked at me with pity and convinced him to walk away, like I wasn't worth his time. After they left, another girl told me she knew that word and that I was right about the character in the story. I was angry at her, too. Why didn't she defend me in class? What good did that knowledge do me now?

The bullying at school increased after that. The boy who had sneered at me in the hallway now mocked me almost every day. This encouraged other kids to pick on me, too. Bigger kids carried me down the stairs, and I'd have to run to make it to the bus. More than once I tripped, with my books flying everywhere.

After the year ended, I told Papa what had happened at school. He was angry on my behalf. If he had known how my teacher had treated me, he would have spoken to her about it, he said. I tried to imagine Papa cornering her and blowing up like he did with you. But strangely, I couldn't. Instead, I pictured him talking to her softly, asserting himself with the gentility of a distinguished suit, his advanced degrees, and his wallet. I relished the image.

The bullying at school didn't cause me to question Papa. The traits that made us stick out now would eventually make us successful, Papa promised. "Nerds will rule the world one day," he always said. He was proof of that. The kids at school didn't understand that Yush and I were destined for greatness, and Papa was shepherding us toward it.

As I STROVE TO meet Papa's expectations, the joy I had once taken from my hobbies faded. Reading, writing, and even painting started to feel rote and mechanical. The fact that things I loved could seem tedious scared me. I read books to extract facts and words, guzzling them like Papa's nutrient-rich Ensure. I doubt that you or Papa noticed my creativity clamping shut, because I barely noticed. I continued to paint and draw—only now I did it to impress the hypothetical white Harvard admissions officers of Papa's imagination.

In high school, I decided to apply to the prestigious Pennsylvania Governor's School for the Arts. The Pennsylvania's Governor's Schools of Excellence were a series of highly selective state-run pre-college scholarship programs offered in multiple disciplines. The art school, once attended by Tina Fey and Kevin Bacon, accepted artists, writers, musicians, actors, and dancers from across the state to study under college professors for several weeks during the summer. Admission into the art program was based largely on one's portfolio, and only a few dozen visual artists were selected each year. Papa wouldn't send me to any sort of sleepaway camp—even the Johns Hopkins summer program, which I had completed online. But I thought he might overcome that anxiety for something as impressive as Governor's School.

During my freshman year of high school, I set up a still life on the kitchen island, and many days after school, I painted for hours. Over the next three years, I painted a self-portrait of me preparing for a kathak performance; I set up candles and diyas and captured the dancing lights reflecting off the granite countertop; I painted a vase of roses from the cover of a *Good Housekeeping* magazine. By now, however, I aimed to reproduce the scene in front of me rather than tap into my imagination.

Papa nurtured my hobby. He agreed to let me attend local college-level art classes in the summer of my sophomore year, where I learned figure drawing. He hung my artwork around the house and even told me that I could paint the basement walls with a mural, if I wanted.

In my junior year, I got into Governor's School. Papa was proud of me. He agreed to let me go, and he even surprised me with a Canon digital camera as a gift before my send-off.

The welcome packet said we could select what we wanted to study over the summer: ceramics, painting, or computer art. I of course planned to study painting. But when Papa saw the list, he told me I had to study computer art. Computer art, Papa said, would position me better for a job as a graphic designer or medical illustrator—something that made real money, something he could respect because it used technology and science.

I was crushed. My excitement over the program turned into resentment. What was mine was not truly mine.

Papa's hot-and-cold support for my art confused me. It wasn't until I saw this dynamic unfold with you that I understood it, Mummy. As Yush and I grew up, you had more time to explore your interests. You took up swimming at a local recreation center, and you and I bonded over new fiction you'd read, like *The Namesake*. But Papa pushed you to "better yourself" by learning more about technology, science, and computers—his interests, not yours. I think you enjoyed some of the extracurricular classes Papa told you to sign up for at the local community college. But Papa got angry if he thought you were not studying hard enough, yet he complained when you had to study instead of cook for him, as he expected you to do. It was as if his support for each of our hobbies extended to the point that our skills fulfilled his image of who each of us should be. I wonder now what more you would have chosen to explore of your own volition. And I wonder what else you and I could have shared with each other through that exploration.

ONE DAY, AT THE end of high school, I decided to confirm what I had long suspected about Papa's feelings toward art. I asked Papa directly: "Do you think art is inferior to science?"

He paused for a moment and then said, "Yes."

"Why?" I asked.

"Tell me, what purpose does it serve?"

I didn't know what to say. I couldn't think of a purpose. Creating art made me feel good and I liked it, but I couldn't quantify, intellectualize, or defend why.

Even though Yush's mind worked more like Papa's, this was something that I didn't have to explain to him. "Your intelligence is different from Papa's and mine," Yush told me once when I felt bad for not being smart in the way Papa wanted me to be. "But don't devalue it just because it is less conventional. It also is one of your greatest assets." Yush made me feel like my art mattered.

If I could answer Papa's question today, I would say this: Art kept my spirit alive. Expressing myself, whether by drawing, writing, or dancing, was an assertion of my existence that enabled me to connect to something deeper than simply what I was expected to produce in the world. Later, when I felt too blocked to create, consuming art broke my sense of isolation and helped me see parts of myself in work created by others. When I forgot who I was, creating art helped me find my way back. Art was my entry point to learning how to love myself. Now I feel sad that Papa might not know what it means to connect with oneself or with someone else in this way.

Chapter 6

Suburban Camouflage

At the end of seventh grade, we moved from the apartment to a five-bedroom house an hour's drive north of Philly. After a decade of training, Papa joined a medical practice. The event was so momentous that, in the year leading up to it, Papa took Yush and me out of school early a few times to observe progress on the construction of our future home. The three of us followed Papa as he walked through the plot of land and visualized the rooms that appeared as a zig-zag of wooden beams: an expansive foyer, a large wooden deck, and a kitchen with granite countertops and floor-to-ceiling cabinets. Papa let me choose the pale-blue shutters and rosy-pink brick, small flourishes that offered the illusion of choice while ensuring conformity as one of the only brown families in a development of neocolonial homes. We had achieved the immigrant dream of suburban camouflage. After we settled into a new home that looked like success, I gushed to Papa, "When I grow up, I'm going to marry someone just like you."

One day, Dadiji and Dadaji would move into the home of their firstborn son. When Dadaji visited that first year, he sat on the deck and cried, thinking of how he had cheated a destiny of servitude in

Haldaur to get to where he was now: a grand house in the American suburbs. I had never seen Dadaji cry. I approached him and said, "You had nothing and built a life for yourself that gave your children even more opportunity. I was born with everything, so I would have to do something that exceeds what I think is imaginable in order to continue what you built."

"Yes," he said, "that is true. But even thinking this way, you have made me proud."

We expanded into wealth as if we'd always had it. I could have bought a dozen pairs of Doc Martens now. You and I went on shopping sprees, and Papa never imposed any limit on how much we spent. Over the next several years, Papa bought a big-screen TV and cable with all the channels and a dozen computers and four cars and a fourteen-foot projection screen for a home movie theater and a professional-grade photo printer and several professional cameras. In the first floor guest bedroom, Papa would later hang a black-and-white pencil portrait of himself drawn by one of his patients. She had contacted the local newspaper, and they wrote a story on Papa's surgical talent. In it, she swooned that she had seen many doctors over her life, but Papa was "just an extremely special person."

Papa enrolled Yush and me in a private school where we met South Asian kids like us, and our academic success no longer made us targets for mockery. In that first year, we thrived: Yush's new best friend threw him a large surprise birthday party that the entire grade attended. By the end of eighth grade, I settled in with a group of friends, won an award for my art, and earned a rare prize in social studies.

We hosted family reunions, too. At Christmas, all the cousins lined up foam mattresses in a row and we played under one roof for a week. One winter, Papa even rented a large tour bus and bought Broadway tickets to *Bombay Dreams,* taking all of us on an unforgettable day trip to New York City. When relatives like Ambika Aunty visited with their little kids, they encouraged the children to follow Yush and me around, hoping that our family's exceptionalism would bless them, as well.

———

ALL OF THIS PERFECTION came at a hidden cost. At home, you were the one who paid the price. Every morning you woke up early to boil fresh chai, make us breakfast, and lay out Papa's work clothes. You diligently matched Papa's tie and shirt with the right suit. This was a fraught process, because if you chose something he didn't feel like wearing that day or a color that didn't match to his liking, Papa yelled at you, ordered you to come back upstairs, and forced you to choose another outfit for him until you got it right. This risked burning the tea on the stove or making him late, and then he might blame you for that, too. Meanwhile, he was nearly an hour late to work every morning, anyway, because he sat at the computer in his surgical scrubs, programming some side project for hours while you prepared everything for him.

At least once a month, Papa stomped around the house and demanded that you cut his nails, even if you were on the verge of sleep. This took at least thirty minutes, as you moved through the tools in a gray manicurist's kit to cut, file, and polish every nail. I never saw Papa cut his own nails. I never heard him offer to cut your nails.

The consequence for speaking up, saying no, or falling behind was Papa's rage. His screaming and insults were so commonplace that I can't remember many incidents with any specificity—what he said, what triggered him, or how exactly you responded. My memories highlight the anger and likely downplay the periods of kindness that followed, probably because none of us addressed the tumult, and therefore the bad moments left a stronger imprint on my mind than the good ones did. I was always on guard for the next rupture of peace, this thing I knew was coming but could never predict or prevent.

I do remember the aftermath of one instance clearly: After Papa berated you in front of Yush and me, you started hitting yourself, punching yourself in the head and yelling that you were stupid and worthless and wrong and that he was always right and so much

smarter than you. Then you fell to the floor and begged for his forgiveness. "Maaf kijiye! Maaf kijiye!" you cried, touching his feet in
frantic motions.

I had never seen you turn violent toward yourself before, and it
scared me. I watched in disgusted silence. Papa said nothing. He
looked down at you and then grunted and walked away. It was easy to
hate him. But in that moment I hated you a little, too, for what I saw
as taking it.

In my mind, when one adult yelled, the other was supposed to yell
back. There was a primal, animalistic equality to sparring. But in our
house, watching you and Papa fight was like watching a war plane
bomb a village. And maybe that's why, rather than being mad at him,
for a long time I was mad at you. I wanted you to rise up against him,
hoping that if you did, the violence would feel less brutally unfair.

In high school, I began talking back to you or standing far away
from you when you dropped me off at the mall, pretending not to
know you in public. I feel ashamed of my behavior now, Mummy, and
I am so sorry for how deeply this must have hurt you. Papa didn't yell
at me, but he said I had to stop behaving like such a "typical American bimbo" acting out at her mom. He had no awareness that I was
imitating the very behavior that he modeled at home. But my treatment of you wasn't simply mimicry, either. It was a clumsy expression
of anger over how mother was raising daughter to learn that to be
good is to betray oneself, to forever contort oneself to fit into impossible, contradictory expectations of womanhood that felt stifling. On
one hand, Papa wanted me to be high-achieving, attending an Ivy
League school and then running a company as a CEO, an extension
of his own greatness. But on the other, I was to serve him, as he expected of you.

One day, while I was at home during a break from college, Papa
came out of his computer room and asked me where the batteries
were kept. I stopped at the top of the stairs and said I didn't know.

"You should be like Mom," he said. "Mom knows where everything in the house is. Why don't you?"

"Mummy moves stuff around, and I'm not even here that often," I said to him. "You live here. You could learn where they are, too."

Suddenly, Papa snarled and marched toward me. For a moment I thought he might push me down the stairs. A part of me wanted him to do it. Maybe then everyone would believe me about the anger I saw at home. I froze. Papa stopped inches in front of me, huffing. Yush came out into the hallway as a referee, inserting himself in the space between us. He convinced Papa to walk away.

YOU WERE NOT, BY nature, quiet, meek, or resigned. You chased mice and roaches in our apartments with the ferocity of an eighteen-wheeler careening down the highway, thwacking them with your chappal without mercy or hesitation. You managed the home, handled the accounting, and organized our trips like a business executive. Papa could walk into a room and know how to fit in. But you could walk into a room and endear people with your genuine ability to listen and respond.

You disarmed others with your playfulness. When we went to Nova Scotia in seventh grade, you exclaimed excitedly, "I want to see a moose! I'm going to see one!" Every time we went on a hike, or even just walked down a regular city street, you announced this, sticking to the bit, getting more and more serious about searching for the elusive, grand moose, because you knew we'd laugh at your insistence. I wonder sometimes if this is why Papa made such a fuss of your "communication skills"—because, despite the cultural barriers you faced, you had an ease with people that eluded him, and this must have led him to feel insecure.

Every so often, Papa compared you to Buaji, stoking your insecurities by saying that she ran the household *and* was a doctor. *She does it all. Why can't you?* I picked up Papa's attitude: On a visit to Buaji's when I was nine, she had set up pumpkins for us to carve. I saw that this custom was unfamiliar to you, but Buaji knew everything about Halloween. You began to help me with my pumpkin, and I said, "No,

I want Buaji to do it." My words wounded you, and you told me later, "Prachi, you really hurt my feelings. I don't like how you spoke to me." I was surprised by your words. When Papa yelled at me, I felt the need to throw up a wall against the onslaught. But when you told me that I had hurt you in such plain language, I felt awful, baring myself to the monsoon of your pain. I wanted to take it back, and I hoped to never make you feel that way again.

As Yush and I became adults, you lamented that you'd taught us nothing. You parroted Papa's words about yourself and believed them. You thought that because your education level or technical skills didn't match his, you were somehow unintelligent or had nothing of value to offer your children. I could never convince you that what you offered Yush and me was so much more essential, not just to our survival but to our humanity. Your consistent, stable love grounded and protected us, particularly as children, acting as a shock absorber against Papa's volatility. Your kindness gave us small pockets of time within which we could learn that we were more than what we produced. I am scared to think about who I would have become without that. What I mean to say is, Mummy, you taught us the most valuable thing of all: how to love and how to allow love in. You taught me that kindness in the world exists, and when I started to lose faith in that, memories of your love reminded me that there are people who are pure of heart. You are one of them.

Chapter 7

Rise, Spirit

Like countless South Asian teens around the world, my first major celebrity crush was Hrithik Roshan, the brawny Bollywood star whose film debut was in *Kaho Naa Pyaar Hai*. Hrithik's biceps outlined the topography of the Himalayas and his dreamy dance moves captivated me. One of my second cousins and I watched the iconic sequence from "Ek Pal Ka Jeena," on loop, in which Hrithik zig-zags his arms back and forth and thrusts his hips forward in rhythmic motions as rain inexplicably pours inside a nightclub called Club Indiana. Hrithik looked absurd, wearing a black mesh top, a bandanna, and tinted glasses indoors, but it didn't matter. We adored him. The two of us stood in front of the big-screen TV in the living room, writhing and wriggling in unison. We pulled Yush into our shenanigans, forcing him to learn the dance with us.

When my cousin left, I continued to practice Hrithik's dance in the living room. I had never decorated my room with anything other than my artwork or prints of Rousseau's jungle paintings, but now I thought about buying a Hrithik poster, like teen girls did in the movies.

I mentioned Hrithik at the dinner table one night. I'm not sure what I said or how he came up. Maybe I was talking about the dance that my cousin and I had practiced. But as soon as his name came out of my mouth, Papa screamed, "You're obsessed! You're acting like an airhead! Enough!" He slammed his palm on the table, in front of you and Yush.

Shame overtook me. I stopped playing the song. I stopped talking about Hrithik. I never dared express any hint of desire over a boy in front of Papa again.

I was too shy to talk to boys. But as I approached high school, Papa's radar went into overdrive. Any social situation involving boys outside an academic setting was now evaluated through the lens of sexual threat. In seventh grade, when my school put on a dance, Papa had refused to let me go. "Who's going to be there?" he had asked. He didn't like the idea of his little girl being around so many boys, where anything could happen.

After Papa said no, I went to my bedroom and fumed. Then I heard you talk to him. It was strange to me that Papa, who had been raised here, restricted me and that you, who had no familiarity with Western dating norms, stood up for me. It was one of the rare times you asked him to reconsider a decision, and it was one of the rare times that he listened to you. I wish I knew what you said to him, Mummy, because Papa never barred me from attending a school dance again.

Papa's messaging implied that if a boy liked me, it was not because he saw my worth but because he wanted to use me for sex. I learned that it was my job, as a good girl, to not let a boy near me. And if I did want to flirt with a boy, or hold hands with him, or kiss him, then I was a deviant opening herself up to a boy's animalistic whims and base urges at her own peril. I was choosing to be used and discarded.

Papa wanted me to remain invisible. But from what I could tell, dating relied upon being seen, noticed, and chosen. America, too, sat high up on a stage, forcing the rest of the world to behold its spectacle. Being seen—well, that was about the most American thing I could think of.

Unfortunately, I was seen as little more than the mule who carried my classmates to an A-plus on team projects. I didn't know how to get people to view me as more than that. At school, Sunil, an Indian American boy, told me that on a scale from one to ten I was a "zero, because Indian girls aren't hot." I wondered: *If even the boys who look like me don't want me, who will?*

One day, as I waited for my bus to arrive, another boy looked me up and down and declared, "Wow, you're so hairy. I bet you have hair all over your body!"

"Ew, no I don't!" I said.

"Yeah right!" he said. Then he grabbed me. This encouraged another boy to pin me down. The first boy pulled my shirt halfway up my back while the other boys gawked and howled at my body. I was giddy that a boy was touching me, humiliated by his intentions, and powerless against his force. My confusion came out as frenzied, pressured laughter, like I was in on the joke. I pointed and laughed at my own body, too, separating myself from my flesh as if it were an oddity on display at a carnival.

I hated that my frizzy, curly black hair, my thick, connected eyebrows, and my brown "chicken legs," as Papa had once called them, announced who I was even before I had a chance to speak. I hated even more that, in my case, the projections seemed to accurately describe me.

When I heard that one Indian American boy at school liked me, I came to loathe him more than I did Sunil, because he reminded me of my own ugliness. When he ate pizza, he brought it up slowly to his face, and his thick, gelled hair shook like pine needles in the wind. On pizza day, I exaggerated his choppy motions, tensing up my neck and face as one robotic unit, slowly opening my mouth, and then shaking my head wildly as I stuffed in the slice. People at the table laughed at my mean imitation. Sunil had let everyone know that he was more desirable than me, and I wanted to send a message that I was more desirable than that boy.

None of us were defined by our physicality or our ethnicity, of course, but I couldn't see at the time that I was lost within narratives created for me by others. Instead, I played into them, no better or different than boys like Sunil. We appeared to one another as avatars of our own racial and cultural anxiety.

MY NEW HIGH SCHOOL had a rule, one that felt designed specifically to embarrass me: Every freshman had to play a sport. In Pittsburgh, Yush and I had played tennis for four summers straight. I struggled so much that, every year, I told kids I'd never played tennis before. They would encourage me by saying, "Oh, you'll get better!" but I knew I wouldn't. To fail at sports, as I did, was another reminder that I could be nothing more than a nerd. I didn't have the coordination for tennis, field hockey, or softball, so I signed up for the last option: cross-country. I could not even run a mile.

The first practice was brutal. We ran up and down hills, sprinting up one, then jogging to a steeper one, then sprinting up that, running back down, and repeating this a dozen or so times, in the peak of summer heat. By the end of practice, I felt as if I'd been pummeled by a meat tenderizer. I went home and crawled straight into bed without showering, caked in fine white salt and moaning in pain. I planned to leave behind this horrid sport as soon as the season ended.

Yush knelt down next to me. "Prachi, are you okay?" He had never seen me so immobilized.

"No," I groaned. "I'm going to die."

My soreness disappeared after a few days, but on the second week of running daily, I suddenly dragged lumber. My legs felt sluggish and slow, with a persistent dull ache, even though the rest of my body felt fine. My coach seemed unconcerned. "You have lactic-acid buildup," she said matter-of-factly. "Take a few days off and drink a lot of water." I followed her advice, unconvinced that anything would improve. My mind was built for school, and my twiggy brown body was simply unequipped to handle strenuous physical activity.

To my amazement, I came back to practice with springs for legs. Over the season, my 5K time dropped to twenty-seven minutes, then

twenty-five, then twenty-four, then twenty-three, then twenty-two.
After races, I taped my bibs next to my bedroom mirror, and by the
end of the season, I found my name printed in the local newspaper's
sports section, which listed the top-twenty finishers of the race. You
took me to a running store to buy lighter sneakers, and the next week
we went back to buy a pair of white-and-pink Reebok racing spikes.
They smelled like old rubber, and part of the glue had crusted over
the white upper. But when I put on these shoes with cold metal that
pierced the earth, I shot off like an arrow in the sky. The man who
sold the shoes to us told me his daughter had times similar to mine as
a freshman, and she ran competitively in college. Suddenly, I dreamed
of running for a college team.

I was a foot shorter than everyone else, so slight that a gust of
wind could rock me. But when I ran, a giant, slumbering spirit
within me came alive, jumping, clawing, screaming, raging forth,
fueling my legs, girding my abs, and pumping my arms to propel me
with a ferocity that I did not know I possessed. My spirit could fly
past boys three times bigger than me, leaving them suffocating in
the smoke of her blazing orange flames. No one could harness her
power but me. Her power could not be taught or indoctrinated or
memorized or copied or appropriated. She was mine, and mine
alone. When I ran, my spirit demanded that others witness me. As I
began to love my body, I understood myself beyond my capacity for
academic performance. I saw that I was so much more than what
others perceived me to be.

MY NEWFOUND LOVE OF running posed a problem for Papa. Running put me out of his sight; he could not control my whereabouts or
trust that someone was monitoring his little girl. After I was out with
a teammate for two hours on a weekend morning, Papa called me up
to his computer room. I stood before him, sweaty and dehydrated.
You stood beside me.

"Why were you gone so long?"

"We ran fourteen miles."

Papa didn't believe me.

"Where did you go?"

"Down to the creek," I said. "We rested for a few minutes and then came back."

"Is that really fourteen miles?" he asked, looking at you.

You nodded.

I could see Papa wrestling with his anger, two parts of himself conflicting: a desire to keep me safe and a desire to allow me to engage in this new constructive hobby I loved. "From now on you're going to carry a phone with you," he said. "You could get raped. It's not safe."

With his one comment, my pride at having run so far turned to shame. The threat of what could happen to my female body overshadowed what I had actually achieved with my body. Papa bought me a soap bar–size Nokia cellphone to carry when on my own, for the express purpose of calling him should I be raped while running.

On another morning, Papa yelled at me when he saw my pink shorts rolled up once, hanging at my upper-middle thigh.

"Unroll your shorts," Papa said.

"What's wrong with my shorts?" I asked.

"Do you know what sexual harassment is?" he said. Before I could respond: "It's when a woman does something to make a man uncomfortable." I rolled my eyes, fairly certain that wasn't what sexual harassment was. I also felt disturbed by the implication. Was my dad telling me I was sexually harassing him?

Papa told me that I only loved running because I loved when boys looked at me running. He said that I ran for male attention. "If you really loved running," he said, "you would run at home on the treadmill instead of running outside."

Insidious doubt crept in; the powerful spirit within me recoiled in fear and shame. When I ran, I felt at peace. But I felt confused that, according to Papa, I wasn't behaving like myself at all.

Papa threatened to pull me off the team unless I began running on the treadmill in our unfinished concrete basement. I tried a few times, but I hated it. I thought that Papa was right—if I really loved running, I should be able to will myself to run on the treadmill every day.

By the end of freshman year, I had qualified to run in the district-level race that fed into the state championship. The night before the race, Papa let me in on a secret: If I ate a candy bar just before I took off, the sugar would give me a surge of energy and make me faster. We didn't have any chocolate bars, so the next morning I grabbed a Quaker Oats chocolate chip granola bar from the kitchen pantry and stuffed it in my duffel bag. Five minutes before the race, I shoveled the gooey, sticky bar into my mouth, savoring the sweet chocolate and sugared nuts that were about to pump my legs with power.

I ran the first mile among the front of the pack, clocking in somewhere in the low six minutes. Papa's secret weapon was working. Then, as I ran past cornfields and into a clearing in the woods at the start of the second mile, I felt a stabbing pain in my lower abdomen. My breathing strained. I wheezed, gasping for air, honking like a goose. I clenched my stomach with my hands and slowed to a trot. With every step, I felt as if an iron fist was punching me in my gut. Dozens of runners passed me. Several asked me if I was okay.

When I crossed the finish line, somewhere at the back of the finishers, I collapsed. I ignored my concerned teammates and walked off into the field, where I cried alone. I had ended such an exhilarating debut season no better than where I had started. I was furious with Papa but just as mad at myself for listening to him. I didn't tell Papa that I had taken his advice, and I didn't tell him that his advice had caused me to fail. Unable to motivate myself to run on the treadmill and ashamed by my poor performance, I barely ran for the rest of the year.

The next year of high school, I joined the team again. I began slowly, starting over, but by the end of the season my pace picked up. Mid-season, a few days after a race in which I had been among the top-ten finishers, Papa yelled at me for more than an hour. There would be so many instances like this in the following years that I can't recall the full details of any specific tirade. But in my journal I wrote about what must have been the first—over getting a B at school.

Papa threatened to ground me, pull me off the team, and take me out of my new school if I didn't shape up. He called me weak and told me I was a failure as I cried, afraid to talk back or defend myself, because I knew it would invite more anger and punishment. He said that from now on I had to be "monk-like," with no Internet, no phone, no friends. He didn't like the new friends I was making—particularly, I think, boys on my team. You both seemed terrified about some vague, abstract fear of drugs and rape—not sex, because as a teenage girl, I was not seen as having the right to choose what to do with my body. Despite your fears, I'd never so much as smoked a cigarette or even held hands with a boy.

Papa's anger was not new, but this was the first time that I did not see any part of his rage toward me as justifiable. And it was the first time that I recall you piling on, berating me the way that he did. Your words hurt far more than what Papa said. After he was done yelling at me, you yelled for another hour. You said hurtful things, things that sounded like what Papa would say. I knew that you didn't mean any of it, but I didn't understand where your anger came from. From you, hateful words sounded clunky and unnatural. It was as if you needed a place to express your anger, and this was the only forum available. I think Papa's words to me gave you a template for your rage. As women who could not express our true feelings safely—our anger and sadness and disappointment, in particular—you and I began to take it out on each other instead.

I wondered if there was something else behind your anger. You had told me once that as a girl you won a local race. The power in my body came from you. For a brief moment, I wondered what you had seen about yourself through running. I wanted to know: Where did your spirit roam now?

———

A FEW WEEKS LATER, after I brought home a few Bs on my next report card, Papa made good on at least one of his threats. Though I
had nearly qualified for state championships, missing entry by just
one spot, Papa pulled me off the team.

My guidance counselor and coach called home. They pleaded with
Papa to reconsider. "Prachi could get an athletic scholarship to college," they said.

The phone call only further angered Papa. "They should be telling
me my daughter can get an academic scholarship, not an athletic
scholarship," he fumed. Papa had made up his mind. Nothing would
change it now.

Just like that, my promising high school athletic career came to an
end.

After I gave up cross-country, my spirit went into hiding, subdued
by shame. I soon forgot about what my body enabled me to do and
how good I could feel in it and again fretted over how much my ugly,
hairy, pockmarked brown face and limbs offended others. My anxiety
became so overwhelming that, even when you took me to Subway, I
hid behind you and asked you to order my sandwich, terrified that the
person working behind the counter would judge me for my mon-
strous, disgusting order of banana peppers, jalapeños, and pickles. I
believed that my ugliness repulsed nearly everyone who was forced to
look at me, and they were just too polite to tell me so.

I thought I had been weak in high school, so as a freshman in college I toughened up. I pushed myself to run 5Ks at my race pace on
a bulky steel treadmill at the gym, blasting Rage Against the Machine
in my headphones while ignoring the TV blaring Fox News in front
of me. After a few weeks I felt a dull ache in my shins. I ignored it and
continued to run on the treadmill, until one day I could not walk
without piercing pain shooting up my legs. A sports-medicine doctor
showed me my X-rays, pointing out multiple hairline stress fractures
in my shins.

Running with such intensity was a recipe for injury, and the treadmill didn't help. "You shouldn't be running those speeds regularly on

a treadmill," he told me. "You should be running outside, preferably on dirt paths."

I was so dedicated to proving that my love for running was real that I didn't realize Papa's threats had never actually been about running. Now I wonder if Papa sensed the confidence running gave me, and whether that scared him. Now I believe that experiencing this raw power from within my own body—just the whiff of it—pushed me to assert my will over the coming years, even when I was told it was wrong.

Chapter 8

Good Girls Don't Have Bodies

ONE DAY, A GIRL named Swapna asked if I wanted to join a dance she had choreographed to a song from the movie *Devdas*. She was a grade above mine, so we didn't know each other well. She needed one more person for a performance at the local Hindu temple, she said. I missed performing Bollywood dances and I wanted desi friends. I knew that you and Papa would approve. I said yes.

Swapna was the unlikely combination of smart, kind, and mellow. Her calmness drew me in. At dance practice, I met her friend Adya, a tall, light-skinned Gujarati girl who went to a neighboring private school. She was Swapna's foil, the bubbliest person I'd ever met, bursting into laughter over the smallest comments. The three of us had an instant chemistry.

Dance practices spilled into hangouts, which rotated among our three homes. At school, Yush befriended Swapna's younger brother, and we absorbed the boys into our group seamlessly. We told one another jokes and stories, mostly, like about the time an uncle gravely cautioned the boys to drink water during a garba, as if the festive folk dance were a marathon: "It's nonstop dandiya! Stay hydrated!"

We laughed, but then Yush couldn't stop laughing. He laughed so hard at the thought of intensely hydrating for dandiya that he fell onto the floor. Then I started laughing harder, until I, too, was on the floor. This is what our time together was like. You asked fewer questions about what I was doing or where I was going when I was with Swapna and Adya, which was good for me, because their parents were far less strict than Papa.

Most Indian kids I knew felt pressured to pursue engineering, medicine, or law, and most Indian kids I knew planned to carry out their parents' wishes. But Adya wanted to become a fashion designer. Swapna wanted to become a novelist. Their parents supported their ambitions. At a time when virtually no South Asian artists, entertainers, or writers existed in mainstream American culture, finding Swapna and Adya made me feel like less of a misfit. Watching them chase their dreams made me believe that maybe I could one day pursue mine, too.

In my senior year, Adya laid my head on an ironing board and ran a clothing iron over it. I struggled to keep my head still as I heard a loud sizzle and felt the steaming-hot metal next to my ear. She insisted this would make my hair pin-straight and shiny: white-girl hair. I put on heavy black eyeliner and mascara, exaggerating my big brown eyes—my best feature, inherited from you. Adya draped me in one of your black georgette saris. We were going to the temple for some event called Parents Appreciation Day, but that was just the excuse for something else: meeting Drew.

Drew, who was now in college, had been one of Adya's good friends in high school. I had met him at a house party the year before, and he'd mentioned to Adya that he thought I was cute. He was tall and blond, with a body cut like the side of a cliff. Boy-band hot. Unlike the other hot boys, however, Drew was nice. And he didn't know that I wasn't cool, because he had attended a different high school. I had been bugging Adya to set us up, and now, tonight, it was happening—well, sort of.

We stopped at a Dunkin' Donuts, and Drew dropped by to meet us. Within a few minutes, Drew told me I was very pretty and then Adya gave me a look of excitement, and I blushed, but thankfully my brown skin did not reveal how flattered I felt. Adya blurted out, "You know, Prachi doesn't have a date to prom," and I shot her a look that said, *Stop embarrassing me!* but also *Thank you, I love you,* and Drew said, "Oh, really? Well, I would like to go with you," and that was it. Suddenly I had a date to senior prom.

I had tricked Drew into thinking I was pretty, but I knew that beneath the makeup and clothes, I was ugly. For the past two years I had been studying "hotness"—the ability to blend into whiteness. I bought makeup, hair products, and other tools to mute my loud ethnic traits. I wrangled my wild curls into barnyard straw with a flat iron, tacked on a heaving bust with silicone-padded bras, and tweezed my lush forest of brows down to twigs. At night when I was supposed to be studying, I started accounts on Match.com and RateDesi.com, a HotOrNot for South Asians. I A/B-tested my assimilated appearance and flirty new personas with adult men. After months of positive feedback, I knew that my efforts were working. I felt brave enough to face Drew.

Maneuvering dates with Drew was difficult because I was not allowed to date. I would tell you I was going to Adya's, and then I'd go to Drew's house. On our first date, he drove us to Red Robin. We shared a sundae and went to the movie theater to watch *Taking Lives* with Angelina Jolie. I felt insecure because I was ugly and Angelina Jolie was one of the most gorgeous women on the planet. I was sure that during the movie Drew would come to his senses and realize that he could have been out on a date with someone who looked like her.

When Drew picked me up for prom a few months later, I expected Papa to interrogate him. But Papa barely interacted with him. Later, though, he asked you, "Why would *he* want to go out with Prachi?"

I think you passed on statements like that as a way to tell me I was always being observed. "Log kya kahenge?"—*what will people say?*—turned into "Log yeh keh rahe hain." *This is what people* are *saying.* When Yush and I took tae kwon do lessons as children, I "kiya-ed" with my whole body, screaming louder and for longer than Yush or any of the boys. After class one day, you mentioned that the moms at the studio had gawked at my loudness. You didn't tell me to temper my voice, but in relaying this to me, you said that my noise embarrassed you. I never kiya-ed that way again. This was usually how we conveyed feelings, too, rarely speaking about them directly and instead telling each other what someone else had said about us, monitoring our emotions and actions based on how we imagined that others perceived us.

I understood why you told me Papa's thoughts about Drew, and I understood why Papa said it. Papa knew what it meant to grow up here. He could have shown Yush and me how to love ourselves in the face of whiteness. But he could not teach us what he did not know himself.

In the bathroom at prom, one of the popular white girls asked me, "Is he your boyfriend?" and I said, "Yeah," even though I wasn't sure of our status. I could tell that I now held an esteem in her eyes that I had not before, like she was reevaluating everything she thought about me.

I learned that when I was seen as the object of desire of a tall white man, suddenly, I mattered. I became visible. People who had overlooked me—including my own father—now noticed me. Soon I relied on the boost I received when such a man wanted me, even if he could not fully understand me, even if when he saw me, he saw conquest or submission or exoticism or domesticity. For a long time that didn't matter to me, because I was using him to perpetuate a fantasy, too. But as one such white man in college told me bluntly: "You're pretty for an Indian girl—but Indian girls can only be nine-tenths as hot as a white girl." Despite my best efforts to fit in, I could never fully belong. Instead, every time I submitted to the fantasy, I strengthened the power of my insecurities. Every time I submitted to the fantasy, I deepened my belief that I had to hide my true self in order to be desirable.

That summer, Drew invited me to his family's beach house. I imagined holding on to his strong torso as waves crashed against us in the ocean or him rubbing sunblock on my back, but I was too embarrassed to tell him that you and Papa would never allow such a thing. You did not even know we were dating. I stopped calling him back. I reasoned that a guy who looked like him probably didn't really like me, anyway.

The truth is, I had no idea if Drew could have appreciated me for who I really was. I never gave him the chance. I couldn't accept myself, so how could I let Drew?

WHEN I FIRST MET Swapna and Adya, I thought of them as the two cool, older girls with driver's licenses who would take me out clubbing. Instead of the club, we frequented Wegmans, the grocery-store chain that doubled as our hangout spot because we couldn't yet go to bars and the mall felt too cliché. We roamed the aisles at night; Adya picked up cans of chickpeas and yelled, "Eat chole!" chasing me while Swapna laughed at us. With Adya and Swapna, I felt like nothing bad could happen.

I had planned to take my first sips of alcohol in Swapna's basement, where she and Adya could take care of me if I got too drunk. I know this sounds bad to you, Mummy, but when I look back on that decision, I see caution. That night, the rain struck the pavement like an army of arrows. We stopped by Wegmans first, where we ran into a friend I'll call Arthur, who sometimes waited at the bus stop with Yush and me. At the grocery store, next to cartons of milk and orange juice, Arthur looked childlike and innocent and less like the hulking bully he could be at school. I thought that being smart was the same as being good, and though Arthur could be cruel, he was well read. Even his cruelty hinted at some secret knowledge about the world that I didn't possess. Embracing the spontaneity of the moment, we invited him over. He rode back to Swapna's with us and later asked if he could stay over, saying his mom would pick him up in the morning.

Arthur mixed the drinks. I chugged the noxious mixture of brandy and Coke as if I'd never tasted anything more delicious. I marveled at how my mind felt weightless and unrestricted. My body felt loose, like

I was in a pool of warm water. That magical elixir subdued the incessant thoughts of how deeply my hairy, twiggy brown body and face must repulse everyone.

I didn't know when to stop drinking. Soon I wobbled and hammed up my dizziness and said, "Oh my God, I'm soooo drunk!" Arthur looked at me with disgust, and I felt embarrassed. We set up pillows and blankets in a row on the floor, the same way that I did when our cousins visited during family reunions. Arthur was to my right and Swapna and Adya to my left. By now the room had started to spin. As we went to sleep, I blacked out.

The memories came to me in the morning, in flashes. After Arthur left, I told Swapna and Adya that I thought something had happened. I had never seen or touched a penis before, but now I had memories of one in my mouth. I somehow knew what semen tasted like. I knew it had happened, but I didn't remember it happening.

You picked me up, and you knew immediately that something wasn't right. The hard, stale stench of alcohol emanated from my skin and my hair. A part of me wanted to tell you. I didn't, because I knew you'd tell Papa. Even now, the thought of Papa's reaction instills fear in my body. Everything he feared would happen had happened.

When I got home, I stayed in bed all day, terrified because I didn't know what a hangover was or how long this feeling would last. Yush kept coming into my room and asking what was wrong, and I told him to go away and leave me alone, that he wouldn't understand. His concern for me only made me feel dirtier. I went into the bathroom, then I fell asleep on the floor, and you came and got me and told me I needed to snap out of it. I said, *Okay, you're right, sorry.* I told you not to worry, that nothing bad happened. I don't think you believed me, but you didn't press me any further.

Using the phone that Papa had bought to protect me from being raped, I texted Arthur. I asked him if what I thought had happened did happen. He said yes. He didn't apologize and I didn't expect him to. I asked him if I was any good. He said no. Too much teeth.

I had been unconscious.

I disgusted myself. I didn't understand how I was so sexually repellent one moment, a sexual object the next.

Though Yush and I talked about almost everything, I hid this incident from him. I had learned that to be a good woman is to be chaste, and he had learned that to be a good man is to protect a woman's chastity. Before I went to college, he bought me pepper spray and told me sternly that I needed to carry it to stay safe. Silently wondering how, exactly, pepper spray would have protected me from Arthur that night, I told Yush I'd carry it if he did. He said he didn't need the spray because he was not a target for sexual violence. While this was statistically true, I didn't know how to tell him why that burden felt unfair. I dropped the tiny canister in a drawer. When Yush noticed later on, he scolded me. "I'm upset that you're not taking this seriously enough," he said. I apologized, putting the pepper spray back in my purse as he watched. When he left my bedroom, I took the pepper spray out and stuffed it in a different drawer—one he wouldn't open.

I imagine that, as a woman, you innately understood what I hid from Yush and Papa, and why. Our womanhood created a bridge between us. Anytime you accompanied Papa to a gala or party, you changed out of your usual khakis and collared shirts to wear an elegant sari. I loved helping you prep. Together we looked through your walk-in closet, each of us pulling out saris we liked. We laid them out on the bed, weighing your options, taking the weather and the event's theme into careful consideration. You and I had the same preferences in food, colors, fashion, and home design, turning us into mirrors of each other.

When we landed on one that we both liked, you began the elaborate process of wrapping yourself. I watched, mesmerized by hands that strummed across the fabric as if you were a harpist. You separated the pleats with ease, while I struggled to pin unwieldy fabric to your bodice without clumping it. We moved to your vanity in the bathroom, where I rummaged through your muted-rose blush palettes and pastel-blue eye shadow, colors that I associated with white women. I tilted your face gently and plucked any stray hairs along your naturally thin brows. Then I steadied my hand to line your pomegranate eyes with kajal and filled in your brows with the same black tint. I stepped back, admiring your beauty, hoping I might look like you one day.

Moments like this form my strongest, most intimate memories with you. I used to believe that was simply because we shared a gender. But now I see a deeper reason: These memories stand out because they are the few in which we were alone, unsupervised by Papa. Free to be ourselves. The rituals of femininity were the only moments between us that Papa did not insert himself into.

I wonder what we would have discussed beyond the outsize influence that directed both of our lives. I can imagine a scenario in which I told you what happened to me that night at Swapna's house. It's possible that you might have blamed me for drinking or become overprotective in response. But these moments suggest that we had the capacity to build our own, separate relationship. The ornamental aspects of womanhood brought us together. Maybe if we could have acknowledged the pain of womanhood, too, we wouldn't have been so burdened by its constraints.

Chapter 9

Dark Space

A FEW TIMES DURING SENIOR year, I invited friends over late at night. I told them to park their cars down the street or get dropped off a few houses away. I ushered them in through the back entrance to the basement, carrying liquor I smuggled down from the china cabinet. You and Papa slept upstairs, clueless that I was drinking and making out with boys two floors beneath you. I feared getting caught, but the risk was part of the thrill.

I think Dadaji noticed that I had been siphoning his scotch and whiskey. He never directly accused me of drinking, but during one of his visits, he said, "Prachi, I am worried about you."

"Why?" I asked him.

"You seem lost," he said.

"I'm fine, Dadaji."

But Dadaji was right. By junior year, I regularly failed tests in almost every subject, including English. I even slacked off in art class. I got a C in precalculus, after which the administration made me retake it. I boosted my grade to a whopping C+. The second go-round, I sat in the back of the room and read *Faust* as my mild-mannered math teacher ignored me ignoring him.

I lived in a beautiful house and attended a swanky private school, with parents deeply invested in my future. I was bestowed with every opportunity that a kid could dream of. Why, then, did I feel so angry?

At home, Papa was a thunderstorm and I was a lightning rod. By the time I was in tenth grade, the same year Papa banned me from cross-country, he erupted over seemingly anything: Getting a B on a test, sometimes even an A-minus. But it wasn't just that. Putting a glass of lukewarm milk back in the fridge. Wearing shirts with sleeves that went past my fingertips. Massaging my temples—or yours—to ease a headache. Not finishing the custard he bought me from a Rita's Italian Ice. All signs of illogical behavior, he screamed. Papa claimed his anger was over my grades, but I felt like this treatment awaited me at home regardless of what I did. One "illogical" move, and I could be grounded for weeks.

I had always loved school. I didn't need a strict parent to push me to excel. But for so long, I had obeyed Papa's rigorous training plan because I believed he was leading me to success. But I was starting to question whether Papa's temper, or his labyrinthine rules, were really about my well-being. I noticed that when I replaced cross country with extracurriculars like tutoring and an entrepreneurial club, Papa didn't threaten to pull me out over my unsteady grades. These new activities supported Papa's image of who I should be. Papa said that I was sabotaging my future, but I felt like he was the one undermining it.

I still wanted to do well at school, but I was too on edge all the time. I couldn't focus. I feared Papa's wrath, though, so I dedicated myself to doctoring my report card. A few times during the school year, I sped home to intercept the mail during my lunch period. I pushed our 1991 Honda Civic hatchback to its absolute limit, praying that its little lawnmower engine wouldn't putter out as I hit ninety miles an hour. I don't remember where you were during the day, Mummy— maybe at one of your classes—but I knew that you weren't home at that hour. I skipped lunch on those days.

While Papa was at work, I created a fake template on Microsoft

Word in his computer room, located conveniently above the garage. I listened for grinding metal as I swiftly issued myself new grades. I never gave myself A's; Papa might suspect something. I carefully opened the manila envelopes, making sure not to rip the edges. I compared my printed copy to Yush's immaculate, straight-A report card, checking the heaviness of the ink on both. I then ran my fake report card through Papa's photocopier until the weight of the ink matched the original. I didn't feel guilty. I felt giddy, using Papa's own expensive contraptions and machinery against him. The next day I'd bring the mail inside after school, open the envelopes before you had a chance to examine the edges, and then hand them to you, pretending they had just arrived. Papa was feeding me a lie, and I felt little remorse feeding one back to him.

When he reviewed my report card, Papa screamed, threatened to send me to public school, and then grounded me for a few weeks. I let Yush in on my secret, and he kept it because he didn't want to witness me "getting my ass kicked by Papa," as he put it. If this is how angry Papa was when I got B's, we both feared what he would do if he saw my actual grades.

I pulled off my charade until the very last report card of the year. You found the original in my purse while I was at a friend's house and handed it over to Papa.

I think I know why you busted me: My defiance hurt you. You had become a casualty in the war between Papa and me. You worked so hard to keep the peace at home. And here I was, poking the bull to get him to charge. My antics made a mockery of all that you had put up with to provide stability. I wonder now if you perceived my behavior as a personal rejection, not just of your efforts as a mother but of my duty within the family. Everyone had a role to play, and everyone continued to play their part, except for me. It is true that I took out my anger in ways that were hurtful. I spat in the face of your sacrifice, and for that, I am sorry.

———

WHEN PAPA FOUND MY real report card, he called me on my cell-phone. I was shaking. *This is it*, I thought. *I will live at home for the rest of my life.*

When I got home, Papa didn't yell. He didn't scream. Instead, he met me with a chilling coldness. This was the paradox of Papa's anger: His temper flared over the smallest things. But now I had done something wrong. I had lied about my performance. I had no intention of telling either of you the truth. I deserved punishment.

Papa didn't raise his voice—not even once. Instead, he lectured me long into the night about how I was ruining my life. At this rate, I was going to be a janitor, Papa said. As Papa spoke, I felt the truth of his words. This time I deserved the words he said, and this time I knew that what he said about me was true. My badness could not be reha-bilitated. Papa had given up on me. I was no longer worthy of his anger, only of his scorn.

Papa cast my rebellion as typical American teen behavior. But, Mummy, real rebels would have laughed at me. I ditched class once—only once—and I had no idea where to go, so I drove to Wegmans, where an aunty saw me. I was so nervous she would tell you that I didn't do it again. When you found a pack of American Spirits in my closet that I had bought to commemorate turning eighteen, you ac-cused me of smoking. I didn't smoke. I did try weed a few times, but I coughed so much that I didn't bother doing it again—I later learned that I have pretty bad asthma.

I resented that whenever I succeeded, Papa credited himself and his Indian values, but when I failed, that failure was uniquely mine, a product of my Americanness. I felt so ashamed that I was—as I put it then—"bad at being Indian." At the time I thought I was abdicating my identity. Now I see that I was asserting it.

Yush and I both thought that Papa's anger stemmed from the pres-sure he felt as a single-income earner and the sacrifices he made to give us a good education—an opportunity that he'd never had as an immigrant boy struggling in a new country, and one that I was now squandering. Papa, too, framed his medical school debt and long hours at the hospital as a sacrifice that, like so many immigrant parents make, was in service of offering Yush and me a better future. But in reality, Papa was not a recent immigrant struggling to make ends meet. His debt was a result of a decision he had made to leave a lucrative career path for one he considered more prestigious, and he had intentionally chosen a partner who did not have a career to compete with his own.

Papa loved quoting Frank Herbert's *Dune* in his lectures, particularly the line "Fear is the mind-killer." Beasts were ruled by fear. Men weren't. Papa would then ask me, "Are you man or are you beast?"

When Papa's lecture ended, and I stewed in self-pity and self-hatred, Yush would creep into my room, look at me, and say, "Come on, Prachi, are you *man* or are you *beast?*" He'd puff up his chest, beat his torso with his hands, and huff like a gorilla until we both laughed.

It turned out that Papa's eerie calm that night wasn't resignation. The moment was an opportunity, like striking oil. A reservoir of fuel that would burn righteous anger for months. That night, he stored the fuel away.

The fire eventually returned. Later, Papa smashed the handle on my bedroom door, breaking the locking mechanism. I had kept my bedroom door closed for, as he put it, "too long." When I began cleaning up my room by picking up my clothes first instead of my books, he screamed that this was why I would never succeed. After I rented a movie he considered too artsy, he berated me in front of you and Yush for what felt like hours and yelled, "At this rate you'll never amount to anything! You'll be a maid for the rest of your life!"

When Yush and I disagreed, we didn't scream or throw things. We did sometimes say hurtful things that we didn't really mean. But we both always apologized, learned, and listened to each other. Yush's love taught me that a fight does not have to become a war that ends in the total annihilation of another.

But I had assumed that, because Yush was not in Papa's line of fire, he had been unaffected by Papa's outbursts. Now I believe that Papa's anger scared Yush deeply. I now think that he saw Papa's treatment of me as a threat of what might happen to him if he failed to succeed in the ways Papa expected. I wonder if, out of a desire to not show his anger the way that Papa did, Yush instead became fearful of expressing any strong negative emotion, turning to humor to mask an anger that he didn't know how else to release. He learned to bury his feelings, a practice that the world bent into habit as he reached manhood.

Though two grades below me, Yush took AP calculus BC the same year I retook precalculus. That summer, he would join a lab at Lehigh University, working alongside physicists and engineers in their twenties. As a high school junior, he enrolled in advanced math courses at Lehigh, competed in a nationally ranked math team, and taught himself how to speed-solve a Rubik's Cube.

Despite this, Yush was popular, I think because he would rather make someone smile than try to impress them. At his high school graduation, Yush pranked the school's headmaster, a white British man. Yush painstakingly taught our headmaster how to pronounce a vaguely Indian-sounding middle name that Yush had made up: "VakaDakaRamaPutna." At graduation, our headmaster unwittingly called Yush Pal VakaDakaRamaPutna Gupta to the stage, and the room boomed with laughter.

Papa's fascination with computers and technology had initially turned Yush off to studying them. He told me that Papa took over his school projects and then Yush felt like what was his was not his anymore. At the time, I didn't understand Yush's hesitation to follow Papa's lead. I viewed Yush's talent in science and math as a gift and wished that, like him, I was naturally skilled in the exact ways that capitalism rewards. I never thought about the toll that his success took on him or what kind of pressure he must have felt to maintain it. I thought Yush—whose name means "glory" in Sanskrit—was blessed. Now I know that he was cursed.

———

By senior year, I had long blown my chances of getting into the sort of college that I had once considered my destiny. But I found a back door: What if I could get into a great school through my art? I applied to Carnegie Mellon's School of Art, telling Papa that I could then transfer to another college within the university and study something serious, too.

Papa supported my application. Maybe he thought my loophole was clever. Or maybe he just thought it would be fun to print slides of my artwork on his fancy printer. But, briefly, we felt like a team: He took photos of all my paintings, and then he carefully cropped them in Photoshop. He asked me for my opinion as he went through the photos, and side by side we assessed each of them in his study. As we worked on the application together, I began to imagine again. I had been so mad at Papa for squashing my dreams, but now I was closer to them than ever before, and he was helping me get there.

At the last minute, as I double-checked my application, I realized that I had misremembered the number of art pieces needed. My portfolio fell short of the required amount. In order to apply, I'd have to create three more paintings within just a few days. I panicked.

"Just use some of Dadiji's paintings," Papa said.

"Isn't that wrong?" I asked.

"It's not wrong," Papa said. "Why is it wrong? No one will know."

"But it's not my work," I said.

"Do you want to get in or not?"

I was shocked that Papa encouraged me to cheat. His suggestion was so casual, as if this was the obvious solution and I had been stupid not to see it. Until now, the small lies he told sometimes seemed harmless: On my thirteenth birthday, Papa took us rafting and purchased me a children's ticket. In my excitement, I had protested, tugging on Papa's shirt to remind him that I was thirteen now—a bona fide teenager. He snapped, "You think I don't know that? Just shut up! I'm telling them you're twelve so I can get a discount!" Earlier that year,

Papa dumped Yush and me at a first-class lounge in the New Delhi airport without paying for admission. He ordered us to pretend we couldn't speak or understand anyone so that we could stay there for free while he and you left to find a ticketing agent. Yush and I saw these little scams as clever ways to upend a system of arbitrary rules enforced by bureaucrats. But Papa pushing me to lie on my college application felt different. Papa said that he valued achievement, but it seemed like he was willing to bend the rules to appear that way—even if that involved cheating.

I was scared of triggering Papa's rage. First, I scrounged for any unfinished works I had, hoping to sidestep Papa's directive. I found two unfinished pieces, which I used instead of Dadiji's paintings. But I still came up one piece short. I then reluctantly sorted through a collection of Dadiji's paintings in the attic. Our painting styles were nothing alike. Dadiji painted large geometric shapes with crisp edges, and I strove for photorealism. I landed on a painting of a thick black tree on a hill, painted against a stylized brown sunset. Out of all her paintings, this was the one that might stand out the least among my work. I added it to my portfolio. I felt ashamed of my application; it was a lie. I never told Dadiji, or anyone else, what I had done.

Months later, Carnegie Mellon sent me a thick packet. You handed it to me with excitement: I had been accepted. Papa said I could go. To my surprise, he even offered to pay the full tuition, room, and board—a sum easily totaling two hundred thousand dollars. I was amazed by Papa's generosity.

But in the next sentence he added, "After that, you're on your own. If you ever need any help or support, don't come to me."

I didn't expect to rely on Papa financially after college, but in his words I heard a threat: Papa might disown me if I pursued art seriously. I didn't want to risk losing more of Papa's approval. A part of me also now doubted whether I could become an artist on my own merit. What if Dadiji's painting was the best part of my application? The accomplishment that was supposed to be mine didn't feel like my own, anymore. I didn't want to launch my dream on a lie.

I said I wouldn't go. I threw away the letter. Finally, I let go of my desire to become an artist for good.

After rejection letters from all the other colleges piled up, I expected Papa to scream, but he didn't. Instead, I sensed a quiet, seething disappointment, like on the night of the report-card incident. Only one other college admitted me: the University of Pittsburgh. Although I would later feel grateful to have attended Pitt, at the time, I felt ashamed. I knew that Papa had not spent tens of thousands of dollars on my private school education to send me to an undergraduate program that he did not consider elite.

JUST BEFORE I LEFT for college, Papa took us out to a fancy restaurant. In the middle of the meal, in front of you and Yush, Papa said, "I can't be there to control what you do, but there are three things you're not allowed to do." I understood that if he found out, or even suspected that I was doing any of these things, he'd pull me out of college and I'd have to live at home. "The first is, you are not allowed to have sex."

My face flushed. I fiddled with the crusted salmon on my plate. I think rule number two was "no drugs," but I had stopped listening. I forget what rule number three was. What I heard instead was, *You may be going away, but don't forget—you are not your own person.*

When I tried to picture my future, I imagined a black canvas. I don't mean to sound dramatic. I didn't want to die. I wasn't worried that my life would end. But I couldn't picture how a single thing would look—how I'd dress, what I'd do, who my friends would be, what I'd study, how I'd spend my free time, where I'd live. Trying to fill that dark space with lightness and distinct shapes and vibrant colors was a futile and dangerous act that would only torture me with possibilities that I knew I could never have.

I don't remember what conversations you and I had about college, Mummy. I hate that Papa controls my memories, too. You and I must have discussed it, but we all understood my education was his domain. Laced with your maternal concern must have been a layer of trepidation as a woman who had never lived on her own, unsupervised, as I was now doing at such a young age. But I did not feel nervous, as you must have. I felt relieved. I was not as excited for a new beginning as I was for a definite ending.

Chapter 10

Shrink and Expand

I MET NANCY ON THE first day of classes freshman year, when I happened to sit next to her in Intro to Psych. We introduced ourselves and she glanced at my doodles and said, "Wow, you draw really well." She nudged the cute guy sitting next to her and said, "Look at her drawing." He glanced over at my sketches of legs and hands, nodded, and then focused on flirting with Nancy for the rest of class. She didn't say another word to me.

Nancy also had the same second period class as me, honors chemistry. Every other morning, we power-walked from one end of campus to the other, barely reaching the lecture hall on time. We had been assigned the same lab group, and then we realized that we lived a few doors down from each other in the same dorm building. Despite this, it took us an entire semester to warm up. Nancy was cold, an observation I brought up later, to which she said, "Well, it keeps away the people who suck."

On the surface, we had very little in common. She was a white girl from a politically moderate Midwestern suburb with exquisite bone structure and a passion for science. But the universe was determined to make us friends, and by the end of the first semester we ate sandwiches at the William Pitt Union almost every day, studied together, and partied together. She told me about her struggles growing up with divorced parents, and I told her about my conflicts with Papa. After freshman year, we became roommates for the rest of college.

I googled her once, and that's how I learned that Nancy had a near-perfect ACT score and had received a full scholarship to Pitt. I knew that she was smart, but I had no idea how accomplished she was, because she had never once talked about her achievements. Later, when Harvard accepted Nancy into a master's program in public health, she rejected it without hesitation after visiting the campus and finding the professors and students to be pretentious. Her decision stunned me.

Nancy had a sense of self that did not waver. I was enchanted by her ability to stay true to who she was. She was not much taller than me and she was not particularly strong, yet she exuded a quiet power. I would study her sometimes to understand how she shored up that power, but I couldn't figure it out. I'd never encountered a woman my age so self-assured.

My friendship with Nancy buffered my insecurity over Papa's claim that I was "illogical," and my friendship with Marin nurtured my creativity and desire to write. I met Marin in English class during my junior year. The class was discussing an intensely vivid scene from Maxine Hong Kingston's essay "No Name Woman," in which she describes feeling haunted by the ghost of her unnamed aunt. Her aunt, a woman the family rarely mentioned, had jumped into a well after being shunned for getting pregnant outside marriage. One classmate raised her hand and said, "It's like that scene in *The Lion King* when Simba talks to his father!" Apparently, my mouth dropped. Marin, a striking woman with bright eyes and onyx hair, almost laughed out loud at my reaction. She sent me a message on Facebook soon after and asked if I wanted to hang out.

Marin was the first friend I made at college who wanted to write, not just as a hobby but as a career. She wanted to be a journalist, she told me. I saw in her an ambition and talent that I hoped I might one day have, too. We fell into a fast, intimate friendship, sharing our favorite books and music and boosting each other's personal dreams and ambitions. As I watched Marin commit to her vision and find success, later landing a fellowship at a prestigious magazine, some small part of me believed that I could navigate a career like that.

Marin and Nancy represented parts of myself I strove to inhabit in an identity that I did not yet own. I felt like they understood who I wanted to be. The friendships I made with them and others in college protected me when, on visits home, Papa told me that I was too selfish. "But if I am really selfish, then that would hurt my other relationships, too, right?" I said to Papa. He conceded that it would, yes.

"But no one else seems to think I am selfish. At least, I don't think they do. I think they like me. . . . If they thought I was selfish, they wouldn't want to be my friends or help me," I reasoned, now questioning whether my friends saw in me the badness that Papa saw.

Papa thought about that for a moment.

"Well, they don't know you like I do," he said. "I know you better than anyone else."

This conversation took many forms, sometimes softly with kind words and sometimes loudly with screams. I always journaled about it, venting my feelings onto the page as my sole witness. I hated myself afterward, wondering why I was so bad and how I could be good again. I thought Papa's anger kept me in line. I thought that the way he treated me taught me humility and made me a better person. I felt ashamed by the thought, but I couldn't shake it—the idea that the reason I was any good at all in the world was because I had a father to exorcize the bad out of me. And without this priestly father, I would have been irredeemably wretched.

In college I set out to find a career path that Papa would respect. I wasn't brilliant like Yush, so I had to find something more practical. First I landed on advertising, a field that combined my artistic talent with business; it would be a career Papa could, if not fully respect, at least accept. I started an advertising club on campus as a freshman. But by my junior year, I became disillusioned with the idea of using my creativity to help corporations sell products. I left the club I'd started. Upon Papa's urging, I thought briefly about becoming a dentist, but I found the number of science classes overwhelming. After a finance professor told me that the writing on my internship applications was too philosophical, I gave up on Papa's insistence to pursue investment banking, too.

I obsessively read Wikipedia entries on writers, artists, and entertainers who had followed professional paths and then quit their jobs to pursue their passions. I became a political cartoonist for *The Pitt News* and took a painting class on campus. I met with the coach of Pitt's cross-country and track-and-field teams and joined as a walk-on athlete, rotating between injuries and practice because I was not used to running forty-five miles per week. I took on a fifth year to earn degrees in both the business school and the College of Arts and Sciences. I majored in English writing and took two journalism classes to see whether I was at all still competent as a writer. I reached dean's list, earned society memberships, signed up for advanced classes, won awards, and befriended several professors as mentors along the way. What looked like overachievement to outsiders was a desire to prove to Papa that I was capable of taking control of my own life. I wanted to find a way to do what I wanted while also making Papa happy.

I thought Papa was in pain because I had been such a bad student in high school. I thought that if I became a Good Indian Girl, our relationship would improve and he would be at peace. I want you to remember that I tried to be that daughter, Mummy. And I want you to know that trying taught me that achieving perfection would not have kept our family whole.

THE SUGGESTION TO NANCY and Marin had been casual: "My family is going to India over Christmas break. Would you want to come?" To my surprise, they both said yes. The idea excited me at first. Then I asked Papa. I was sure he'd say no. I realized, after I asked him, that I had hoped Papa would say no.

I was uncomfortable when non-desi friends came over if Papa was home. One time during summer break from college, when a white friend dropped by, Yush, my friend, and I watched *Da Ali G Show*. Papa entered the basement, poised and charming in front of company. He lingered in the corner of the room and watched the show for a few minutes. I remained tense as he stood there. When my friend left, Papa came up to my room and screamed at me. Watching that garbage show was a sign of how irrational I was, he yelled, more evidence that I would never be successful. He didn't say a word to Yush.

I was nervous about my best friends seeing my family life so intimately, and I was nervous about what Papa might find when seeing me with these white friends up close. I felt a dissonance that I could not yet articulate, a tear in what W.E.B. Du Bois called the "double-consciousness" of race, not knowing how to meld my distinct identities. I understood these two versions of myself as Indian—my home self—and American—my outside self. I was anxious that either I would not be Indian enough for Papa or I would not be American enough for Nancy and Marin. Ultimately, I'd be outed as a fraud by everyone I cared about.

Weeks before the trip, Nanaji died. I didn't know how to comfort you. I was too preoccupied with reconciling the warring parts of myself. You met your grief for the loss of your father alone, without our support, burying it to accommodate my friends and host them among your mourning family.

EVERYWHERE I WENT, PEOPLE saw me as Indian. But India was the only place in the world I felt American. The specter of India loomed so large over my life, yet my entire actual lived experience with a vast country of over one billion people and hundreds of spoken tongues was probably no more than about three months, total. I do not know how long we stayed when you took me as a baby, when I learned the Hindi that I can still speak in choppy waves.

The savory smell always hit me first: a mix of roasted peanuts, exhaust fumes, and the slight sweetness of paan that conjured memories of the home you grew up in. I loved waking up to the imam's daybreak call to prayer from the nearby mosque. I never got tired of seeing the aggressive monkeys, flying armies that Yush lured in with fruit despite your warnings not to tempt them. Our cousins taught us how to fly kites with glass-coated strings, and we spent hours trying to cut down the neighbors' kites high in the air above us. At least once during every visit, we broke into a spontaneous dance party, where all of my aunts, uncles, and cousins blasted the latest Bollywood songs.

I noticed that, despite the traditional patriarchal structure of your home, the women had power over their domain. In my American imagination, "homemaker" was a belittled title. But Mamiji, your sister-in-law, ran her house like a naval captain. Mamaji, my uncle, respected her authority. The kitchen was treated as a place worthy of reverence. None of my cousins seemed particularly obsessed with school or success, either. The culture that I associated with being Indian, the culture of my home, was so different from yours.

By this trip, I was only a few years younger, at twenty-one, than you were when you emigrated to Canada. You had now lived outside India longer than you lived in it. Your relationship with your motherland was complex, so much so that I think you struggled to talk about it. It must have been so bittersweet and even painful for you to visit, catching a glimpse of a parallel universe that held both your past and your alternate present in one view; a place that, like you, had changed so much that neither of you could fully recognize the other anymore; yet simultaneously a place that saw and loved you in a way that your other, permanent home never could. Your grief, like all grief, forced you to hold contradictory emotions at once: longing and repulsion, relief and agitation, freedom and entrapment. I was too lost in my own anxieties on that trip to be there for you, Mummy, or even to consider what you felt as you processed your father's death.

———

WE SPENT A FEW days with your family before showing Marin and Nancy the Taj Mahal and, later, the serene backwaters and tea plantations of Kerala. I had been so worried about what Papa might see about me when I was with my friends, but during the trip I began to see Papa through Nancy and Marin's eyes. I was embarrassed by what I saw. Papa rushed us into the van, yelling, "Jaldi jaldi jaldi!" and then the five of us would scurry in—and wait on Papa for another fifteen minutes. When Marin bought a pair of leather shoes, he lectured her on how to break them in, as if she had never before worn shoes. During one family dinner, when a few of our relatives had fasted, Papa yelled at the waitstaff over bringing them, in his opinion, the wrong kind of fruit. He grumbled, "This is not how we do things in America. No one there would stand for this!" What I had once admired as Papa's assertiveness, I now perceived as arrogance. I worried that Nancy and Marin would see Papa as a walking, talking stereotype.

As we drifted past palm trees on a boat in Kerala, Papa told all of us about some distant relative who had dated a man in secret for three years and then, after he proposed, said she'd break up with him if her father didn't approve. Papa said that daughter was good and sensible. Back at the hotel, Nancy scoffed at this privately and said, "If someone kept me a secret and then told me after three years that they'd break up with me if their parents didn't approve, I'd break up with them." I agreed with Nancy but knew I could never voice such a thing to Papa, and I was confused over whether this attitude and criticism was "American" of me or not.

I had at first viewed the cognitive dissonance I experienced as strictly about Indian versus American identity, a gross oversimplification that reduced my understanding of myself—and of culture—to a monolithic set of immutable traits. I didn't yet have the language to articulate the complexity of my feelings. My struggle to become my own person was complicated further by trying to understand what part my cultural heritage played in my identity, a heritage that was overshadowed by Papa's expectations of me and underscored by our liminal place in American consciousness.

TOWARD THE END OF the trip, Papa knocked on my hotel room door. You stood beside him. Yush wasn't with you, so I knew already that I was about to get in trouble. You were on my right and Papa on my left, and as we walked on the beach in Kerala, Papa told me that he was worried about where I was heading in life. He said I should be like Nancy, who was logical and rational. He told me that Marin, who aspired to become a writer, will "never be successful," as he put it. I kept quiet, looking down at my feet moving through hot sand. I wondered if he said this because he really believed it or to instill doubt over my own judgment and ambitions. You nodded in agreement, though I don't think that you believed much of what Papa said. I think you were hurt that I had focused more on my friends than on you, and so you went along with Papa's harsh words.

When I came back, I was agitated. I didn't see in Marin what Papa claimed to see, but I didn't want to tell her what Papa had said, so I felt as if I had to distance myself from her. Later, I took Nancy aside and told her that Papa wanted me to be like her. She laughed. "Your dad would hate to have me as a daughter," she said.

"Why?" I asked.

"Because I would tell him exactly what I think, and I don't think he'd like that." Then she asked me, "Why do you act like a child when you're with your dad?"

"What do you mean?" I said, getting defensive. I received her question as judgment from a white woman who didn't understand anything about the stress of navigating life with two different identities. Nancy had crossed a line that she wasn't supposed to cross.

"You pretend to not know things that you know. You ask him questions when you already know the answer to them. You're smart, but around your dad, you play dumb."

The truth of Nancy's words hit something deep inside me, a place

that I had numbed. In that moment, I felt humiliated—but also recognized. Something I had put to sleep had been awakened, and I
could not ignore it.

It turned out that Marin, too, had been concerned by the extent to
which I shrank myself. She later told me that when I got sick on the
trip, I asked Papa what juice to order to help ease my cold. I didn't
even remember this interaction or think it was strange until I saw it
through the eyes of my friends. Throughout college, when I went to
Pitt's healthcare center, Papa expected me to call him from the office
so the doctor could run the diagnosis and treatment plan by him.
After that trip, I stopped telling Papa when I got minor colds or went
to the health center, no longer wanting to consult him for decisions
that I knew I could make on my own.

WHEN WE RETURNED HOME, as Nancy and Marin loaded up the car
for the ride back to Pitt, you pulled me aside. You said that I had
treated you horribly in India, that I had ignored you and didn't care
about your grief over Nanaji's death, and I was too self-absorbed and
selfish. Your words stung me.

Finally, I broke under the tension. I had felt conflict with Papa for
years. After that trip, in which my friends observed a dynamic that I'd
never quite been able to articulate, I decided I didn't want to make
myself small to appease Papa anymore. I could no longer maintain
the façade of existing in two ways, and on the drive back, as I fumed
and vented and cried, I resolved to fight to be true to myself. That was
a commitment I would break, and make, and break again many more
times. I didn't feel empowered by my decision. I felt ashamed.

I struggled to determine whether the behaviors in Papa that I found
distasteful stemmed from differences rooted in culture. While cultural
norms certainly played a role in what Nancy and Marin found different about our family's dynamics, I think that what they pointed out to
me as concerning was not simply code-switching or differences of
collectivist cultural norms. At college I existed to others not as a

daughter or as a sister but as an individual, and they had each been alarmed by the degree to which the woman they knew was diminished around Papa.

As an immigrant woman who did not work beyond the home, you relied largely on Papa's network of friends and family to get by. You did not have access to an independent support network of friends as I now did. Nearly everyone in your community was organized toward preservation of the family unit, even above individual well-being. Your social acceptance depended on your ability to play the role of the perfect wife or perfect in-law. I wonder what you would have seen about yourself if you had a separate group of friends—maybe through a job or an outside hobby—who saw you not as a symbol but as a full person. I wonder if Papa discouraged you from pursuing independent activities for precisely that reason. Later, you did work outside the home, at Papa's medical practice, but you remained under his watchful gaze.

By virtue of your role as mother, wife, and immigrant, the self-exploration that benefited me in college was not a privilege extended to you, at least not unless you upended your entire world again and risked losing the community you had created in an isolating new country. It brings me so much shame to consider now if there was a part of you that held this against me, jealous that you had to lose everything to make certain choices for yourself, while I had the privilege of knowing I'd still have the support of my friends if I walked away. And, although it was you who made a decision to search for more opportunity, it was I who benefitted from that sacrifice now. A part of me wondered if I was living your dream, deferred.

AFTER THAT TRIP, I began to intervene when Papa laid into you, preparing to absorb the anger that he reserved for you. On visits home, I saw remnants of Papa's rage: a water faucet he'd smashed; a wine stain on the ceiling from a glass he'd thrown across the room; a broken garbage disposal. You had put chicken bones in the trash rather than down the compactor—which was illogical behavior, according to him. Then he threw the chicken bones in the garbage disposal, which is what broke it. You had to oversee the repair. I don't know how you coped.

One time I stepped in between you two just as tension escalated. "Don't talk to her like that. It's not okay," I said to Papa.

"Prachi, stay out of it. Don't come between me and my wife," he growled.

"She's my mom, so it's my business, too," I said.

Then you said, "Prachi, stop. Stop. It's okay," annoyed at me for having made a tense situation worse. I left the room, angry at him and frustrated with you.

It didn't occur to me then that you probably didn't feel safe with me, either, because even while I was resisting Papa, I was guilty of buying into his depiction of Indian born-and-bred women as meek and subservient, judging you and stepping in as your American savior. Papa routinely told you that you were incapable, but by seeing you as someone who didn't have a voice, I treated you as powerless in our household, too. It was too hard for me to accept that, on some level, you made a choice to tolerate his behavior and to later redirect your anger toward me. It was too painful for me to consider that a part of you chose to accept mistreatment rather than to leave, that you later chose to protect him instead of protecting me.

You were raised in a conservative household, but it was clear from the choice you made to leave your country that you sought a different life. Though many women are taught that their job in marriage is to support a man and make him happy, I wonder if you believed that more deeply and profoundly than I could ever understand. Maybe that idea became the guidepost around which you navigated a new place, a new marriage, a new country, a new life, as you attempted to orient yourself here. Whatever the reason, you made choices aligned with that belief—the idea that a man's happiness is the foundation of a family's happiness and unity—and based on that, I see how my eventual refusal to bend to my father's will was interpreted as a disavowal of family and disrespectful to you as both a mother and wife.

One time, after a fight, I told Papa soberly, "Papa, if you continue to talk to me like this, I don't know if we'll have much of a relationship when I'm older."

He didn't scream or yell. "Is that a threat?" he asked, braced for an escalation.

"No," I said, quickly backing off. "I just think that when I'm on my own, if that doesn't change, it will strain our relationship."

"But you'll always be my daughter," he said. "Nothing changes that."

Chapter 11

Good Judgment

By my second year of college, I was still not allowed to date. But I was desperate for a boyfriend, and while living at home that summer, I found one. A stranger named Chuck had messaged me on AOL Instant Messenger, thinking I was the sibling of a friend who shared my last name. I suspected that this was a lie. Chuck had gone to my high school, though he graduated just before I entered, so we had never met. He likely used that as an excuse to contact me randomly, but I didn't care.

Chuck ate what I called a caveman diet: beans straight from a can and unfiltered organic juice from Trader Joe's. He smoked a lot of pot and idolized dead white philosophers. But he told me I was beautiful and he planned romantic dates, and that was enough for me to want him. Yush covered for me when I took long day trips with Chuck. Or I'd say I was sleeping over at Swapna's, and you would start calling me at eight A.M., suspicious, but asking no questions other than, "Where are you? Come home." I'd rush back, hoping Papa wouldn't notice the miles I put on his car or the unknown address in New Jersey that I plugged into his GPS.

Chuck was white and therefore didn't understand why I needed to hide him. He introduced me to his parents, and he was understandably hurt that I had no intention of doing the same. I was not willing to sacrifice my already tenuous place in the family for what I saw as a summer fling. I tried to break things off before I went back to college. He drove over to our house to beg me not to, which terrified me because surely you and Papa would notice. Within minutes I agreed to continue seeing him, in part because I was flattered by the romantic gesture and in part so he would leave quickly.

That same year, during his senior year of high school, Yush got a girlfriend. You had her over for dinner, and Papa let Yush go on dates. Papa let Yush run cross-country, too. He said it was because Yush had good grades. I felt it was because Yush was a boy.

When I got back to college, I pleaded with Papa that I be allowed to date. My grades were good now. I was pursuing a serious career path in business. I hoped that if he agreed, then I might no longer have to lie about my relationship. But Papa said no, I was still too young and immature, and I needed to focus on school.

He changed his mind a few weeks later, after he heard that my second cousins in India had started dating. Papa was surprised by this development and did not want to appear narrow-minded to relatives in a country that the American media described as "third-world." I then, very tepidly, attempted to tell Papa about Chuck, but I immediately felt uncomfortable. I had to justify to Papa what made this man worthy, but I didn't know how to quantify that. I couldn't say that he supported my desire to write or that he was romantic. I knew Papa wanted to hear that he was destined for a successful career and came from a successful family. Papa said if I wasn't proud of him, I should break up with him. It was the logical thing to do.

I listened to Papa and broke up with Chuck. I hid my heartbreak from you both. You probably thought my moodiness was more American self-absorption. "I am disappointed in myself for being this way," I wrote to Yush in an email. "This is pathetic."

Within hours, Yush wrote back, telling me that I was strong, that I was allowed to cry, that I was not weak for hurting. He said that whenever I felt low, I could always come to him. He wrote a list of qualities about me that he admired and promised to always remind me of how much he loved me.

My love for Yush overflowed. Knowing I had Yush's support didn't make my pain go away, but now it felt like it wasn't mine to carry alone. His understanding made my heartbreak more manageable. "Sometimes . . . most times, I don't know what I would do without you," I wrote back. "It's you and me, forever."

Yush joked that I'd find the perfect man by sorting through a list of résumés and that, if it were up to me, I'd have men apply to be my boyfriend like I had applied to college. This was true at the time. I still clung to the belief that a person's worth lay in their achievements and social status. I needed that to be true because, otherwise, I felt like a failure for no reason. Otherwise, Papa's punishments meant nothing. And I needed my pain and confusion to mean something.

I understood that I had to marry my next boyfriend. By permitting me to date, Papa had allowed me to choose a partner, with the understanding that he retained final veto power. I wanted to be wanted, and I wanted to be treated well, and I wanted to wait for a man who I knew I could bring home to both of you.

During my senior year, a few friends convinced me to come out with them to the saddest bar near campus: the balcony of a Qdoba restaurant on Forbes Avenue. We ordered the unsavory fishbowl, a clear plastic vessel full of Windex-blue liquid and four straws. If even two people drank from the bowl at the same time, their heads nearly touched. We loved it. My friends had invited a friend from medical school, and he brought with him another classmate, Thomas, a tall, handsome man with fluffy brown hair.

After drinking the fishbowl, I contemplated going home, but as we walked down the stairs, one of my friends said, "Thomas thinks you're cute!"

I found this surprising. Thomas had barely talked to me. I suspected that my friend only said this to convince me to stay out. It worked.

We walked over to our favorite spot, Booms, a grimy campus dive that sold dollar Yuenglings and played hip-hop. I followed Thomas to the bar, sidling up as close as possible without actually touching him.

"Do you want a beer?" he asked.

"Sure," I said.

"It's a dollar," he said, pointing to the sign. He paid for his beer but didn't offer to pay for mine, and then he walked away.

I found his aloofness refreshing. He wasn't mean or pushing me away. He seemed comfortable on his own, and I liked that I couldn't sense any pretension or performance from him. We returned to the group and made small talk as we danced. Before I left, I wrote my name and phone number on a napkin and shoved it into Thomas's hand. "Call me," I said. "I'm serious." He said he would. I was certain that I'd never hear from him again.

A few nights later, as I was leaving class, I got a call from an unknown number. Thomas and I talked for forty-five minutes, and he asked me out on a date. He took me to a nice Thai restaurant off-campus. He called me to schedule a second date. I never had to worry if he'd call when he said he would. He read *The New England Journal of Medicine* cover to cover and looked up studies to learn about conditions and disorders. His interest in medicine seemed genuine, motivated by a humble passion and earnest curiosity. He cared about my interests, too. When I shared my love of writing with him, he subscribed to *The New Yorker* and added it to his weekly reading. I thought that you would like him, too, Mummy, and after I got to know him, I knew why. He treated his mother with a tenderness that suggested he would speak to you with a similar level of affection and respect.

I believed Papa would like Thomas, too, though perhaps for another set of reasons. Even while Papa criticized aspects of Americanness, he had molded us to succeed in white America. Thomas, in many ways, personified that success: He was the son of a doctor, and he was at the top of his medical school class. He came from old money—a family full of former politicians, lawyers, and surgeons, all with Ivy League degrees. Though I discovered his family's history much later, Thomas already represented a part of white America that we could never have accessed on our own.

In our third week of dating, Thomas came to pick me up after I'd spent the day running around campus, finishing and submitting essays without eating a solid meal. As I was getting ready for the date, I nearly fainted. Nancy let him in. He found me sitting on the bathroom floor, eating pickles and drinking pickle juice straight from the jar, with no makeup, and my hair half straightened, half frizz. I was sure that once Thomas saw how hideous I looked without makeup or silky straight hair, he would lose interest in me. Instead, he knelt on the bathroom floor and made sure that I was okay.

After a month of dating, he paused while walking me back to my apartment. "If we are going to make things official, there's something I want you to know about me," he said.

"What's that?"

"I have depression."

"Oh," I said. "That's okay."

I thought that just meant he got sad, sadder than most people did, a little more frequently. I didn't ask him any questions about depression, I didn't know anything about depression, and I didn't attempt to learn anything about depression.

After dating Thomas for six months, I told you and Papa about the relationship. Papa wanted to meet him right away. He came to spend a weekend at home with us. We stayed in separate bedrooms, of course, and Thomas made guacamole with Papa. In the morning, we planned to go for a walk at the outdoor mall. As I was getting ready to leave, you intervened and said, "Prachi, let's go—just you and me."

"But Thomas wanted to come," I said.

"No, he can't come. Papa wants us to go so he can talk to him alone."

"That's not fair," I said. "Thomas can do whatever he wants!"

Thomas overheard and said, "It's fine, I don't mind staying back."

"I'd rather not leave you alone," I said.

"No, Prachi, let's go. Papa wants us to go."

You were uncharacteristically forceful because Papa had told you to get me out of the house so he could talk to Thomas man-to-man. Not wanting to start a fight in front of my new boyfriend, I relented. As I sifted mindlessly through dresses at Banana Republic, I fumed about how Papa had gone behind my back. He could have told me, *I'd like to talk to Thomas one-on-one,* or he could have just said whatever he wanted to say while we were all together. But this felt manipulative. You thought Papa's antics were over the top, but you also felt like I was overreacting. *Papa wants to talk to Thomas. Just drop it, Prachi.*

While we were gone, Papa sat Thomas down and interrogated him the way a father does in a Lifetime movie: *What are your intentions with my daughter? What are your plans for your future? Where do you see this relationship going?* When Thomas relayed this to me, I was livid. I apologized, worried that Papa's intensity would make Thomas reconsider our relationship. I, for one, would not want to marry a partner whose overprotective parent butted into our affairs. I was so grateful when Thomas seemed unbothered. "It was fine. I answered his questions, no big deal."

This would become my favorite trait of Thomas's: He let things go. Nothing would come up, days or months or years later, to be repurposed as a weapon. He was go-with-the-flow, live-and-let-live.

As much as I appreciated it about him, I didn't know how to be like that. Sometimes I took his nonchalance as not caring about me or not loving me, and I would act out in the ways that felt so familiar to me to test his love, pushing him away and calling him names that Papa had once called you or me: *selfish, worthless, useless.* But even then, Thomas was patient with me. When my temper spiked, he remained calm. When I cooled down, he spoke to me about not making "a mountain out of a molehill" and not using mean words to express my feelings. As I saw this goodness in him that I lacked, slowly I found a new man to serve as my God.

I was grateful when the weekend I brought Thomas home ended without incident. As we left, Papa pulled me aside and said, "Mom and I wanted to give you and Thomas our blessing for marriage." I was a little taken aback: I wanted Papa's approval, but I had not expected that Papa would actually bring up marriage upon the first meeting. But I also felt relief. I knew then that I could fully release myself to Thomas and that my judgment was finally good.

Chapter 12

Homecoming

YUSH ATTENDED CARNEGIE MELLON, living about a mile down the street from me at Pitt. We saw each other every week, at least once if not more, and his friends became mine and mine became his. During finals week my junior year, when I got severely dehydrated from the flu, Yush came over to my apartment between classes to check up on me. I could not walk, I could only crawl. He camped out on my bedroom floor and helped me get to the bathroom, nursing me to health with gallons of Gatorade and Miyazaki films he downloaded on his laptop. I am sure it comforted you and Papa to know that we were there looking out for each other.

Although Yush had initially hesitated to study programming, in college he discovered tech projects that had the potential to change the world's future. He joined the Google Lunar X Prize challenge to build a spacecraft and land it on the moon, ran a hackathon on campus, and learned to program his own operating system. He maintained a stellar GPA while taking the hardest courses the school offered in computer science and electrical engineering.

But as college progressed and his course load increased, Yush turned away from his social life. Like me, in high school he had discovered a natural talent for running, which enabled him to run for Carnegie Mellon's cross-country team. When he dropped out after freshman year, I urged him to reconsider. I encouraged him to ask out one of my friends, a pretty Indian American woman who had a crush on him. He dismissed both as a distraction.

He lived off a diet of pasta and five-hour energy drinks. He devoured cookies, milk, and beer before bed to pack weight onto his wiry frame—an effort to bulk up, he said. He mused that the overwhelming majority of men in his computer science classes meant that women were less capable in science than men were. I gently pushed back, but my own lack of talent in math and science didn't exactly support my case. I found his insecurities and growing bias against women troubling, but at the time it didn't feel like Yush was changing much. It felt like he was blasting off into the heavens, accelerating along the trajectory of his destiny.

The summer that I graduated from college, Yush rented an apartment in Venice Beach while he interned at SpaceX. He coded software for a space capsule that delivered cargo to the International Space Station, but Swapna and I joked that he made fireworks, because that was about the most complex projectile we could fathom. One night, Elon Musk took the employees out for drinks. Yush bought him a shot at the bar, toasting by quoting Buzz Lightyear from *Toy Story*, "To infinity and beyond!" Musk laughed, knocking back a shot on Yush's command.

America was a year into its deepest economic fallout since the Great Depression. As most of my classmates watched their futures collapse, I had accepted an offer from a prestigious management-consulting firm. Thomas narrowed down his top residency program choices to cities where I could transfer offices, putting New York City at the top of his list. As I secured my future with Thomas, embarked upon my new career, and witnessed Yush's rise, I felt as if everything in our lives was following the course that Papa had charted for us.

But this confused me, too. I had succeeded both in spite of Papa and because of Papa. I didn't know how to reconcile the shame I felt when I wondered to what extent the traits that made Papa so hard to get along with were traits necessary to attain the kind of stability and security that I now enjoyed. What if I needed his anger to motivate me?

To CELEBRATE MY NEW job, I planned a ten-day vacation to Prague with Swapna, which I paid for with my signing bonus. A few weeks before the trip, I reviewed my schedule with Papa over the phone. I planned to come home two nights before my flight, and after the trip I'd spend another week at home with you and Papa.

"I think you are cutting it a little too close," Papa said. "You need to do all of your packing. Mom and I know what goes into packing, and you can do a better job here."

"How do you mean?" I asked. "I don't really understand."

I thought that maybe Papa would offer a checklist of essentials to pack. Instead, Papa's temper flared. "Why is it that you never respect what Mom and I have to say?"

The stakes of the conversation had just changed. We were no longer talking about logistics or packing. I was now caught in an earthquake, struggling to find footing as the ground rumbled beneath me. I realized later that Papa had wanted to spend more time with me at home before I left for my vacation, but he didn't actually say that.

My confused, rushed responses further angered Papa. As I relay it now, the conversation sounds so absurd that it almost makes me laugh. But at that moment I shook with righteous rage. The angrier Papa became that I would not bend, the more rigid I became, every bit as stubborn as my father. Then Papa threatened to call the police and report that I was driving a stolen car.

"Go ahead!" I fumed.

"That's it, I'm laying down the law!" Papa screamed. "You *are* coming home on Sunday. And if you don't, you're not going!"

"You can't do that!" I yelled back. "I paid for the trip with my own money!"

"I don't care! You're not going!"

Then I did something I'd never done before: I hung up on him. It felt forbidden and scary. Good Indian Girls did not hang up on their fathers. But it was also a luxury. Now that I had a job, Papa couldn't threaten to cut off my phone access, or forbid me to apply to jobs that he didn't approve of, or warn that he'd stop paying my tuition—all threats that he had made in high school and college to keep me fully dependent upon him. Hanging up gave me a surge of power. Stemming the fight really was as simple as pressing a button.

A few minutes later, you called me. You urged me to do Papa's bidding. In the past you had helped me avoid Papa's wrath, but sometimes you carried out his orders like a soldier. This time you felt like his co-conspirator, applying a similar pressure. In this instance, your desires aligned with Papa's.

You pleaded with me to come home earlier. You said that I had hurt Papa and that you were trying to calm him down, but this was so hard for you and you needed my cooperation. Your words tugged at my heart, but I would not budge. I must have been on speakerphone, because as I spoke to you, I heard Papa screaming, "Shut up! Shut up! Shut up!" at me.

It is hard to convey the intensity of those screams. It was an uprising; a deranged, feral, guttural yell of an animal trying to escape from within the body of a man. Then Papa grabbed the phone and roared, "I don't want to see you! Don't come home!" I hung up on you both again.

I could have obliged. I have thought many times about why that felt impossible to me and why that impulse—the one that I had internalized as selfishness—served as the instinct that saved me years later. In that moment, Papa wanted me to react not to his literal words but to his anger. Even as I felt pathetic and childlike, defending myself in a rundown apartment that my father paid for, through a phone he had bought for me, I knew that something larger was at stake. Had I retreated, I would have validated Papa's belief that bullying me was an appropriate way to get what he wanted. If I buckled now, I would be inviting into adulthood the very treatment that I had tried so hard to escape as a girl. I would be setting a precedent that I was still his to control.

You called the next morning to say that Papa was up all night, really hurting, and said that I didn't respect him and that if he couldn't be a father to me then he would have to cut me out of his life. You said that you didn't want to cut me out of your life but you would do that if things didn't change. I didn't understand where any of this was coming from.

I learned later that Papa had rammed his head through the bathroom wall that night, repeatedly, leaving a gaping hole. The next day you had to find someone to patch up the drywall. You must have been so angry with me: I had the power to stop this, and I chose not to.

I felt like a routine phone call had opened a tenth circle of hell in mere seconds, and now an indestructible tie had somehow been severed. Yet I had never been so sure that I didn't deserve to be treated like this. I was a good kid now. I was upholding my end of the bargain that—for years in high school, yes—I had reneged on. But my current success gave Papa so much to brag about. He even bragged about the money he saved by not sending me to an Ivy League school. I was far from perfect, but I was indisputably the sort of daughter that you both could finally be proud of in the Indian American community.

Looking back, I realize that this was the incident where I began to wonder if Papa's temper and controlling nature were indicative of something extreme, a potential sign of an illness that none of us knew how to address. It was the first time I questioned if something else was at play, far beyond the image of strict Indian fathers that people around me had dismissed as cultural or the anger that Yush and I assumed was a byproduct of the stress of a sole breadwinner. I had never before heard of Papa turning his anger inward, and I had never heard you this scared.

Yush advised that I give Papa time to cool off and return the car Papa had let me borrow so he couldn't use it to threaten me again. I followed Yush's advice. I wrote Papa a letter to try to reason with him.

Papa emailed me a response, saying that I would never understand him. You called to tell me my letter was horrible.

I told you I wasn't coming home. I hung up on you again. Any empowerment I felt from hanging up the phone on either of you had disappeared. All I felt now was deep shame, confusion, and sadness. I had followed the rules. I had done everything I was expected to do. Why was this happening?

It was after this incident that I first sought Buaji's advice. I had never been particularly close to my aunt. I had been wary of her, reminded of Papa's stories about how angry and selfish she could be, that she had once been a feminazi. But Buaji and Papa had set aside whatever differences they had as teenagers for the sake of family now. If anyone could help me navigate a relationship with my father, I thought, it was my aunt.

Buaji thought that perhaps Papa was acting out because he was stressed by all the change. His little girl was growing up, something that must have been bittersweet for him. Her advice: *You can only control your own actions. Act in a way that you can be proud of, and you won't have any regrets.*

Every morning from Prague, I called home to say that I was safe. Papa would answer, say, "Okay," and then hang up. He didn't speak of our fight, and neither did I.

When I came home ten days later, Papa didn't acknowledge me. When I entered a room, he drifted past without a word. It almost felt worse than the yelling. At least when he yelled at me or called me stupid, he acknowledged my existence. Now I felt like I didn't matter to him at all. I took a Greyhound bus back to Pittsburgh the next morning. I don't remember much about the following weeks, except that what should have been the most exciting summer of my life now felt like the worst summer, and I didn't understand why.

A week before my birthday, Papa sent me an email. There was no trace of the enraged man who seemingly hated me. Instead, I recognized my other father, the loving father who doted on me. "I go to bed every night thinking of you and wake up every morning thinking of you and whenever I get a free moment, I turn to you," it read. "I'm sure that the last month has been more stressful for you. Perhaps it is time for a new beginning. Let me know what you think."

I knew that email must not have been easy for Papa to write. When we spoke on the phone, he said he was sorry. Then I said I was sorry, reflexively, because I thought I was expected to apologize to him, too. I tried to recall a time that I had ever heard Papa apologize or acknowledge wrongdoing to anyone but could not think of such an instance. The small gesture filled me with so much hope. The knot of anger within me immediately unraveled. I chalked up the incident to stress and believed his rage was a thing of the past. I knew that, going forward, Papa would treat me with respect, recognizing that I was finally the daughter that he had needed me to be. I flew back the following weekend, and the three of us sat as a family, flipping through my slideshow of photos of Prague.

I was home.

Chapter 13

Discovering Aliens

I worked as a business technology analyst, specializing in information management. I couldn't explain to you what this title meant or what my job entailed, though, because I myself had little idea. After a week of training in Pittsburgh, the new-hire class flew to Orlando, where hundreds of recent college graduates filled a convention hall and learned about how impressive the firm was and how impressive each of us was for being hired by the firm. During that first month, I spent ten-hour days staring at PowerPoint slides in conference rooms alongside colleagues who struggled to absorb the information thrown at us. After I put in six more weeks making PowerPoint slides from home about terms I would ultimately never understand, in September, the firm placed me on a project in Boston.

Travel was a part of the job: I would spend my weekends in Pittsburgh, flying to Boston for the project, where I'd stay at a hotel from Monday through Thursday. I had been brought in for an urgent, mysterious task, but no one told me what that was. After an entire week, I still did not understand the project or my role on it, yet I was there until ten o'clock every night. On Friday evening, things became even less clear. The partner leading the project told the analysts to cancel our Monday-morning flights; we'd have to come up Sunday. "It doesn't matter how much it costs, just do it," he said. We estimated that Sunday's work, whatever it was, would cost the client an additional ten thousand dollars. *This is it,* I thought. *All of my new training and knowledge will finally be put to use.*

We spent Sunday reformatting Excel spreadsheets. For six hours, we adjusted font sizes and colors and added borders to tables. This is when I realized that, while the firm promoted itself as an elite institution for only the best and the brightest, I had not been hired for my advanced knowledge, my depth of experience, or my riveting intellect. I had been hired because I was an overachiever who had aged out of a grading system and needed a new system within which to prove my worth. In this way, I suppose I had found the perfect job for me.

THE CALL CAME THREE nights later, around midnight. I was asleep. I didn't recognize the number. I ignored it. The phone rang again. I picked up, irritated but concerned. Why would anyone call so late?

"Prachi, this is Gabe, Yush's friend. We found Yush's suicide note—"

I knew that Yush's friends often played pranks. Yush told me that he sometimes ran a "fight club" in his room, where he and his friends would wrestle or take swipes at one another, imitating Brad Pitt from the movie. I think he probably exaggerated swapping a few playful jabs with friends, but the idolization of violence still worried me. Yush dismissed it as "a guy thing" that I wouldn't understand.

But this time they'd gone too far. I got angry. "Gabe, if this is some sort of joke, it's not funny," I said, my voice cracking with worry.

"It's not a joke." Gabe's voice was urgent but calm. "Yush wrote a suicide note. His car is gone. We're looking for him with the police. Have you heard from him?"

I started hyperventilating. I tried to think about how I could help.

"Do you know his license plate number?" Gabe asked.

"I don't." I got mad at myself. How could I not have memorized his plates?

Gabe told me they'd keep looking and give me updates.

Yush was trying to kill himself—or maybe he was already dead—and I was pacing back and forth, hundreds of miles away, in a Westin hotel room. The following minutes were agony. I left Yush voicemail after voicemail, crying into the machine, telling him how much I loved him, *please don't do this, don't leave me alone in this world, don't take away my best friend. I need you,* I said. *I love you so, so much.* The machine cut me off. I called again. The machine cut me off. I called again. I had no idea if Yush would ever hear those messages. I was alone, and my fear strangled me.

I called Thomas and woke him up. He was calm. He was always calm. Sometimes I wished that he would get angry or scared on my behalf. I asked Thomas if I should call you and Papa. "Of course," he said. "They're your parents." In my panicked state, I had hesitated because I wanted to somehow bring Yush to safety before I involved you both, even though, of course, I could not. I did not want to call you, Mummy, to tell you that your son was missing and might, in that very moment, be killing himself.

Ultimately, I called. Papa at first didn't understand what I was saying, and then he said he was on his way. You both drove to Pittsburgh in the middle of the night.

I don't know how much time passed, but Yush called me back. I had never cried so hard, and I hoped to never cry like that again. Yush was laughing maniacally, like a cartoon villain. There was something so off and so distant about his voice. Dark, sinister, twisted. He kept laughing. "I'm fine," he said. "Don't worry, Prach, I'm fine."

Hours earlier, Yush had visited the top of the Cathedral of Learning, the tall tower on Pitt's college campus, where I'd sat in class two years before. He had planned to jump from the top, but the windows were barred shut. He then drove to a gas station and filled up a carton with gasoline. He poured the gasoline over his body somewhere in the woods behind Carnegie Mellon, among the trails we had run through together countless times. When I was calling him, he was debating whether to light himself on fire.

The campus police found him and took him to the emergency room, where he was treated for gasoline contact burns. Yush later told me that he had purposefully not reached out to me that day. He knew if he heard my voice, he wouldn't be able to go through with it. My voicemail saved his life. If my phone hadn't been charged, if it had been on silent, if it had been in my bag, if cellphones hadn't existed, my little brother, my only sibling, my best friend, would have been dead.

The next twelve hours were hell for all of us. I was shaking all over. I was crying, but my face was too weak to move, and I emitted these almost choking sounds. I needed to wait out the time but didn't know what to do. I took a long hot shower and stood there, my tears melding with the water, trying to understand what happened to a boy I thought I knew everything about. After my shower, I sat down with my laptop to research suicide. I spent a long time crafting an email to my project manager about why I needed to leave, but I didn't know how to tell anyone what was happening, because I didn't understand it myself. Yush was not dead, but he was not really alive, either. At least, not in my mind. Something seismic had shifted for all of us, and I didn't know what it meant or why it happened or what came next, but I understood that nothing in our world would ever be the same. When sunlight returned, I went to the airport. It would be another six excruciating hours before I was in Pittsburgh with you and Papa and Yush.

On the plane, tears poured down my face, and my nose ran, and my whole body shook. An older white woman sitting next to me asked if I was okay. I shook my head no and she asked me if I wanted to talk and I said no. Nancy, who was Catholic, had once said she believed suicide was selfish, and in that moment I worried that if I told people my brother tried to kill himself, would they think less of him—or of me? I didn't understand anything about suicide, but I knew that Yush was not selfish, and I could not bear the thought of anyone thinking that he was.

When I got to Pittsburgh, I collapsed on the bed in your hotel room. I sobbed into the comforter as you sat next to me with your hand on my back. It was strange how calm Papa was, and it bothered me. *Show some emotion; this is not the time to repress it,* I thought. Papa told me that it was important that when I saw Yush, I did not cry. Yush should not know how sad I was, because it would make him feel guilty, and Yush needed us to be strong.

The two of you had arrived as Yush was admitted to the psychiatric center that morning. Yush later told me that when he saw Papa, the father we both related to through intellect, Yush had little reaction and felt little emotion. But when he saw you, the mother who made room for our self-expression, he cried in your arms, his first emotional release. And when Yush saw me that afternoon, he crumbled. Our bodies folded into each other. He shook wildly, sobbing into the side of my head, and I held on to him with such force that he could feel, in his bones, that I would never, ever let him go.

It took everything I had to not lose my composure, but I didn't let myself cry in front of my brother, as Papa had commanded.

Now I wish that I had sobbed and let my tears funnel into a stream that carried Yush ashore. I needed Yush to know that he was my world. I needed Yush to know that I would crumble without him, too. I needed Yush to know that crying was not weakness. I needed Yush to know that around me, he never had to pretend to not be sad. And I, too, needed to know that my sadness was not a burden on my brother, that it was an outpouring of the love we shared.

Yush stayed at the ward for the next two weeks. I planned my entire life around the two brief windows of time during which I could see him: once in the morning, and once in the afternoon. I had walked by the drab building countless times on the way to Thomas's apartment but never really noticed it before. The women at the front desk began to recognize me. "No one comes by to see the family this often," they said. "You're a really good sister," they said. *If I were such a good sister,* I thought, *none of this would have happened.*

Before entering the ward, we had to place most of our belongings in lockers. This included anything that could be used as a weapon, like pencils, shoelaces, keys, and coins. One of the few things allowed inside were books. But what kind of book do you buy someone who maybe wants to kill himself when he's stuck in a place where he definitely can't kill himself? I spent hours at Barnes & Noble trying to pick something, but nothing felt right. I bought six books, settling on a haphazard collection that included *Through the Looking-Glass* and *The Hitchhiker's Guide to the Galaxy.* I knew that Yush probably didn't feel like reading much, but I needed him to know that I cared.

Yush slept in a small room with a twin-size bed. He wore sweatpants and sweatshirts without laces, and socks but no shoes, because he didn't leave the floor for two weeks. It seemed like a prison, but Yush said that the staff was kind, and he seemed to be relieved to have a break from functioning in the real world. I wanted to cocoon myself around my little brother and wrap him with warmth and keep him safe forever.

Yush didn't want to think of the people in the ward as friends, exactly. The more he talked to them, the more he wondered how he could have ended up there—with people who came from horrendously abusive families and had real problems, he said. Yush took some assessment test, and the psychiatrist told him that he was probably the smartest patient he'd ever tested, another fact that made us feel like Yush was an anomaly, as if his intelligence meant that he should have been able to logic himself back to sanity.

At first you felt guilty, as if you had caused Yush's mental illness because one of your brothers had schizophrenia. We didn't talk about my uncle much, so I don't know how you viewed his mental health and I don't know how witnessing your older brother's dramatic, heartbreaking change—from someone lively, smart, and funny, like Yush, to the heavily medicated, foggy uncle I saw briefly on the few trips we had taken to India—affected you as a girl. But once, when we were in college, Papa told us that you had been engaged to a man before him—a fact that stunned me for many reasons: because breaking off an engagement was so defiant, because I had thought of you as so traditional, because I was still learning new secrets about you. You said that you ended the engagement when you saw how the man's family treated his mentally ill sibling, keeping him locked in a room and away from everyone else. Their actions were not unheard of in the context of the oppressive stigma and shame that mental illness carried in India, but seeing this disgusted you. Nanaji respected your wishes, even though I am sure publicly breaking an engagement must have damaged his reputation and yours. It must have been terrifying to watch your son and fear that, yet again, you might lose a man you loved to an illness you did not understand.

Papa felt guilty, too. He told us, for the first time ever, that he believed his family had a history of depression. Maybe that's what caused Yush's unhappiness, he said. Papa's façade of omniscience cracked and he broke down, asking me if he'd been too hard on Yush. I had never seen Papa doubt himself before, and it made him finally seem human to me. As he confided his fears, I cried and I said, "No, Papa, you've given us everything, you're a perfect dad."

Ultimately, I don't know how you made sense of Yush's suicide attempt or his mental health. While I think it's likely that Yush had a genetic predisposition toward depression, I believe that the pressures that led Yush to consider taking his life were complex and not summed up simply by genetics.

Over the next two weeks, Yush told me how he gradually lost touch with reality. All summer he had been working long hours to make sure everything was correct for his part in a capsule that would be launched to the International Space Station. But when he ran his code, something failed. He hunted for the bug for weeks, he told me, breaking apart his code and putting it back together again and again, unable to find the error. At the end of the summer, he learned that the mistake was not in his code but in someone else's, causing Yush's to fail upon execution. He realized this only after a colleague had fixed their code, after which Yush's software suddenly ran smoothly. Yush had beaten himself up over a mistake he assumed was his, literally breaking himself to fix something that was never broken. He believed that the stress triggered psychosis. Yush knew that success wasn't worth his sanity. When he was offered a job at the end of the internship, he turned it down without hesitation. He lost his mind and almost his life, but his flawless code ended up in the International Space Station.

He had known that he needed help. A few weeks before the suicide attempt, when he returned to Pittsburgh to begin his senior year, Yush made a series of appointments with the college therapist. Unbeknownst to me or Thomas, he swiped a few of Thomas's antidepressant pills from a bottle in Thomas's car. But none of us—including Yush's therapist—had picked up on how unwell Yush was or that he was on the verge of a psychotic break. That is how good Yush was at meeting the expectations of others.

He began to imagine that he was a vigilante meant to fight for justice. He walked through neighborhoods with high crime rates in the middle of the night and tried to intervene in fights. He concocted a plan to fly to South Africa, which had one of the highest murder rates in the world. He struggled with violent, intrusive thoughts. Eventually, his delusions turned against him, and he believed that he was the true evil in the world. He thought that the world would be a safer and better place without him in it, and so, that fall, he decided he had to end his life. To him, it was all very logical.

I don't have access to Yush's medical records, but according to my journal entry, Yush was diagnosed with psychotic depression and medicated with an antipsychotic and an antidepressant. On one emotional-assessment test, he scored high for repressed anger. This meant that he didn't know how to express his anger, so he became an expert at holding it in and directed his rage at himself instead. He laughed at inappropriate times, often at very dark, morbid things that were not meant to be jokes. He felt antisocial and disconnected from others. Life wasn't meaningless, he said, but he just didn't fit in; he was not connected to the world, while everyone around him seemed to be. He slept in odd increments, no more than four hours at a time. Silence made him uncomfortable. He was changing, but I didn't know to what extent the change revealed a true self that he had always repressed or a self that was buried under severe depression.

Yush told me that high school was the last time he had felt truly happy—a time before he found computers, when he had a full life, with hobbies like drumming and cross-country and reading fiction and dating girls. He had been naturally good at this thing that society rewarded him for, but I'm not sure that he ever really wanted to compete or excel. I remember when Papa pushed him to apply to one of the prestigious Phillips Academy boarding schools, but Yush didn't want to. Papa was adamant, because the school was an entryway to the Ivy League. Yush reluctantly interviewed. I remember, Mummy, that when a letter arrived securing a spot on the waitlist for Yush, you intercepted it and showed Yush in private. He told you he didn't want to go, and you agreed. You threw it out, and none of us told Papa. At the time, I scolded Yush for passing on an opportunity for success that I would never have, a chance to be among the truly elite. But Yush was happier at home. I think Yush would have been happy with a simple life. What I think he didn't feel sure about was whether, if he chose that simple life, he'd still be loved and respected.

Looking back, I see that, by tossing out Yush's letter or buying me clothes that we both knew Papa wouldn't approve of, you carefully chose when and how to apply resistance to Papa's expectations. You subtly exercised your influence within our family system. In these moments I see your resilience. Now I see that your decision to endure, too, was a deliberate choice.

IN THE FRAGILE MONTHS that followed, you and Papa and I worked as a team. Papa rented an apartment down the street from mine, close to the Carnegie Mellon campus, which we furnished with a glass-top dining room table and large sofa that I found on Craigslist. You and Papa spent every weekend in Pittsburgh to be with Yush. I reached out to Yush's friends regularly to keep tabs on him. I called you and Papa every week, sometimes multiple times, to let you know how Yush seemed to be doing. Yush probably resented that we treated him like fine china that could break at any moment, but we didn't care, so long as he was alive.

For the first time ever, I felt that you and Papa needed me. The following months cemented my deep belief that there was nothing more important than family and that the four of us, despite our differences in the past, were committed fiercely to one another's well-being. I knew then that I never wanted to be too far from you and Papa or Yush. I left the project in Boston and asked to be placed on something in Pennsylvania, so that I was never more than half a day's drive from any of you.

But a part of Yush had closed off, even to me. I didn't know how to express concern or show care for him without poking at an insecurity. I sensed, for the first time ever, a distance between us: each of us sizing up the other to assess whether this person was telling the truth or hiding something, because each of us feared that if we admitted how we really felt, the other might withdraw.

As dedicated as we were to one another, we were bound by shame. Days after Yush's attempt, Chachiji, Papa's sister-in-law, had called to ask me about my new job.

"Hey, Chachiji!" I answered cheerfully, as Papa drove.

He mouthed, *Don't say anything.* I nodded, already knowing that whatever was happening to Yush was to be kept a secret. I happily recounted my new job, splitting myself from the pain of something I didn't yet understand. We didn't know how to control the stories that others would tell about Yush or us, and so it was best not to say anything at all. We put up a wall between ourselves and everyone else while pretending there was no wall at all.

Success was supposed to make one immune to struggle, I thought. I had long understood that mental illness didn't happen in high-achieving Indian American families like ours. In fact, both Yush and I had believed that part of what made us so successful was this ability to clamp down on our feelings and not let them out all the time, the way white people did so gratuitously. In my simplistic understanding of the world, it was this unfiltered outpouring of feelings that caused white families so much strife, and it was our emotional discipline that enabled us to work hard and succeed.

None of us knew then that what Yush dealt with was not an anomaly but a tragically common symptom of the pressures he faced. We didn't know that Asian American college students are more likely to deal with suicidal thoughts and attempt suicide than white students—straddling multiple cultures, experiencing racism, and living up to narrow expectations of achievement exerts extreme stress on the mind and body. To navigate those pressures, Yush and I learned to repress our feelings and forge onward, as Dadaji did, as Papa did, as you did. None of us knew that this very survival tactic compounded our pain.

There was no way for us to talk about any of this, because we did not know these problems even existed. We found out about a problem like most families do, when it became so big that it exploded in front of us and we could no longer avoid dealing with it. And we dealt with it the way most families do: quickly and quietly. We swept up the mess, put things back as best we could, and continued to live in the same way, as if nothing had ever happened. We didn't know that by trying to forget, we were more deeply committing ourselves to the very circumstances and problems that had caused the explosion in the first place. We didn't know that we were teaching Yush not to resolve his pain but to find more-creative ways to hide it. Now I wonder what decisions Yush would later have made if he had been encouraged to talk about his mental health, rather than feel pressured to stay quiet.

Despite having missed a full semester of college, Yush would graduate on time, with honors.

But as our family struggled to find some sense of normalcy, I began to question the idea of normal. Yush's best friend, who also lived with depression, said, "This is a dumb analogy, but it sort of fits. It's like in *Men in Black*. If you don't believe in aliens, you walk around like everything is normal. But once you become aware of depression and how it lies to your mind, it's like you know about the aliens. You can't go back to the way you used to think, and you can't believe how uninformed you were." It was not the most eloquent analogy, but it captured my sentiments. For the first time in my life, I began to wonder what else I had failed to see because I had blocked it from view.

Chapter 14

Jekyll and Hyde

T HE SPRING THAT YUSH graduated from college, you shattered your knee on a hike with Papa. As you recovered, I requested to work from home to look after you while Papa was at work. But on my first night back, while you were still in the hospital, Papa and I got into a fight.

It began the way they often began. "I can't even talk to you or make suggestions to you, so I don't try," Papa complained to me. "You completely ignore my experience, always assuming that you know better. You trust your judgment over mine," Papa said.

"I do make decisions based on my judgment. What kind of adult would I be if I didn't do that? You do that, too," I said.

"When I was your age, I listened to my parents and was a lot more respectful of their wishes than you are," Papa responded. "I cannot say a thing to you, because you do not care about what I have to say. In fact, it happened recently."

Papa went on to list an example of how I had ignored him: when, on a brief visit to Montreal over the winter, I didn't explore the city's expansive underground mall as Papa had suggested.

I remember that trip. A few months after Yush's suicide attempt, our family went to Chachiji's house in Ottawa for a family reunion. Buaji's daughter, my cousin Priya, wanted to tour McGill's campus, where she planned to apply for undergrad. As we left the house for the two-hour drive, Papa said that you and he would like to join us. Papa took a long time to get ready, making the rest of us late. Once we arrived, it was too dark to tour the campus. Papa parked at the underground mall and told us he wanted to show us this impressive network of subterranean stores. None of us wanted to see a bunch of shops. As the oldest cousin and as his kid, I voiced the group's wishes and said, "We want to walk around outside a bit before we have to get back. We'll meet you here in an hour."

Papa said that he was furious at the time, but you calmed him down and said, "Prachi never listens. She always does whatever she wants to do. Just let her go."

"You made me feel this small!" Papa screamed, rage rushing up like a geyser as he recalled a memory from months ago. "You had to have your way, even though I'm the one who knows Montreal! I'm the one who knows what to see!"

"It's not an affront to your authority," I said. "So what if you know Montreal better? We saw something we wanted to explore. What's the big deal?"

"You made it a big deal!" Papa bellowed. His anger, now unleashed, had to run its course. "I have the experience and you don't! I know what to see and you don't. You don't know what you wanted to see or didn't, because you had no idea what was there!"

I tried to keep my voice steady and calm. "I'm sorry, but I don't think that's really a fair example," I said. "The purpose of that trip was—"

Suddenly, Papa grabbed one of the wooden chairs from the kitchen table and lifted it over his head and smashed it against the floor. He bashed it again and again until the chair was no more than a pile of splintered wood, all the while screaming that I was a stupid, selfish, worthless, arrogant idiot.

I was amazed by the damage Papa's small frame could inflict upon such a sturdy chair—it was like the superhuman strength mothers shored up to save their child, except in reverse. He yelled at me to get out of his house, but I was already running. I grabbed my bag, stuffed it in the car loaned to me by my company, and fled to the apartment in central Pennsylvania that my company paid for. I drove in the dark and called Nancy to tell her what had just happened, still in shock, shaking with adrenaline. By the time I got to the apartment, Papa had emailed me to tell me that I was a hypocrite.

I had thought that Papa would be proud of the woman I was becoming. But as I graduated from college and got my first job and began to exercise the autonomy that comes with being a financially self-sufficient adult, Papa seemed to resent my independence, becoming enraged when I held different opinions or made decisions that strayed from even the most minor advice or suggestion. I was offering my family my highest form of love, commitment, and care, and I felt like not only was it not enough for Papa, but he viewed my love as a failure to the point of rejection.

I began to call Buaji more frequently, both to seek advice and to vent. I felt dirty and selfish sometimes, talking about family that way, even though what I told her was true. But Buaji never made me feel like what I said was wrong; she didn't inhale it like gossip, and she didn't sensationalize it by getting livid on my behalf. She listened. And I didn't know that I needed that so badly, but I did. I needed someone to hear me, really hear me, and tell me that what I felt was okay to feel, because I didn't trust my own senses. And I needed to know that, despite all the material comforts I enjoyed and all the gifts that Papa bestowed upon me, what I experienced was difficult, and I wasn't bad or weak for thinking so.

Through these repeated phone calls, I changed my opinion about my aunt. I looked for it, but I couldn't see the bad in her that Papa had always cautioned me about, and as she continued to offer me advice that helped, I began to rely on her for emotional support. As we built our own relationship, I reevaluated everything that Papa had always said about his mean sister and her conniving husband.

Yush was angry at Papa and tried to reason with him, but when Papa wouldn't budge, Yush asked me to forgive Papa. I emailed Papa a few days later to ask him if we could put aside our differences for your sake, so that I could come home and be with you while you recovered from your knee surgery.

"You're a good kid," Yush told me.

"Thanks," I said. "I wish Papa felt that way."

Papa did not respond to my email. I emailed you to explain why I hadn't stayed through your recovery, but I didn't hear back. For a week I called you every day, but you didn't pick up. I wonder what Papa told you and the other aunties who came in my stead about why I never visited you.

One month passed, and still I heard nothing from you or Papa. For Mother's Day, Yush and I decided to surprise you anyway. I came with Thomas, and the three of us brought you a cake and flowers. We entered through the deck, where we found you sitting in the sunroom with a cast on your leg. You lit up. "What are you doing here!" you said with excitement. Then Papa came downstairs. He marched toward me.

"What are you doing here?" he said to me. The same words, but they gave me a chill.

"It's Mother's Day. I wanted to—"

"Get out of my house!" he screamed. "How dare you come here. You are not welcome here!"

Papa walked closer. I fled. Papa stopped at the deck and looked on, overseeing my departure.

"I'm sorry you had to see that, Thomas," he said.

"It's okay," Thomas said dismissively, not wanting to engage with Papa's temper. I was hurt that Thomas didn't defend me. His calmness, the quality that had once attracted me to him, now frustrated me. I wanted him and Yush to be visibly angry on my behalf. Instead, I felt like roadkill cleared by a brother and a boyfriend who plugged their noses as they carried away the rotting meat.

More than anything else, what you said next hurt me the most.

"You should never have come," you said, crying. "Prachi, why did you come?"

OVER THE NEXT FEW weeks, after Yush graduated and prepared to move to California for his new job at Intel, conversations with him revolved not around our own lives but around Papa's volatility and how we could intervene or suggest that he seek help. Yush and I both decided that, because something about me seemed to enrage Papa, it was best for everyone that I maintain my distance from him. It was the only viable solution.

I worried about the stress that playing peacemaker was placing on Yush, who was still only months into his own recovery. He was eager to move forward and begin a new chapter of his life. But managing Papa's rage kept pulling him back into chaos, unable to focus on himself as he transitioned into adulthood. I began having intense recurring nightmares in which Papa berated me in front of the family and everyone, including Yush, piled on, and then I would accidentally kill Papa somehow, like by running him over with a car as I backed out of the driveway. My nightmares horrified me.

A few days before the Fourth of July holiday, I got a call that would justify Yush's and my paranoia. I heard your frantic voice on the other end. I had been at my desk for less than an hour that morning. I don't remember your exact words. I remember that the call was short, and when I hung up, I tried to hide the tears on my face. I must have walked into my boss's office, but I don't remember what I said to anyone at work about why I rushed out. Along with my grief, though, I also felt shame. I was sure that, with two family emergencies in my first year, I'd end up getting fired. Within ten minutes I was in my car, on the highway, speeding home.

You had found Papa unconscious on the living room recliner, frothing at the mouth. His heart had slowed to around thirty beats per minute. The paramedics arrived just in time. Papa had gone out for a long drive alone the night before, stopping to pick up a prescription he had written for a heart medication. He ingested nearly the entire bottle, and then he settled into the recliner to die. When the paramedics showed up, they asked you if he had taken anything. They had only a few precious minutes to intervene. You hesitated. You had found the bottle of pills in the car, but you were afraid of showing them. You didn't want them to take away his medical license. *Log kya kahenge?* Yush was shocked, then angered, by how you muzzled yourself over concern for how we may be perceived. If Papa died, his medical license wouldn't matter. Yush, who was living at home for a few more weeks, retrieved the pills and showed them to the paramedics.

I left the office crying, but when I got onto the open highway, driving under a cloudless cobalt sky, I felt giddy. I blasted Ludacris on the radio and danced in the car seat, shaking my hips and bobbing my head. Mummy, I am ashamed of how light I felt in that moment and what it says about me. I could be generous to myself and explain it as hope, the belief that Papa hitting rock bottom might level out to something better. Or it could have been something ugly—that my nightmares were really fantasies coming to life, that I hated my father and was happy he was suffering now. But I think what I felt was liberation—a belief that no matter what happened next, the four of us would finally start being honest with one another. Our pain was out in the open. We could no longer hide it. Going forward, there would be no more secrets.

When I saw Papa that afternoon, he was unconscious in a hospital bed in the ICU. The doctor said that he was stable and likely to recover. The pills Papa ingested had an antidote. For the first time I could recall, Papa looked at peace. I feigned tears, but when I saw him, I wasn't sad. I was angry. Angry that it had come to this, when Yush had asked Papa to seek therapy, and when Yush and I had offered to go to family therapy, too. I was angry that Papa had pushed us away instead of considering our pleas. But I also began to feel hopeful. He had not died. Our family had been given another chance.

I could no longer pretend that everything was fine, and neither could you. I called Papa's siblings, my Chachaji and Buaji, and as I sat in the parking lot of an outdoor mall, I unraveled. I opened up about everything we had deliberately hidden from them in the past year: Yush's suicide attempt, Papa's volatility over the past several months, and now his suicide attempt. The next day Buaji flew from her home in Winnipeg to stay with us. Papa remained unconscious in the hospital, where just a week ago he had been treating patients.

After a few days, Papa moved to the hospital's psychiatric facility. Yush and I visited him in a large cafeteria with a thin carpet and tables for patients and visitors. Papa appeared frail but oddly dignified. I had trouble looking him in the eye, not because he was wounded but because I knew he did not want me to see him that way. I spoke first.

"Why did you do it, Papa?" I asked, as Yush sat beside me.

"Do you really want to know?" he said, looking only at me.

I nodded.

He paused. Without breaking eye contact, he told me: "I can't seem to live with you. I'd rather be dead than have a daughter like you." Papa's eyes stayed fixated on me. I looked down, holding back all the feelings that suddenly coursed through me. I don't remember how long we talked or what else was said.

As I walked back to you and Buaji in the hallway, my mind turned into static. In disbelief, I repeated what Papa had said to me, the words making me angrier and angrier. My agitation agitated you.

"Prachi, please—" you said, motioning for me to stop complaining, as if I were irritated over a delayed flight or canceled dinner reservations. You expected me to not be angry or hurt. I wanted to feel rage, but instead I felt numb.

Buaji told me that what Papa said to me was manipulative. She said that I was not responsible for his attempted suicide. Intellectually, I agreed with her. But I didn't know how that knowledge should change my behavior. There is nothing more final than death, no binary clearer than breathing and not breathing. From that point onward, I was terrified that if I said or did something to set him off, Papa would attempt suicide, and the next time, he would succeed. Though I didn't believe I'd done anything bad, that didn't protect me from the reality and severity of the crisis we were now in.

For years you'd kept your distance from Buaji, as Papa had cautioned. But that week, riddled with anxiety, you could no longer maintain the façade of perfection, either. You told Buaji that Papa called you stupid and useless and worthless every day. I had seen Papa talk like this to you; I knew this to be true. But for a long time I didn't know—and I didn't want to know—what else you went through: that Papa used the threat of self-harm to control you. *He tells me all the time that I'm stupid and useless and I can never live without him, and that if he kills himself, I won't know what to do and I'll be all alone,* Buaji recalls you confiding. On previous occasions he'd taken large doses of sleeping pills and told you to look at what you'd done, that he might not wake up because of how you had hurt him. You stayed up at night watching him sleep, terrified that his next breath might be his last. Maybe that's why you had been slow to react when the paramedics arrived—you had seen Papa harm himself before, and you thought he'd wake up.

You and I thought, separately, that Papa had hurt himself because of something we each did. Neither of us understood that blaming us for his self-harm was a form of abuse meant to coerce us into doing what he wanted. Papa needed help beyond what we could provide. Neither of us knew that we couldn't save Papa. But for years, each of us would continue to try.

I CANCELED PLANS TO visit Swapna and Nancy in Chicago that week, telling them just that "something came up" and I couldn't go. I gave no indication that I was dealing with something difficult, yet I was angry that they didn't seem to care about what we were going through, as if they should have somehow figured out what we'd all worked so hard to make impossible to figure out. Holding on to my resentment was more comfortable than telling them the truth, which would open me to potential rejection or judgment. I could handle the pain of disappointment better than I could handle the feeling that maybe my friends wouldn't understand.

Days later, after Papa told us that he had been diagnosed with depression, he began to insist he was fine—more than fine. Now that he understood what the problem was, he was back in control. Yush and I were both alarmed by what seemed like a performance to say what he needed to say to get out of a place that he felt was below his dignity. We spoke privately with one of the nurses who had been administering Papa's care and begged her not to release him yet. She told us that she agreed but that there was little anyone else could do unless he was at risk for suicide.

Papa's suicide attempt had revealed to all of us the depth and severity of his pain, but it was Papa's extreme denial of his suffering mere days later that terrified Yush and me. We had dismissed Papa's behavior in the past as machismo, or as an immigrant dad under stress, or as a little strict and controlling due to his own cultural values, but now we believed these explanations to be severely lacking. We suspected that "depression" didn't fully explain or describe what Papa was dealing with, either. We believed that the way Papa engaged with others fundamentally interfered with his—and our family's—ability to function.

Yush and I wrote a letter to his doctor, in which we expressed concern over releasing Papa without a more thorough investigation of what ailed him. "You may have observed this on your own, but in our conversations with him at the ward, he has expressed that though he is aware of his depression now, he thinks he has reached a solution and is fairly confident that he can fix this," we wrote. In our letter, we connected the dots between traits that at first seemed like a difficult personality and something destructive that required serious professional intervention. "We wanted to be sure to share what we know with someone who can help him—because we have tried to reach him and cannot," we wrote. "We fear that if he does not change, he will reach another episode similar to this one."

The doctor overseeing Papa's care did not respond to our letter. Papa returned to treating patients within weeks. To ask Papa about his mental health was to rip open a scab and let the blood flow all over again. And more than anything, I wanted to keep the peace. We again performed normalcy. There was a genetic, chemical imbalance, and now that he had medication, everything had been fixed. Just like that.

In the following months, however, Papa began talking to relatives about depression. Against a culture of secrecy and shame over mental illness, particularly for men, opening up about depression was an act of bravery on Papa's part that helped others find a way to address their mental health, too. I marveled as Papa transcended stigma, bending the titanium rules of log kya kahenge with his hands like a superhero—something you or I could never do.

But Papa spoke as if he had been cured, and could now offer others the same cure. He seemingly saw depression everywhere, in everyone, and tried to influence their care regardless of whether they expressed having any symptoms or asked for his help. When one of his cousins was going through a divorce, he insisted she was depressed and booked an appointment for her at a local clinic without asking her permission. She went, out of a sense of obligation, and the doctor assessing her said she wasn't depressed. Papa even suggested writing a prescription for antidepressants for you. Papa was not a psychiatrist, and you were not his patient. His eagerness to prescribe serious mood-altering substances—which would have been a clear violation of his medical license—alarmed Yush and me. Yush confronted Papa over his willingness to write prescriptions for antidepressants, and they got into a fight. I don't know if Papa wrote any prescriptions for you at that time or not.

The day that Papa came home from the psych ward, he was con-templative. Papa asked me to sit next to him on the couch. He told me that he didn't really mean what he had said to me. He confessed that he felt like Dr. Jekyll and Mr. Hyde—and that something about me "brings out the Hyde" in him. I did not know what to do with this information. I believed that Papa regretted his words. But it seemed like he wanted me to accept that I would be his verbal punching bag and not take it personally or ever allow it to create distance between us. As he spoke, I listened quietly, scared to respond. I shoved my feelings down, and my numbness deepened.

Chapter 15

Numb

AFTER YUSH MOVED TO California to start his first job, I spent most of my weekends in New York City with Thomas, who was in his first year of residency. We had been together for about three years and had talked about marriage. But during residency, Thomas's depression flared. He didn't have time to see a therapist, he said, so I dedicated myself to taking care of him. I wanted to keep things peaceful and my needs small so that he could do his important, lifesaving work as a doctor. I thought this is what it meant to love someone well.

That winter, Thomas and I went back to Pittsburgh for a weekend visit. He made dinner reservations at my favorite restaurant, an upscale Asian fusion spot. We rarely went out to fancy restaurants, and when we did, we always split the bill, so when he told me he was taking me out, I suspected that he planned to propose.

After he paid and we left, I thought maybe the proposal wouldn't happen that night after all. The temperature hovered around freezing. Thomas had a bad cold and felt feverish, but he suggested that we visit the Cathedral of Learning on Pitt's campus. "Now?" I asked. "Can't we go tomorrow?"

"No, I really want to go right now," he said. I wondered why he was so insistent. We drove down to campus and walked for another ten minutes to the majestic tower. Thomas led me to a stairwell, stopping at the fifteenth floor. I recognized the spot immediately.

In our first year of dating, I had surprised him with a Valentine's Day picnic. I'd brought a bottle of wine and glasses and taken him to that same spot, where a tiny window opened to a terrace on one of the towers. No one was allowed there, of course, but the window had not been barred shut. Thomas barely fit and had to wiggle his way through, but once he reached the terrace, we marveled at the view. The entire city stretched out before us, still and sparkling in the night.

When we arrived at the same window three years later, it was bolted shut. Flustered, Thomas said, "Let's go to the top."

Thomas was referring to the same window that Yush had once sought to jump from. I didn't want to go there, and I was hurt that Thomas didn't seem to remember that. But I didn't say that to Thomas. I could tell he was anxious. Instead, I told him that I knew the windows up there were also shut. "Let's leave," I said.

Thomas insisted. I suppressed my anxiety. We arrived at the thirty-fifth floor. He walked over to both windows and tried to pry them open. I tried to stop thinking about whether Yush had done the same thing.

After he tested both windows, Thomas said, "Let's go for a walk."

"Thomas, it's so cold and you're sick!" I said.

"Let's just go for a quick walk."

I had grown irritated. I teetered down the sidewalk on three-inch heels, shivering in my thin wool coat, gray leggings and a long silky top. Thomas walked ahead and then stopped in front of Heinz Chapel, the stone building behind the Cathedral of Learning.

"Wait, I want to look at this," he said.

I stared at the red door of the chapel that we had each seen infinite times, wondering if Thomas's fever had made him delirious. Then Thomas got down on one knee. I saw a sparkling diamond, the ring I wanted, and he said a bunch of words—something about beautiful and smart and wanting to spend the rest of his life with me, I think, but I couldn't focus and I couldn't hear anything and I gave him my hand and he put the ring on it and then he paused and he asked, "Is that a yes?"

"Yes! Of course, yes!"

In building a life with Thomas, I could see a familiar trajectory: We would get married and then move to the suburbs and raise a family with two children by the time we were thirty, like you and Papa did. I had picked out a list of names for our future children—names that would fit into American society but also be distinctly Indian—and I knew that I wanted to take Thomas's last name. The idea of starting a new family of my own with Thomas buoyed me in the face of our family's chaos. I thought that he could save me, like a raft floating past in an ocean, giving me a place to rest as my own family drifted farther away. Marrying him would cut me out of our family's dysfunction and place me in a new home that would be forever safe, secure, and stable.

I had always dreamed of having a large desi wedding. But now I was certain about one thing above all else: I did not want Papa to pay for our wedding. I feared that he would use that as justification to exert more power over me during married life. I had learned by now that I could not pay the steep, hidden cost of Papa's generous and usually unsolicited gifts. Thomas and I decided to pay for a small wedding ourselves. We planned to celebrate our engagement with a few friends at a local dive bar.

Over a nice dinner at a restaurant, I told you and Papa about our engagement, and you both lit up. But Papa ran with his excitement, as if he was the one getting married. Seconds later he was already planning the party: who he'd invite and where to start looking for venues.

"Thomas and I want to pay for the wedding," I said, interrupting Papa's daydream.

Papa laughed. "It's a nice sentiment," he said, "but it's just a sentiment. Nothing more."

The father who had screamed at me for taking advantage of him financially now treated my ability to support myself as a mockery. I was angry.

But I had not seen Papa happy in years. Terrified that if I pushed too hard, Papa might hurt himself, that night I proposed a deal: He could do whatever he wanted for the engagement party, and Thomas and I would manage and pay for a small wedding. Papa agreed. I was proud that I'd brokered a compromise and staved off a crisis.

I WORKED AMONG A group of men who proudly self-identified as bros—one even went by the nickname "Bro King." They lived in central Pennsylvania but reveled in their big-city lifestyle, unironically raising their BlackBerry work phones in local bars while yelling, "Mansh! Mansh! Mansh!" in a huddle.

"The Mansh" was short for the Mansion, an ordinary suburban three-bedroom home in which they hosted *Jersey Shore*–themed dance parties in a dingy concrete laundry room. These were the exact type of men Papa had tried to shield me from and the very men I avoided in college, too. It felt ironic that success meant working alongside them now. To make my bleak reality slightly more palatable, with their permission, I started a blog ridiculing their antics.

Managers on my project worked nonstop. They lived in other cities but spent most of their weekdays in central Pennsylvania, drinking with these twenty-something bros every night. It seemed to me that success meant giving up one's time, health, and relationships to make a rich corporation richer. After seeing how stress from work had affected Yush, it felt vital to not let my job take over my being. I no longer sought to rise within the firm. Instead, I wondered why I had been taught to make my ambitions so big yet keep my imagination so small.

I declined many after-work drinks and dinners because, every so often, I would get a call from you, frantic that Papa was suicidal. The calls weren't frequent, but the fear of receiving one in front of my co-workers isolated me. One time, I had just sat down at a large table in a sports bar with half a dozen colleagues, when I heard from you.

"I think Papa's going to do suicide," you said through sobs.

"What's he doing? What's he saying?" I tried to keep a steady, calm voice, so as not to call attention to myself, but a co-worker noticed my expression fall and gestured to ask if I was okay. I waved her off. As I felt hot tears coming on, I blurted, "Sorry, I have to go." I rushed out before my dinner arrived, without offering an explanation.

As I walked to my car in a nearby lot, numbed by the cold winter air, I let my tears flow. You described erratic behavior, Papa getting angry or violent. Rage swelled up within me on your behalf, but I felt so helpless. I tried to distinguish, through the phone, whether the behavior was in fact escalating to the point of self-harm, as you feared, or whether it was more of Papa's commonplace anger that all of us had witnessed growing up. My effort to gauge which reaction was more harmful was futile. I validated your anger and fear, and then I criticized Papa with an eagerness that shames me now.

On the flip side, in these moments Papa called Yush and described you as volatile and screaming insults at him. Yush and I would receive contradictory sides of the story, then we'd call each other, attempting to triangulate the issues at home, both helpless because we couldn't do anything from so far away. When we spoke to either of you again, everything resumed as normal.

Later, you'd call me up and say that Papa was angry about what I had said to you and that he didn't like us talking to each other. You had embellished or misrepresented my words, telling Papa that I said I hated him, even though I didn't say that. I felt betrayed.

"Why did you tell him that, Mummy?" I asked you.

"Prachi, don't get mad," you said, getting defensive.

Then I'd call Yush and vent to him about how much your behavior confused me: You treated Papa like the enemy one moment but were fiercely loyal to him the next. Eventually, after this cycle happened a few more times, I snapped at you. "If you don't want me to hate him, then don't talk to me about how bad my father is!" I yelled.

I am sorry, Mummy, that I didn't understand that your back-and-forth was a reflection of how confusing it was to live with him. Without Yush and me at home as buffers, Papa was now your entire world. You felt responsible for his well-being, but you were also so angry at him for hurting you. I wonder if your decision to tell him some version of my thoughts was a way to share your own opinion passively, which was safer than directly saying that his behavior hurt you. We were all drowning, unintentionally dunking one another below the surface in an effort to lift ourselves up in a raging ocean.

I HAD OPENED UP to only a few friends about what was happening within our family. With everyone else, I projected the image I was supposed to project, and so long as I did this, no one had any reason to think that something might be wrong. This is what I believed it meant to be okay: the ability to convince everyone else I was okay. But with the shortened days of winter, as I saw sunlight only as patches of light gray on my dark-gray cubicle wall, I felt increasingly unstable. For a few hours I'd keep my emotions at bay. Then, with a single comment or thought, in my head I raged at everyone who made me upset. Papa's denial of the severity of his mental illness was destroying this family. I felt like I couldn't talk to you about anything anymore. Worst of all, Yush and I were being forced to take sides. I told Yush that we couldn't let our parents polarize us. This would ultimately prove to be impossible.

It seemed to me that everyone around me was unstable and it was my job to make sure that everyone was okay. I needed help, too, but you, Yush, Papa, and Thomas were already struggling with so much. Finally, I reached out to HR.

Angie, the woman who approved my time off, had once said something about therapy. She'd simply listed the options available to me as an employee: My company covered six sessions of talk therapy. But no one had ever suggested therapy to me before, and I so deeply craved some acknowledgment of the dysfunction in our family, and

Angie spoke to me with such a sweet, concerned manner that I felt as if she cared for me.

At first, I had dismissed therapy because I wasn't suicidal or battling life-impairing mental-health issues, and I thought therapy was really only for addressing serious issues like that. But now I needed to talk to someone—anyone—about this reality that I hid from the world. I booked six sessions with a white woman who appeared to be only a few years older than me. I described to her my family dysfunction. It felt good to talk to someone and have my emotions validated. At the time, I thought that was all therapy could offer me.

ULTIMATELY, I LOST MY composure over a pizza. Just before I left work at seven P.M.—which was early—my boss asked me to order pizzas for the team members who stayed behind. I called in the order and then went back to my corporate apartment and ate what had become my usual dinner: handfuls of shredded Colby and Monterey Jack cheese straight from the bag and a half bottle of Yellow Tail shiraz. I turned on *Law & Order: SVU* and numbed out. One hour later, my cellphone rang. It was my boss. He sounded irritated. I had apparently messed up the pizza order. I ordered a chicken and veggie pizza, not a chicken and onion pizza.

After all the year had wrought, that phone call undid me. I was so livid that I could not sleep. I had reached my limit with family, with work, and with feeling horrible. All of the anger that I had repressed came rushing out. I paced around the living room and then wrote in my journal, gripping the pen hard, sloppy handwriting flowing. I stayed up all night writing and rewriting an email to my boss. In my rant, I noted that he never seemed to ask the men to order food for the team. I did recall, however, a male co-worker scheduling parties at the strip club after work. I was never invited to these—not that I wanted to go.

As daylight approached, I emailed my letter to a male co-worker I trusted and asked him to make sure it wasn't offensive. I didn't include the line about the strip club. I sent the email to my boss and cc'd his boss, telling them both that from now on the men on the team could place orders for themselves.

I had never done anything like it. I was not especially good at my job. After more than a year, I still didn't understand much about data warehouses, SQL queries, or databases—information I had been expected to learn at work but had neither the interest nor the ability to focus on. Mostly, I expended my energy on suppressing my feelings. But I knew that the project suffered a shortage of workers and firing me would cause my boss far more work than he wanted to deal with.

In a private meeting, my boss told me that it was offensive that I had called him sexist. He said he was not sexist. I said okay. He never asked me to place food orders for the team again.

I left the office early that day, still fuming. I didn't like who I was becoming. I complained about my boss every day, but in a way I also needed him to be a jerk, because otherwise I had to face the real source of my pain: that I felt like our family was falling apart, and I couldn't do anything to stop it. I needed one domain within which I could change or control my circumstances. I decided that I needed to leave this project and go feel human again.

It all happened quickly after that. Angie from HR said I would likely qualify for unpaid leave because of what I was dealing with at home. This meant that I would still have a job and I would continue to have health insurance for two months.

I talked it over with Thomas. He supported me. I told him I wanted to try to become a writer. I did not write anymore, except for that bro blog. I didn't know how to write what I really wanted to write about. Writing demands conviction. But the last thing that I could put on my page was me—not that I even really knew who that was. I prided myself on my ability to be a chameleon: to change myself to reflect what others needed of me when they needed it. This, I thought, was the quality that made me unique—that was what made me *me*.

But I knew that, for as long as I could remember, writing helped me make sense of the world. My journal was the only place that felt safe.

I believed that deep within me was something I needed to coax out for my own survival and that writing would help me do that. I wondered if it was possible for me to feel the way I did when creating as a kid, or if that was a relic of childhood I had to give up as part of being an adult. I didn't know the answer to these questions, but I knew I had to find out.

I know, Mummy, that you once kept a journal, too. I have a vague memory of a comment Papa made in passing when I was thirteen or so, so faint that I thought I might have conjured the detail out of a desire to feel closer to you. But I don't believe I could have imagined it.

Even then I felt that there was something significant about you writing. I had struggled to see myself in you beyond our shared physicality. This tiny detail suggested that more of me came from you than I'd realized and alluded to a rich emotional life unknown to me.

"You know, Mom used to keep a journal, once—when she first moved to Canada," Papa had said.

"Mummy, why did you stop writing?" I asked you. I wondered if the day you stopped writing, you stopped believing that your story could ever matter.

You said nothing.

"I don't know," Papa said, answering for you. "One day she ripped it up and threw it out," he said, shrugging. You remained quiet, blank. "You should start writing again," he said offhandedly. You looked away.

Ripping up a journal is ripping up a soul. Shaken by the violence of the act, I wanted to know everything: when you started keeping a journal, how often you wrote, why you wrote, what you wrote, why you stopped. What Papa dismissed as an inexplicable fit of hysterics was, I imagine, a response to something sinister that he did. But you would not tell me then, and I know that these are questions I cannot ask you now.

———

A FEW MONTHS AFTER Thomas and I got engaged, I forced myself off the project by applying for the unpaid leave of absence. I didn't tell you or Papa about my plan.

I feared that if I continued to follow Papa's expectations, I'd end up as isolated and angry as he was. He had raised Yush and me to see the world as a place where our accomplishments, money, and social status defined our worth. The events of the year had prompted me to question this outlook. I saw that, despite all that Papa had accomplished and how intelligent he was, happiness and peace were strangers to my father, and that same drive for achievement had nearly killed my brother. I needed to prove to myself that I was capable of living beyond Papa's shadow and that happiness was achievable some other way—or at least that it was possible to live without feeling this horrible all the time. I was miserable at my successful job and did not see anything particularly extraordinary about the work I did, only that we created a work culture that told us how extraordinary we were to mask how unhappy we all were.

The day I left the project, a colleague approached me and asked me what I was going to do with so much time off. It wasn't a question.

"You're going to be so bored," he said. "You're going to feel so empty. You'll see."

I laughed—a real, deep laugh. The thought that this job was supposed to give me purpose in life was so absurd that I found his comment hilarious. "No," I said, "I'm going to finally be happy."

He looked at with me with pity and then walked away.

Chapter 16

New Beginnings

Dᴜʀɪɴɢ ᴍʏ ᴛᴡᴏ ᴍᴏɴᴛʜꜱ of unpaid leave, I bought a four-by-six-foot canvas and wedged it between Thomas's desk and the couch in our cramped Manhattan apartment. I studied a five-by-seven photo I'd taken at a rocky beach in Maine, and over the next few weeks I channeled my emotions into brushstrokes on the expansive canvas. I started at the top with enthusiasm and dreams of emulating impressionist masters, but once I got down to the monotonous brown rocks, the painting slipped far away from the majestic visions in my head.

Soon I gave up, rushing through the bottom and hoping no one would notice my shoddy workmanship. When friends came by, they remarked, "Wow, did you paint that? That's amazing!" I nodded sheepishly, embarrassed by how good they thought it was, knowing that I had barely put in effort, knowing that this would not pass in any solid art program, knowing that they probably left unsaid *for someone who isn't a real artist.* I felt like my art was a cheap party trick that I used to impress other people and manipulate them into liking me. I put my brushes away again. I desperately wanted to create something good, but I didn't know what that meant. I was trying to get in touch with the part of myself that could express, but after a childhood of learning how to suppress, I didn't know how to do that.

As my time off drew to an end, an adviser from the firm reached out to talk about getting me on a new project. I responded with rote, saccharine enthusiasm that, yes, I was excited to be back. But I delayed the first call as long as possible, and then, when the day came to return, dread, anxiety, and fear took over my body. I wanted to cry. I wanted to do anything other than go back to an office and perform some charade. I couldn't do it. Any of it. I knew then that I had to quit.

I didn't tell you any of this because you would tell Papa, and I didn't want Papa to know, because he might pressure me to change my mind. I couldn't tell either of you that watching our family self-destruct had pushed me to quit my stable, successful job and blow up the life that both of you had worked so hard to help me attain.

My worst-case scenario was still one of immense privilege. I had enough savings to survive should I not be able to find a new job immediately. I knew that if I didn't make it as a writer, I'd likely find another job in another industry someday. I knew that I had Thomas's support throughout it all. I knew that I would be fine.

The following Monday, I put on a miniskirt and walked across the city to the company's headquarters. On the elevator, a middle-aged woman in a business suit looked me up and down and said, "Do you work here?"

"Not anymore!" I exclaimed, not attempting to hide my joy. I returned my company laptop and left the building.

LIKE ME, AFTER A brief foray into the corporate world, Yush quit his job to pursue his passion. He wanted to use his creativity and intellect to solve deep societal issues as an entrepreneur. Not long after I left the consulting firm, Yush moved back home to build a platform that allowed anyone to create interactive digital textbooks and share them with others—his solution to democratize and increase global access to education.

Yush's presence at home comforted you. You could observe his mental health without intruding. But I worried about his isolation. I encouraged him to live on his own, in a city, and establish his own life. He worked nonstop on this product. He did not date, most of his friends lived elsewhere, and he did not make any money. While the platform he coded was technologically impressive, Yush had no business plan for the company and little sense of who would use his product or why.

When Yush met an obstacle that could not be overcome by intellect alone, he applied brute force to move it. He created an algorithm to mass-email professors about his platform, treating the issue as simply one of numbers. When his solution failed, he sat bewildered as to why most professors ignored random emails from a recent college graduate who claimed to have solved the problem of inaccessibility of higher education. He called me, frustrated.

"Yush, you live in the basement of your parents' house. Would *you* take you seriously?"

"Hmm," he said, "I see your point."

A few days later, he called to tell me that he spent his last two hundred dollars on a headshot for his LinkedIn profile. I laughed.

"Why did you do that?"

"To look more professional," he said. If the problem was that people didn't take him seriously, Yush thought having a headshot—a symbol of professionalism—could fix it.

One weekend, Yush, Thomas, and I rented a cabin in the woods near the Pennsylvania–New York state border. Just before the trip, Papa told Yush that he had scheduled an appointment for Yush with his new psychiatrist. You mentioned to me that this man had altered Papa's diagnosis. We talked about it in whispers, understanding that this knowledge was forbidden to pass between us. I didn't know how Papa felt about his new diagnosis or what his treatment looked like or whether he believed in it, though, because he never spoke to me about his mental health. We acted as if there was nothing to acknowledge.

Yush had followed his own treatment plan in Pittsburgh. But Papa saw them as bonded by this chemical monster in their brains, and occasionally he tried to influence Yush's healthcare. He'd scheduled this appointment with his new doctor in the middle of our trip, without Yush's consent. Then he pressured Yush to go by saying that his money would be wasted if Yush didn't attend. I was furious and told Yush that he did not have to go if he didn't want to. To avoid a fight with Papa, Yush said he'd just get it over with.

When Yush came back, he was disturbed. "He told me I was bipolar within the first ten minutes and tried to prescribe me lithium," Yush said. "I'm really worried about why Papa thinks he's so good."

I checked online patient reviews of the doctor, and rating after rating corroborated what Yush had told me: a condescending psychiatrist who diagnosed patients with bipolar disorder within minutes. Yush confronted Papa about his concerns and relayed to me what sounded like the most heated argument they'd ever had. Papa screamed at Yush the way he'd often screamed at me, and he threw something at Yush.

Years after this, Yush would experiment with serious mood-stabilizing drugs, going on and off them at his own discretion, one of his later girlfriends told me. He had become skeptical of the entire institution of psychiatry. When I look back at Yush's meeting with Papa's psychiatrist, I wonder if that was the moment when Yush decided that the outside world could not help him, that he would have to rely on his own intelligence to come up with solutions for his mental health.

AFTER TWO YEARS OF misery, our family had something to celebrate. Relatives were flying in from all over the country for the extravagant engagement party that you and Papa had planned at the local country club. You took me to Edison, the New Jersey town filled with South Asian clothing and grocery stores. I chose a flashy pink and teal mermaid-cut lehenga with gleaming rhinestones, glass bangles, and golden jewelry. On the day of the party, a caterer set up a dosa station on our backyard deck to host lunch for our relatives ahead of the evening's festivities. You wrapped yourself in an ornate silk sari with delicate gold jewelry, looking like a queen.

That night, Dadaji welcomed Thomas to the family. "I greet you all on behalf of my father and mother, who were both born in this little village in India at a time when there was no electricity, radio, trains, or telephone. I greet you all on behalf of my Nana, my mother's father, who was born sometime near 1880 and lived his entire life of ninety-five years in the same village. I am sure that he never imagined his descendants will someday invade America," Dadaji said. "In all these eighty years, I have never been more happy than today."

Family and friends filtered into your royal court and watched you and Papa coronate me a princess. Thomas and I posed for photos on the lawn on an unseasonably warm, sunny fall day. Guests funneled in and out of a photo booth that you and Papa had rented, posing with silly hats and stuffed animals. More than one hundred people crowded the dance floor to a mix of Bollywood songs, top-40 pop tunes, and classic hits.

We continued the party at a local bar, where Papa paid for everyone's drinks. I cozied up to Papa on an oversize leather couch. Under dim lighting, buzzed from alcohol and the grandeur of the celebration, I overflowed with gratitude.

"Thank you, Papa," I said. "This means a lot to me."

Papa smiled softly and we hugged. You sat close by, feeling the comedown of an exciting but exhausting day. You loved Thomas, and I'm sure you must have felt less concerned about me, knowing that I was marrying into a kind, stable family. I'm sure you were glad, too, that father and daughter were getting along again.

———

THOMAS AND I BEGAN to consider locations for the wedding. When I showed Papa a venue for seventy-five people, he said, "That's too small."

"But we made a deal," I said. "The engagement party was for you, and Thomas and I want a small wedding."

"You can't have a wedding that's smaller than the engagement party," he said. "How will it look if our friends and family at your engagement aren't invited to your wedding? Mom and I will be humiliated."

I was too scared to fight. The wedding was the only thing that seemed to bring Papa joy. I didn't want the happiest event in my life to be marred by the drama and crisis that I now expected in our family affairs. Wedding planning involved too many intimate decisions, each one creating room for conflict and misunderstandings that could spiral into a complete breakdown. I was terrified of becoming the daughter whose wedding was so stressful that it caused her father to harm himself, and I didn't want to place that kind of stress on you, either.

Thomas and I talked it over with his parents and agreed that it was easiest to accept Papa's wishes. His parents said they'd chip in, too, so that we would still get some say in the decision-making process. It wasn't so hard to fall into the fantasy. We found a historic estate on a pastoral lawn. You bought me two bridal lehengas with so much beadwork that each weighed about ten pounds. I again got swept up in the excitement.

AFTER QUITTING MY JOB, I had spent the summer trying to get in touch with my creativity again by taking improv, sketch writing, and cartooning classes in New York City. I was shocked by the cost of journalism school. I did not know if I could ever pay back student loans on a journalist's salary. The investment seemed too risky. Instead, I decided to live off the savings from my two years of work and make breaking into journalism my full-time job. I would give myself two years to build a network and land an internship and get something—anything—published. If I couldn't do that, I would lay the dream to rest, I decided. I told you both about my plan to become a writer only after I had quit, when it was too late to change my mind. Maybe by then, however, neither of you was too concerned. I was engaged to a doctor. It did not matter much what I did for my career because, in your eyes, I would be looked after regardless.

Marin—my friend from college whom Papa had deemed unsuccessful—was now a journalist at a prominent magazine. She had introduced me to a former colleague who worked at a New York City media start-up. I had no media experience, but I offered to help with the analytics side of the company, hoping to eventually write for the website and learn more about the industry. I was supposed to get paid, but the start-up founder stalled each month. By the end of the summer, a few months before the engagement party, I was laid off from a job that had barely compensated me.

That fall, I briefly wrote freelance copy for a failing ad agency. My bosses once told us to walk around the floor several times in opposite directions, as often as possible, to make it look so busy that investors would rent the floor. During a vacation with Thomas's family the following winter, I learned that I had been let go.

Later, I responded to a Craigslist ad seeking screenwriting interns for a production company run by a convicted con man who had reinvented himself as a Hollywood producer. He looked like an egg resting on toothpicks and routinely proclaimed things like, "This script will be the next *Citizen Kane!*" and "Vitamins are more addictive than heroin—it is a fact!" I saw several half-naked European girls who looked barely sixteen walking through his Tribeca condo. During a break, the producer showed a nude photo of one of them to another male writer and said she was his girlfriend. I heard, a few years later, that he had assaulted one of the women in the internship.

That year, as I struggled to find paid work, the weight of my decision to leave a secure, stable job finally crushed me. One of my copywriter co-workers, a balding man with a monotone voice, told me that

I'd never make it through the doors of a good agency without impressive names on my résumé. A silver-haired woman at the media start-up, who'd worked at a large cable news organization, said that I couldn't break into media because I wasn't an Ivy League graduate. I spent four weeks devouring *Lost*, years after everyone had watched it, wondering if I had damaged my life beyond repair.

My ignorance and idealism protected me. My stubbornness and ego pushed me. But more than anything, a self-righteous refusal to bend to Papa's worldview motivated me. I had risked everything and staked my identity on the hope that there was more to life than competing and performing. Backing off now felt like an admission of defeat, resigning myself to the idea that Papa had been right about the world, about me, about everything, and I could never be more or any different than what he said I was. To me, this transition was not about a job or even a career. It was about an approach to life and who had control over how I lived mine: me or Papa. I had given myself two years to make an earnest effort, and I was going to see it through.

Just as my hope faltered, Marin introduced me to an editor at *Gawker*. I applied for a summer internship there. After interviewing me, they asked me for a five-hundred-word writing sample about my consulting experience. Those five hundred words took me three full days to write.

A few weeks later, *Gawker* offered me an internship.

The internship was unpaid. But when I found out, I jumped up and down on the bed like a child. I had made it. I knew now that the toughest step had been accomplished. I had a foot in the door. Now that I was in the room, they would finally have to see me.

Chapter 17

One-Way Street

As I BUILT A new life for myself in New York, I often went home to Pennsylvania on weekends, eager to spend time with Yush and plan the wedding with you and Papa. During one of my visits, Dadaji called to check when he should schedule plane tickets to stay with us. Papa hovered nearby. You answered the phone and quickly handed it to me.

"Talk to Dadaji," you whispered. "Ask him to come on a different day, because we'll all be at Swapna's wedding." I was confused as to why you couldn't just tell Dadaji this, but I said okay. As I spoke to Dadaji, Papa overheard me.

"They can come any day they want to," he interjected.

I thought maybe Papa didn't understand. "Dadaji called to ask for a good day to come. I told him any day except Saturday, since Swapna's getting married that day."

Papa repeated himself, this time aggressively. "You don't get to tell my parents when they can or cannot come to my house. You don't live here anymore."

I was taken aback. "Relax, Papa," I said. "They're also my grand-parents. Dadaji doesn't mind coming on a different day."

Dadaji booked tickets to arrive a few days after Swapna's wedding in mid-July. By the time Dadaji and Dadiji came, however, I would be long gone.

THE MORNING AFTER SWAPNA'S wedding, as I laced up my sneakers for a run, Papa came downstairs and asked if he could talk to me about something. I understood that this was not a request. I nervously followed Papa into the sunroom, where you had set up trays of fruit and bread and served us tea. Papa told me that he wanted to talk to me about my behavior. I had disrespected Papa by telling Dadaji when to come, Papa said, referring to the phone call from several weeks ago. I struggled to understand how this had been disrespectful. I looked to you to back up the fact that you'd asked me to tell them. Instead, you said, "No, Prachi, I didn't say that."

I was confused.

"But, Mummy—"

"No, no, Prachi."

I realized then why you handed me the phone that day. You knew Papa would get angry, and you didn't want to be blamed. You had set me up to take the fall, and you denied it now because you were scared of how Papa would react. You had long ago stopped being my lookout. Now you acted as Papa's henchman. I felt betrayed, but I wasn't angry with you. I was sad. I understood that it was a survival strategy. I could leave. You had to stay.

I apologized in a way that was careful not to accept wrongdoing but also to acknowledge that Papa felt hurt.

"I am sorry that you felt disrespected by that," I said. "That was not my intention."

My apology appeased Papa at the moment. But he was still searching for something. He switched the subject.

"Why are you so close to Thomas's parents?"

"What do you mean?"

"Mom and I have seen the way you talk to them. You don't talk to us the same way, with the same respect. You call them more than you call us."

What was I being accused of—not loving him enough? Of loving my future in-laws too much? I had distanced myself from Papa cautiously as a way to prevent blowups, not because I didn't love him. I limited our time together; I avoided getting into extended or in-depth conversations; I withdrew from conversations or I agreed robotically. Seemingly benign interactions could be repurposed months later as examples of how horribly I had treated him, and I did not want to supply him with more ammunition. We hadn't had a fight in months. I thought my strategy was working. But now Papa had picked up on the distance between us and accused me of not caring about him, without any awareness of his role in creating the existing dynamic.

"You should treat us with more respect," he said, "the way you treat Thomas's parents."

After a few more attempts to evade Papa's line of questioning, I began to sense that this "talk" would not end until I admitted wrongdoing, a form of submission, an emotional laying my head at his feet to beg for his forgiveness. Papa would raise bogus claim after bogus claim until I conceded that I was wrong and bad and selfish and disrespectful. I didn't know how much longer I could tiptoe around his feelings. I was also profoundly hurt by the suggestion that I didn't love my parents enough, particularly because I had tried so hard to be what Papa needed me to be. It was painful that my best ability to express love was received as rejection, and it made me feel like, no matter what, nothing I did would ever be good enough for him. I responded as carefully as I could.

"Respect is a two-way street," I said. "And I think it's a little hypocritical—"

It happened in a flash. Before I could finish my sentence, Papa growled and grabbed the white Corelle tray in front of him and smashed it over the back of my head. I screamed. White shards fell over me and raspberries plunged into my T-shirt, seeping into the fabric as a permanent stain. My brain froze, but my body moved fast.

"It's all the same," I said breathlessly, my eyes rolling around, searching, nothing making sense. "Nothing has changed, nothing has changed, I need to get out," I said to myself, out loud, to no one.

In my memory, the next few seconds play out slowly, because I still can't reach the next moment without reminding myself what happened in the previous one. Each action is so illogical, so disconnected from reality, that to move forward in the memory I have to remind myself of the events and words that led to this specific moment and then work up to the next. I think you are screaming, or crying, and I am just running. Papa is screaming insults at me, calling me arrogant, stupid, and worthless.

I ran out of the sunroom and into the kitchen, trying to reach the garage to flee the house. By now I never fully unpacked while at home. I always left my backpack by the garage door, because I knew I might have to run away without notice. I could walk three miles to the bus stop beside the highway, where I'd catch the next ride back to New York's Penn Station. I was just a few feet from the door when Papa lifted a large steel saucepan from the stove and hurled it at me with perfect aim. I ducked. The saucepan crashed into the wooden cabinet just behind me, then hit the floor with an explosive bang. A deep gash ran through the cabinet door instead of through my skull. Papa, huffing, stood at the other side of the kitchen, lips pressed into a thin line, eyes homed in on me. I didn't recognize the man glaring at me. I kept running.

To my surprise, it was not Papa but you who chased me now. You blocked the garage door. I was trapped. I ran into the bathroom to shut myself in until Papa cooled down. As I tried to close the door, you threw your body between me and the doorframe and pleaded with me. "Prachi, why are you doing this to us?"

I yelled for you to move out of my way, but you had cornered me. Papa barreled toward me. I had to get out.

I pushed you aside, and then I grabbed the kitchen phone. I held it above my head and waved it around like a gun. "I'm calling the police!" I screamed at Papa. My hands were shaking, as was the rest of my body, but I steadied my fingers well enough to dial 911. I held the phone up and let it ring.

Suddenly, Yush burst into the hallway. He had been asleep in the guest bedroom next to the bathroom, jolted awake by the crashing of the pots, the cracking of the wood, and the cacophony of our screams. He emerged to find me hysterical, fruit splattered on my gym shirt and my running shorts, with a phone in my hand as a shield against Papa. I didn't know it then, but this would be one of the last times that the four of us would ever be together as a family.

"Should I tell the police to come?" I yelled, asking Yush what to do. The operator was already connected on the other end, but I didn't respond. Papa didn't speak.

"Put the phone down," Yush said in a measured voice, motioning with his hands as he looked from side to side at a crazed woman and an eerily calm man. I didn't know if Papa was gearing up for a second fight or if he was finally backing down, but I was not going to stay to find out.

"Let's go," Yush said to me. Yush escorted me to his car without saying another word to you or Papa.

"He's such a good man, he's never hurt anyone," you cried as I entered the garage. "He only gets like this when you are around. Why did you have to call him a hypocrite?"

And then came the words that continue to haunt me: "How can you leave me?"

I wanted to cry, *How can you expect me to stay?*

BEFORE YUSH DROPPED ME off at the bus stop, he tried to explain, clinically, that "there's just something about you that sets Papa off."

He told me to not take it personally. He insinuated that I must have done or said something to trigger Papa's violence. Yush hadn't witnessed what happened, yet he blamed me for provoking Papa, as if I was equally responsible.

If I had stayed, and if the police had arrived, would they have pressed charges? What would have happened to you if Papa was arrested? Or would the police have looked at me, a frenzied brown girl with no visible marks, and at him, a calm, presentable doctor, and concluded that I was just making it all up? Regardless of the outcome, I would have been held responsible for our family's public embarrassment, which was the most unforgivable act of all.

I boarded the bus back to New York with disheveled hair, wearing gym clothes with raspberries smeared across my shirt. I tried to call Buaji and tell her what happened, but the bus driver yelled at me for talking on the phone. I hung up, feeling dejected. I was twenty-five, living with my fiancé, but at that moment I felt like a stupid girl trying to be something I was not. The welt on my head turned into a large purple bump, hidden underneath my thick hair. I had an upset stomach all week. Had I not yet started to move toward the life that I wanted for myself, I am sure that I would have sunk deeper into that feeling of worthlessness.

Four days later, on my twenty-sixth birthday, Papa sent me a one-sentence email that read: "I'm very, very sorry for what happened on Sunday." I wondered how a father who had so many creative words for how wretched I was seemed to have so few words to express remorse.

I forwarded his email to Yush, went to the *Gawker* office in SoHo, and focused on writing a blog post. Yush responded with an email saying I should forgive Papa. The sorrow and regret in his email was genuine, he said. I was annoyed at Yush. What kind of behavior was I supposed to tolerate and ignore and get over? What about how this affected me? I was not a rubber band that could just snap back into place. And if Papa's violence escalated as I did better for myself, how bad would it get going forward?

Papa had said before that I wasn't letting him be a father, that I would more readily listen to a stranger's advice than to his own. It made me sad that this was his understanding of our relationship, one in which he imposed his will and I did his bidding, no questions asked, and it surprised me because he had, at least when I was a girl, taken such pride in my outspokenness and had encouraged me to think critically and independently. But as a girl, I had inhaled his speech like an intoxicating scent. I upheld his divinity. My confidence and feistiness were cute, nonthreatening quirks because, at the end of the day, I remained dependent on him and I did as I was told. The tragedy was that I believed that if Papa wasn't trying to control me, if he could have learned to see me not as an object but as an individual, then we could have shared the love that I knew we felt deeply for each other.

Some part of me wanted to accept Papa's apology. It was just a plate, just a small bruise. I had overreacted. I was not truly in fear for my life. So many fathers are brutally violent; some are completely absent; some sexually abuse their children; some never show even a sliver of kindness. Was I such a princess that I couldn't handle a few scratches from a father who otherwise doted on me, who had paid for my education and given me all the tools to succeed in this world? Papa was flawed, but what person isn't? Thanks to him, I had a better setup for life than most people ever get.

When I called Buaji, she didn't sound as shocked as I expected her to be. "Was I wrong to call the police?" I asked her. As she heard doubt overtake my voice, she told me that, no, I had done nothing wrong. I was not to blame. She believed me, she said, because she had once been me.

Buaji revealed that when she was nineteen, in a sudden fit of rage, Papa hurled a tempered glass plate at her head during dinner. It shattered against the wall behind her, missing her by a few centimeters. Dadiji and Dadaji had looked on helplessly, while Fufaji, her then-boyfriend, lunged at Papa. Though soft-spoken, Fufaji was twice Papa's size, and in that moment he asserted his physical dominance. "If you ever do something like that again, you and I are going to have a problem," he said to Papa. You were there, Mummy, watching the entire episode unfold as Papa's new bride. I wondered if this explained why Papa didn't like Fufaji—because, in Papa's eyes, Fufaji had emasculated him in front of you. You never mentioned any of this to me.

Maybe you had forced it out of your memory, the way you would block out what happened to me at our home that summer.

When Buaji told me about that incident, it was as if someone had cut a tiny slit in the wall that separated my reality from the façade that Papa projected to the world. I could peer through that slit and see a part of my own experience. Somebody else saw what I saw, too. Maybe my senses weren't deceiving me after all. But it was just this little slit. I didn't know how big that wall was yet or what remained hidden on the other side.

Years later, Buaji admitted to me that she had felt nauseated after talking to me that day. What happened once was happening again. She wondered privately: Had it ever stopped, as both she and Fufaji had long assumed?

In the past, I had written long emails trying to bridge the gap between Papa and me. I had accepted his apologies, however meager and rare they were. This time, I had nothing left to say. I wanted more than a "sorry." I wanted accountability.

I waited for something more substantive.

A few days later I received a typed letter from someone named Susan. In it, she introduced herself as Papa's therapist. I didn't know Papa was seeing a therapist, but this made me hopeful. The letter was dated a day after my birthday, a day after he sent me the apology. Maybe the therapist was writing to ask me to consider attending family therapy, as Yush had suggested to Papa before. Maybe she was offering to mediate a conversation. I would have agreed to that. If Papa could acknowledge that he was not a perfect dad, our relationship would have improved. It would, at the very least, have been an honest one.

The letter was only two paragraphs long. In the first paragraph, Susan explained that she had been informed of the "current difficulty" between Papa and me. She did not detail what these difficulties were. Then she wrote that I was not "to discuss with or inform any other person" about Papa's "problems or treatment" or anything "relating to such matters" without his "express written permission." Absent his written consent, "it is required that you maintain confidentiality," the letter read.

The letter infuriated me. I interpreted the notice as intimidation, like a cease-and-desist letter from a lawyer, intended to prevent me from talking about my own experiences. It seemed that Papa cared more about preserving his reputation than about mending our relationship.

Again, I did not respond.

A few weeks after the letter arrived, I received an email from Papa. There was no mention of the therapist's letter or of the incident at home. It was about the wedding.

"I'm not sure how we got involved in an even larger marriage," it read. "Mom and I have decided that we should return to what you told us to do originally. We have done our part for celebrating your marriage to Thomas and will let you take care of the wedding itself. This is your chance to plan and have the wedding in your own style."

Out of context, the email appeared loving and considerate. But when I read it, I felt my sanity slip. Papa was reneging on the deal that he himself had manipulated into existence. He was no longer paying for our wedding, despite having booked a venue and chosen caterers on a budget that he knew Thomas and I could not afford. I was crestfallen that the wedding I had become so excited about was no longer a possibility. But what angered me more was how Papa phrased it: as if he was performing a favor to us.

Again, I did not respond.

When I called Yush to vent over how Papa had manipulated the wedding, Yush thought that I was acting spoiled. "So you won't have a big wedding—so what? Why did you expect Papa to pay for such a big wedding in the first place?" he said.

Yush's reaction hurt my feelings. I realized that, although Yush held me responsible for Papa's behavior when Papa lost control, when I complied with Papa's wishes or accepted his gifts out of a desire to maintain peace, I was not similarly responsible for Papa's feelings but instead seen as taking advantage of Papa. Yush viewed my concern of triggering Papa as a convenient excuse to get what I wanted. I knew then that I could not continue to use fear of Papa's reaction as a way to justify my own behavior, because it was a battle that I could never win. I had to do what I believed was right, regardless of the impact it might have on Papa. But that was easier said than done. I would continue to struggle to act on that belief for years.

A few weeks later, a *Gawker* editor forwarded me a job opening at a different national news outlet and encouraged me to apply. I applied and interviewed and accepted the job, in disbelief that suddenly, a little more than a year after leaving the consulting firm, I was a working journalist. My gamble on myself had paid off. The welcoming of the internship and the journalism job, in contrast with how I'd been cast away from home that same summer, reinforced that my instincts were leading me in the right direction. I was onto something and going somewhere, and I couldn't let Papa's anger drag me down now.

Still, I wanted to lash out at him the way he did at me. It didn't feel fair to take it quietly and then also show him grace when I had been given none, all for the sake of family, which increasingly felt like a farce. I continued to rely on Buaji for advice, and she continued to encourage me to take the high road, no matter how Papa behaved. For a long time, I was frustrated by advice that seemed to cater to a double standard: I was expected to be calm and rational, but no one dared challenge Papa's anger.

But that summer, after I refused to participate in Papa's escalations, I realized what taking the higher ground had enabled me to do. Deep down, I had always feared that I was just like Papa, because, like him, I was hot-tempered, stubborn, and highly critical. I insisted that the world exist the way I wanted it to, and when it failed to meet my expectations, I got righteously angry. It was only in not lashing out that I was able to prove to myself that I wasn't the same. Had I mirrored his reactivity, I would have become further confused and convinced that even as I despised him, I was just like him, seeing his behavior in my own reactions to him. I would lose the ability to distinguish who I really was versus what I was reacting to, and boundaries between us would vanish, as I had seen happen between him and you.

I had originally listened to Buaji because I respected her. But that summer, I began to see how owning my reactions and behavior liberated me. By not responding to Papa's tantrums, I took myself out of them entirely, to the point where I could recognize the absurdity of his actions. I started to understand the directionality of the movement, how it traveled from one source and then stopped at another. His outbursts were a pattern—not an anomaly. I didn't understand what caused his anger, but I was no longer willing to submit to the repetitive cycle.

Thomas and I lost the wedding venue and postponed the wedding indefinitely. I didn't want a wedding at all if this was the cost.

I knew that this decision would hurt you deeply, Mummy. I knew that you wanted me to forget and move on. It is what you had done. But, Mummy, I couldn't. A part of me wanted to call you, reason with you, plead with you to see my perspective. But I knew that you didn't want to hear any of it.

I was angry with you, too. I didn't see you as the casualty in the war between Papa and me anymore. I felt as if you had firmly chosen a side, and it wasn't mine. You didn't protect me anymore. I understood now that you protected him.

That November, Thomas and I decided to elope. We didn't tell anyone about our plans. We rode the subway to the courthouse in Lower Manhattan to apply for a marriage license. But when we got there, the courthouse was closed. Veteran's Day.

We went home and tabled our wedding plans for another date. It didn't matter. We had time now.

Chapter 18

Broken Hearts

I HOPED THAT YOU WOULD reach out so that we could build our own, separate relationship, but you didn't. Maybe you were still mad at me for leaving you at home with him alone. Maybe you were angry that I was not willing to endure for you what you had endured to raise me.

I wanted to belong somewhere. I wanted to be around people who thought I was good. I reached out to my Chachiji in Ottawa and asked her if we could get the family together over Christmas. Papa and you had planned a vacation to Aruba, so neither of you would be there. Maybe the warmth of joking and laughing with my cousins could help me feel like I wasn't such a mistake.

One by one, all the families confirmed attendance. Then Yush told me that Papa had changed plans at the last minute: He'd decided to come to the reunion that I organized. I wondered if Papa did it to assert his authority over "his" family and push me out. I worried that he would succeed. I knew that some of my relatives watched the precarious relationship between what they saw as a generous father and an angry daughter with concern, afraid that my disobedience would spread to their own good children.

After consulting with Buaji, I decided to send Papa an email. Our relationship was not likely to ever become close, but perhaps we could agree to maintain a safe distance to enjoy each other's company in whatever form we could both handle.

I drafted the following email:

> I hope that you are doing well. I have missed you and Mummy a lot over the past 6 months and think about you frequently. I love you both and miss you both. I know that you are planning to go to Canada this month, and I was wondering if you are willing to move past what happened this summer, then maybe we can see each other there. I don't want there to be any drama or rehashing of the past; I just want to try to be able to enjoy each other's company. If you are okay with this, then I will plan to come when you are coming. Please let me know.

I read the email many times, making sure that nothing I wrote could be interpreted as angry or passive–aggressive. Yush and Buaji said it was a beautiful email and they were proud of me. I sent the email to Papa and waited for the response.

The response was brief. Just one line, and it shattered me.

> Broken hearts don't mend so easily.

Yush told me that you wrote the email, Mummy—not Papa. I wish I didn't know that. Papa's anger I could tolerate. But the fact that you blamed me for our family's undoing . . . The pain of that could break me. I told Yush that I didn't want him to play intermediary between you and me and Papa. I didn't want to find out information third and fourth hand and taint my precious relationship with him. If you or Papa wanted something from me, you could tell me directly, I said. Yush agreed.

That night, Yush confronted you and Papa. "You're more interested in being angry than being a family," he said to the two of you.

The confrontation led to a fight, he told me, where you and Papa stormed out of the house. Afterward, Yush agreed that it was time to move out of your basement.

Still, Yush wanted me to forgive and forget and move forward. Over the past year, he'd seen firsthand the toll that running Papa's new medical practice was taking on both of you. You had recently joined the practice to help out. "They're going through a rough patch," Yush said. "It gives me more empathy for Papa."

Yush believed that we owed Papa a certain amount of respect for all that he had given us. I thought that, too, but I could never quite agree to the level of deference Papa expected, especially since I felt it was founded upon a myth: Papa acted as if his success was self-made. But Papa couldn't have accomplished so much without your willingness to support him and stay at home to raise us. We were expected to honor Papa's sacrifices, but did not offer you special treatment for all that you had given up to look after us.

Papa had sought a bride who'd been raised to support her husband and one who, specifically, did not have a career, bypassing the need to consider the complicated questions that arise when two people earn income in a household. Yush seemed to assume that because you had been raised to not expect to build a career or pursue outside hobbies, this meant you never wanted them. I saw things differently: that, even if you did want to build a life for yourself beyond our home, you lived in a household where you could not safely express such a desire. What Yush perhaps saw as natural order, cultural tradition, or even just your own inclination, I saw as a double standard and an inequality within our home that did not have to exist, even within the confines of culture.

I am not sure when exactly this took place, but I think it was during that summer. I needed to stop by the house to pick up a few belongings, including a pair of gold platform pumps I had bought for my wedding. Yush and I both knew what would happen if I dared come home while Papa was around, so Yush snuck me into the house one afternoon while you both were away. When I went to my bedroom, I noticed that photos of me in the main hallway had disappeared. Old magazines covered my dresser, replacing my jewelry boxes and artwork. I searched the closets, but I couldn't find any of what I had come to collect. I held back my tears and told Yush how much it hurt to see evidence of my erasure. I felt as if Papa had cut me out of the family, and now both of you were trying to forget that I had ever existed. Yush shrugged. "It's just a photo," he said. Then he looked at me and recoiled. "Wow, are you crying?"

At the time, I took Yush's callousness personally, resentful that he could not extend compassion to me, especially after how I had supported him. It felt as if there was a limit to the degree and amount of time I was allowed to hurt, and that did not go beyond whatever amount Yush deemed rational. But now I suspect that Yush's reaction wasn't personal. Rather than using feelings to understand what stories he told himself about the world around him, Yush used rules and logic to decide which emotional responses were valid and which were not and then aligned himself accordingly, turning the world into 1–0 binaries: If this is true, then that must also be true. I think that Yush was afraid of his feelings, because that emotional current swept him up somewhere scary and alone, so he clamped the spigot shut. This stunted his ability to respond to my emotions, which had begun to overflow. He saw my emotions like the threat of a tsunami's rising tide, under which he'd drown.

Yush wanted his loving family back as much as I did. But to him, that meant I had to revert to my former role: to readily accept and always forgive mistreatment, and to never take it personally. Yush was right. This was what it would take to have our family back. The problem was, I didn't want to sacrifice myself like that anymore.

AFTER RECEIVING THAT EMAIL from you and Papa, I told Buaji that I wouldn't go to the reunion, because I didn't feel safe. Then her son, my cousin Dev, called me.

"I talked to Mom and I was thinking—I can rent a hotel room. I'll stay there with you," he said. "We can drive to the house if you want to see everyone, or they can come hang with us. If things get dicey, I'll get you out."

I was floored. Dev was the cousin closest to Yush and me in age. He and Yush attended space camp together as kids, and when we entered adulthood, the three of us organized separate get-togethers for the cousins. I figured he would encourage me to attend, but I didn't think he'd offer this much support.

When I attempted to open up to one white friend about what had happened that summer, he said, "But your dad threw you such a nice engagement party. How could he be abusive?" An Indian American friend invoked the "tiger parent" stereotype, saying, "Come on, he's just strict. What Indian dad isn't?" A close Indian family friend told me, "But your dad's such a cool guy. How can you just stop talking to him? You should involve him more." Again and again, I was told that what I called mistreatment was a misinterpretation of the lengths to which my father had gone to ensure that I succeeded. When I refused to accept that explanation, several relatives and family friends pulled away from me, casting me as ungrateful for what my parents had sacrificed. It felt as if success was so paramount that no one was willing to consider whether its pursuit could come at a personal toll.

Later, I found out through my relatives, Papa would say that I made up the events of the summer. I exaggerated a small fight, which they could believe, because Papa was so generous, and I had long appeared so angry and ungrateful. When Dadiji found out, she scolded me. "How could you call the police on your own father? You're crazy," she said. She swatted my head right where Papa smashed the plate on me. I broke down and cried in front of my young cousins. Buaji stepped in and said, "Mom, can you imagine how scared she must have been to feel that she needed to call the police on her own father?" Dadiji said nothing back.

I had expected a similar response from Dev. Instead, he took my words at face value, believed me, and turned that belief into action at the expense of his own comfort. Dev's kindness felt revolutionary for another reason, too. The quiet acceptance of my truth, particularly from a male relative, revealed that the dynamics within our family weren't simply expected cultural gender norms, as the quick dismissal by others had implied. A part of me felt like all of this was too much. I was being melodramatic, and Dev was indulging my tantrum. But another part of me felt seen, wanted, and loved.

"If you rent that hotel room and stay, then I'll go," I said, fighting back tears. "Thank you."

Within hours, Dev had booked the hotel room.

WHEN I MET PAPA in person in Ottawa that winter, we both pretended that nothing was wrong. But we avoided each other. If he was in the room, I'd slip out or stop speaking. It was a performance I knew well, though in the past my acting had been automatic. This time, it felt forced. Now I chafed underneath the mask I wore.

You did not acknowledge me. You barely looked in my direction. I was used to this silent treatment from Papa, but from you, Mummy, it was unnerving.

I realized that Papa would not lose his composure around so many adults. I told Dev that he could cancel the hotel reservation.

After a day or two, Papa approached me. "Can we go somewhere and talk?"

I stiffened. I had promised myself that I would not let my guard down again, not unless something had changed. Emboldened by the number of adults around us, I said, "No, I don't want to go anywhere."

I shook as I said it, terrified of the consequences of speaking my mind.

"Okay, we can just talk here," he said. He remained calm. His tone was gentle, kind, loving—confusing.

"Beta, I don't want to be this far from you. No matter what, I will always care for you. You're my daughter," he said. "Whatever happened, I'd like to put the past behind us."

I was surprised by Papa's words, but this time I did not let myself find solace in them. I still felt angry that a plate to my head could be dismissed as "whatever happened." Papa had rejected my loving gesture from a month ago and now presented himself as the bigger person.

I looked to my side and saw that you were watching us closely through the doorway. After months of ignoring me, you finally spoke to me, too, as if I had always been your beloved daughter, as if nothing had caused a rift, as if nothing had happened at all. I held back my anger. After Papa's gesture, you began to speak to me again. But I didn't feel the same warmth from you that we shared in my childhood. Your love felt restrained.

Papa hugged me. I limply hugged Papa back and said, "I want that, too." It wasn't a lie. I did want that. But I knew that what I wanted was not likely to materialize. In fact, I was now certain nothing would change. I saw the cycle resetting, preparing to begin anew. I promised myself that this time, I would not participate.

Chapter 19

Terminator of the Male Ego

As the demands of residency took over Thomas's life, he folded inward. When he wasn't at the hospital, he caught up on much-needed sleep, read academic studies, or watched sports. He had little bandwidth to extend himself beyond that. As he retreated, I followed him and neglected myself, because that is what I had seen you do, because that is what I thought a good woman does for the man she loves. But I increasingly resented that, while I worked so hard to fit into his world, he expressed little interest in understanding mine. I explored New York with friends Thomas didn't know, ate dinners alone or cooked for just the two of us, and sat next to him in silence while he cheered for teams that I didn't care about. Oftentimes, any attempt to express my true feelings or needs created tension between us, which interrupted the peace we both so desperately craved. I relied on my friends for support in navigating my career change and family conflicts, sharing less and less of my inner life with Thomas.

After four years together, I told Thomas that I wanted to work on improving our connection. He agreed to go to couples therapy. The therapist assigned us homework of touching and talking, but the exercises were a chore to both of us. I fantasized about other men. I developed crushes on any man who told me I was beautiful or who paid attention to me in ways that Thomas did not. The expensive engagement ring on my finger—the one that I had picked out and wanted so badly as proof of our love—now called to mind a brand, signaling that I was a man's property. I was expected to take his name and remake my identity for him without him giving up anything for me. He didn't expect me to give up so much, but my resentment burned anyway.

I had pursued marriage so aggressively because I believed that Papa's plan for me would make me successful, stable, and happy. But in the past year, I'd started to think deeply about what I wanted from life beyond meeting Papa's expectations. I had been so intent on marrying Thomas, but now that marriage was imminent, it no longer seemed satisfying.

Confused, after nine months of little progress, I met with our therapist alone. I asked her if it was normal to feel trapped at twenty-six. I asked her if this was just what happens in long-term relationships. She said, no, relationships did not have to feel like this. I hoped that she was right, but I didn't believe her.

Our engagement had stretched from one year to two years, and finally one day Thomas came home with an ultimatum: "I need to know if you still want to marry me," he said, "and I need to know by next month."

I had originally believed that Thomas was drifting away from me, but I realized then that I was the one who had pulled away. I did not know where this current was taking me or how to get back to him, but I no longer wanted to fight against it to try. When I saw that our life together was enough for Thomas, but I wanted so much more, I knew I could not marry him.

I didn't call you to tell you that I ended the engagement. I am sorry, Mummy, I know that I should have. But after you and Papa denied the events of the summer, I felt rejected. And I didn't know how to explain any of this to you, a woman who had given up everything—a country, a language, an identity, a family—for a stranger. I couldn't tell you plainly that my decision came down to a lack of intimacy, particularly since I had never seen that sort of connection between adults when I was growing up, and I was not even sure if it could exist within a marriage. I didn't know how Papa would react to the news: whether he'd scream at me or support me or ignore me. I could not withstand any more pain, so I stayed quiet.

When Papa found out, he sent me an email. It was the most loving, kind email I had ever received from him:

> As you might expect, Dadiji just called me to tell me what happened. I can only imagine what you are feeling. I want you to know that Mom and I love you very much and don't ever want to see you hurt, especially not in this way. Please call us. Our differences are easy to bury in the face of something this important. You have a home with parents who care. Please let us help you and support you in any way we can. Nothing can change the fact that you are our daughter and we will always care for you even if we don't see eye-to-eye on some issues.

Papa articulated the words that I had longed to hear from him for years. In that email, I saw the Papa of my childhood, who doted on me and fostered my confidence and spoke to me like I could do anything. I wanted that Papa back desperately.

But his email didn't bring the relief or joy that I thought it would. I felt only more pain.

Under the spotlight of Papa's love, it was easy to feel chosen. When I turned twenty-one, Papa had booked a dinner cruise around New York City. He bought tickets for several of my friends, too, treating us to wine and cocktails and photographing us like celebrities ascending the stage at the Oscars. He loved taking you, me, and Yush to fancy dinners and hosting over-the-top celebrations, no expense spared, for the people he loved. But that adoration could sour into hatred in mere seconds, with little warning, making the kindness seem like a lie. It was this cycle that hurt so much, the sense that he could express care only when he could play the hero.

Sometimes I let myself imagine what it might be like to know Papa as your nieces and nephews in India did, or as the aunties and uncles here did—the family friends and relatives from both sides of the family who got the best of Papa without having to deal with the painful parts. He was so generous with time and money and attention and care, and the intense admiration and loyalty and devotion he received from them fueled even more kindness and generosity on his behalf. When one of your nephews in India wanted to get married, Papa helped him find a bride, stepping in as a secondary father figure. When your other nephew was diagnosed with terminal cancer, Papa hosted him and his sister in America, paid for his healthcare, and took them on a tour around the country. Whenever relatives from India visited, Papa went out of his way to extend them support.

But his relationships with relatives, even yours, were so centered on Papa's benevolence that you couldn't maintain ones of your own. You turned into a background character in his star performance. I doubt any of your relatives would have been willing to hear a single critical word against the man who bestowed so much upon them.

I didn't want to cut Papa out of my life. But I believed that relying on him for emotional or financial support would pull me back into an unhealthy cycle of dependency, and I had to figure out how to take care of myself. I had no backup plan. I had no Thomas and no longer felt like I had you. I had only a new job, a few months of savings, and a deep knowledge of what I didn't want for my life.

I found a roommate on Craigslist. I'm sure that you were concerned that I was living with a man I did not know. In that apartment, I finally became the ruined woman of Papa's nightmares. I ruined myself with men I knew and men I didn't, allowing myself to enjoy a pleasure with my body that I never had felt before.

———

WHEN I WAS GROWING up, my assumptions about the world blocked me from ever having to question why the world you and I lived in was the way it was. But when I was just being myself—even when I was not trying to prove some point—I was still wrong somehow. Too loud or too outspoken or too opinionated or too independent—traits that Papa had encouraged when I was a girl but found threatening as I became a woman. It was only because I did not fit into his world that I began to ask why I did not and why I could not.

Questions are dangerous. Questions lead to dissent. Why was Papa's rage dismissed as a logical response to stress, but when I expressed any hint of anger, I was told I was being too emotional? Why did no one else see the dynamics in our family as I did, and was I crazy for finding them unfair? I had grown up understanding that men need sex and pleasure, but why did it feel so wrong to seek these things for myself, too?

That year, as I distanced myself from Papa, embarked on a new career, and broke off an engagement, I finally had the freedom to safely explore the answers to these questions. The change was gradual, and yet, when my transformation began, I did not feel as if I were changing into someone else. I felt like I was coming back to a self that I had abandoned.

I had never thought of myself as a feminist. I had believed, as I had been raised, that women had achieved equality already, so everything happening now was just female supremacy. But now I worked in the progressive media, among co-workers who wrote about abuse and assault. Beyoncé sampled author Chimamanda Ngozi Adichie's definition of "feminist" in a hit single. I had never read a single feminist text, but I had a lifetime of resisting and surviving the patriarchal norms these women openly criticized. I began to call myself a feminist, too, as a way to honor my values and figure out how to return to myself.

That label helped me understand why so many people supported Papa's version of reality over mine. For the first time, I read literature that described the dynamics of our home not as love or duty or tradition, as I had understood them, but with harsh, unforgiving words. Domestic violence. Emotional abuse. Gaslighting. I had thought of abuse as purely physical: brutish fathers who came home drunk and battered women black-and-blue, never showing their families a shred of kindness. What I read offered nuanced depictions of emotional and psychological abuse, in which people of all genders were capable of genuine care and affection but maintained control over loved ones through a constant but abstract threat of violence and culture of secrecy. The labels and definitions offered me a new frame for understanding my experiences within our family, turning my fuzzy feelings into concrete shapes with names from which I began to form a language. Realizing that our family dynamics matched with established patterns observed again and again by others allowed me to recognize myself in something beyond my microscopic view of the world. The literature validated my sense that what you and I experienced at home was not something either of us had to accept.

While the readings empowered me at first, they ultimately shamed me into a deeper silence. Everything I read revolved around white families. I knew that I couldn't take these resources to you or Yush, though I couldn't quite articulate why that felt impossible. At the time, I interpreted my sense of isolation through the colonizer's story: I felt as if these progressive white women had all this information that could help us but we couldn't access it, because we came from some regressive, backward place.

Now I understand my isolation differently: I grew up surrounded by white people, alienated from my cultural heritage and its history. My understanding of both was so limited that I assumed I was alone, that no one in South Asian American communities felt like I did. They of course did, but many didn't feel safe talking about these issues openly, either. I thought our family was an aberration and therefore hyper-dysfunctional. When these white women empathized with me, I believed they accepted me when no one else ever would.

But, while I read about similar dysfunction in their homes, I knew that their solutions wouldn't work for you. I didn't understand why not, though, and I assumed yet again that this reflected some inferiority on our family's part. Years later I found resources that contextualized our home life within the American immigration system, colonialism, and the caste system. The interventions that worked for white women did not consider the various structural, racial, or cultural barriers that immigrant women of color faced in accessing help, assuming also a familiarity and cultural acceptance of divorce. The South Asian–specific resources articulated the double bind that trapped you: You bore the burden of maintaining the cultural image that predicated our communal belonging in America, but your ability to project this perfect image was then used against you to delegitimize your own feelings. So long as you portrayed the image you were expected to portray, was anything really *that* bad at home?

I didn't have many people to help me make sense of what was happening at home or the dissonance that I experienced as shame. In an effort to comprehend the rift in my relationships with you and Papa, I began to describe Papa as abusive in conversations with Yush. This created a barrier between us. Yush viewed the label as judgmental and reductive. "I see it as a terrible relationship, and he can be abusive," Yush said about my relationship with Papa. "But I see you demonizing and not acknowledging the good stuff, too. At the end of the day, he has your back."

"I always thought that was true about Papa," I said. "But now I don't think so."

"Well, you don't exactly have his back, either," Yush said.

From Yush's perspective, I had taken from Papa when it was convenient for me and rejected him now that I no longer needed him to survive. I felt like Yush didn't understand that the care he received from Papa did not extend to me.

Yush still believed that Papa's "wartime personality" was ultimately a good thing. Papa might fail to show up in the everyday, but in a crisis Papa would sacrifice anything to save someone he loved. Yush saw himself this way, too: levelheaded under duress and truly at his best when solving problems, a burden of masculinity that women did not bear because society did not expect them to function as providers. But I didn't see things that way.

In our family, loving someone meant rescuing them or letting yourself be rescued by them. But when I needed help to cope with work and the chaos at home, no one in our family had the capacity to support me, because everyone was dealing with their own, bigger problems. As I rescued myself, I wondered if that could be a form of love, too: the ability to take care of oneself well enough to not require saving.

"In a crisis, I'm not going to call the person who isn't reliable day to day," I told Yush. "I will call the person who knows how to show up for me consistently. Besides," I said, "I don't need you or Papa to solve my big life problems. I just want to enjoy life with you."

As I FELT ISOLATED from you and Papa and increasingly distant from Yush, Dadaji surprised me by calling to say, "For the first time, you are not under the control of a man."

"What do you mean?"

"You were under your father's control, and then you were with Thomas. Now you are free," he said.

I thought Dadaji would be ashamed of me. I thought he would be angry that I had left a good man and embarked on solitude instead of marriage. I assumed that he'd be disappointed in my inability to have a good relationship with my father, the eldest son whose accomplishments had made him so proud. That was how Dadiji seemed to feel. When she got on the line, she said, "Prachi, don't be too strong, or you won't find a husband."

I was too scared to ask you how you felt, Mummy—whether you agreed with Dadiji or not.

But Dadaji didn't seem to find my independence concerning. In fact, he supported my self-exploration.

"Prachi is Goddess of the Rising Sun and Destroyer of Darkness. And you have given it a third meaning!" he said.

"What's that?"

"Terminator of the male ego."

I laughed.

"I feel sorry for the poor fellow who tries to stand in your way!" he said, laughing, too. "The problem with humanity," Dadaji continued, was "the belief that the man should have the upper hand."

"Do you think that?"

"Think what?"

"That men should have the upper hand."

"No, no," he said. "But that's what others think—that woman should be happy because she is called Goddess."

Dadaji would become the second person in our extended family to identify as a feminist, a label that meant, to him, that women should have access to education and the same opportunities as men. When I asked him about his transformation, he connected the suffering of his childhood to his mother's low status in society. "I have seen how difficult it was for her to live after she became a widow. And I have seen how difficult it was for women without education," he said. If his mother had had the same rights as his father, Dadaji would not have become a foster child, he would have been spared from poverty, and his family would not have been split apart.

Despite this insight, Dadaji was a controlling father and husband for most of his life. When I asked him how his upbringing may have been different if the women around him had equal rights, Dadaji fell silent. "Very difficult question," he said. Then, with some soberness: "I might have reacted in the wrong way, thinking that an injustice was being done to me."

It was his grandchildren, he said, who introduced him to what he called "the modern world." Removed by a generation, he was able to see his granddaughters not merely as future mothers or an extension of himself but as individuals who should move through the world unencumbered and unafraid. On previous occasions, he'd cautioned me against marrying any man who expected me to stay home to cook and clean for him—even though Papa expected that of you, and Dadaji had once expected that of Dadiji.

While I had always measured myself against Dadaji's sacrifices as an immigrant and respected him as the patriarch of the family, he did not hold his sacrifices against me. He did not cast any of my decisions as a rejection of Indian culture or of my family. If we could bridge the expansive generational and cultural gap between us so effortlessly, maybe the wrongness Papa saw in me wasn't something innate to me. Maybe it didn't mean I was not Indian enough or too American, and maybe, just maybe, I didn't need to meet so many conditions or work so hard to be worthy of love. Maybe love was simpler than I thought: Maybe it was a willingness to witness someone, to be curious and empathize with them, as they are.

I asked Dadaji if he was disappointed that I didn't become a banker or a lawyer.

"No. Why would I be?" he said. I tried to explain to him the pressure many Indian American kids felt to become these things, but he didn't understand. He told me that it was always obvious to him I should become a writer.

"I figured you were just confused," he said. "But you found your way back."

Maybe we both did.

Chapter 20

Parts Unearthed

THE WINTER THAT I broke off the engagement with Thomas, Papa had reached out to me with such kindness. I'd wanted to accept his support so badly, but I knew that it wouldn't last. Instead, I told him that I needed some time and that I would get in touch when I felt more stable. I meant what I said. Papa said he understood. He said he'd be waiting for me when I was ready.

Maybe he interpreted my extended silence as an act of war, because a few months later I realized he had responded with his own: I had been excommunicated again. Some time over the summer, Papa shuttered his medical practice in Pennsylvania, sold the house I'd grown up in, and bought a condo in Toronto near where he grew up. Neither of you called to tell me this news. I found out about the move by happenstance, when Dadaji called me to say hi. Over the course of that year, this is how information trickled down to me in the family. I was a tumor that had been surgically excised and discarded. But this time, I did not know why I had been cut out.

I was confused. Building a medical practice was a decades-long dream that Papa had achieved only in recent years. We had all assumed that he would run the practice through retirement. After a lifetime of moving, our family had finally settled into a community. Dadaji was surprised, too, but then again, Papa had always been impulsive. "Who knows," Dadaji said. "Maybe it will be good for him. Maybe he'll finally learn to relax."

Papa had told family friends and distant relatives that he was moving to Toronto to look after Dadiji and Dadaji. When I ran into one of the Indian uncles in the community, the father of a boy I'd had a crush on in middle school, he expressed admiration at what a good, dutiful son Papa was. I forced a smile, saying, "Yeah."

It is hard to put into words how much the news of your move and the loss of nearly all evidence of my childhood—particularly the sudden way in which I lost it—devastated me. For years, I would avoid friends from high school. I couldn't explain to them why visiting felt so painful. *My parents moved* didn't really capture what had happened—that Papa made a unilateral decision and cut me out of the family to the degree that not only was I not personally informed, but I knew that I would have been forcibly removed from the premises if I attempted to visit.

Thankfully, I had kept my journals with me since college. But I lost nearly all of my artwork, awards, books, and photos. I wondered if those drawings and paintings, some of which had earned me a coveted spot in Governor's School, ended up in a Goodwill, or maybe a landfill, or maybe on the walls of some neighbor or family friend. I mustered the courage to ask Papa once, years later, and he just said he had no idea what happened to my artwork, as if it had evaporated.

You did try to save my things, including some of my paintings and photo albums, for which I am grateful. Over the next few years, neighbors and aunties would contact me to say that you'd left boxes behind for me. Ambika Aunty, the relative of Papa's who had encouraged her children to play with me when I was younger, reached out to deliver a few of them. She lived in New Jersey, just a short drive from my East Village apartment, and I thought that in the Indian tradition of treating a relative like a daughter, she might invite me to her home or attempt to meet with me in New York. Instead, she called me one day to schedule a drive-by delivery. She and her husband pulled up to the curb. He grumbled about how I hadn't been able to find him a better parking spot. They both stayed in the car with the hazard lights blinking as I took out the boxes and dumped them on a puke-stained sidewalk. I slammed the trunk shut and waved an awkward goodbye. They left and did not reach out to try to see me again. I understood what it meant. I was bad now, so best to keep away from me.

For years, the boxes sat in the back of my closet. When I finally gathered the courage to open them, hoping to find my artwork, racing bibs, or yearbooks, I found mostly old clothes that didn't fit me anymore and outdated costume jewelry. I don't know why you chose these things to pass on to me, and I cannot imagine the stress you must have been under as you attempted to pack up your home of more than a decade within weeks. But the things that really mattered to me were not things that had any resale value. They were just scraps of paper or canvas that could never matter to anyone else except, I had thought, my family.

Seeing my childhood tossed out felt deeply cruel. I thought that maybe Papa orchestrated it, insisting that most of my artwork be thrown out because he wanted to drive that knife into my wound a little bit deeper. But then I had another thought: I wondered if I was making it about me when it was not about me at all. What if I was simply collateral? That thought hurt me even more—that Papa was so careless with the evidence of my childhood not to hurt me but because it didn't matter to him. Had it ever mattered?

I would not be able to write or paint anything authentic for years, plagued by that question. I would struggle to believe that anything I created could ever really matter, because it didn't seem to matter to the people who were supposed to love me the most.

———

IN THE FALL, A few weeks after you and Papa moved into the new condo in Toronto, Buaji called me. She told me that you had threatened to jump out of the car as Papa drove down an eight-lane superhighway. When you arrived at the condo, you refused to go upstairs, afraid you might jump from the balcony. Papa called Buaji's twenty-one-year-old daughter, Priya, who studied at a local university, for help. As you struggled with thoughts of suicide, Papa dumped you with Priya because he said you were too hard to deal with.

Priya took you to a local psychiatric clinic, but when you looked around and saw that you were lumped in with visibly distressed people, you forced a façade of perfection and downplayed your symptoms. You told the clinician treating you that you were just stressed due to a move, nothing more. But you refused to return to Papa, so Papa asked Buaji to take you in. Papa then went off to take a solo vacation to unwind and recover from the stress of dealing with a wife who was too hysterical, he told Buaji. I felt helpless throughout, relying on Buaji, Yush, and Priya to tell me what was happening, because Papa still wasn't talking to me, and you told Priya that you refused to speak to me until I "made up" with Papa.

You arrived in Winnipeg, where Buaji lived, with a bag full of pills, some prescribed by psychiatrists and some prescribed by Papa. Fufaji, who was also a doctor, found you an Indian psychiatrist. She told him to stop giving you those pills immediately and took over your care. Fufaji hired a home aide to stay with you while he and Buaji worked, so that you wouldn't be alone.

Papa thanked Buaji and Fufaji for taking you in, but almost immediately he became frightened of losing you. After you began to stabilize, a few weeks later, he insisted that you return to Toronto. Your psychiatrist strongly advised against this. To appease Papa, over the next several weeks you flew back and forth between Winnipeg and Toronto on weekends. In Winnipeg, you met with the psychiatrist regularly, and she recommended you take self-assertiveness and self-esteem classes. As you recovered, in frequent phone calls and during

your brief weekend visits to Toronto, Papa could sense your confusion. The invisible split deep within you was now visible at the surface.

After refusing to speak to me for around a year, you reached out to
me from Buaji's home. In regular video chats over Skype, I could see
that you had space to think and feel. You began to wonder who you
really were and what you wanted and how to figure that out. You
didn't know up from down or down from up, because to live with him
was to live in a world that was constantly spinning on an axis he controlled, and you never had a chance to steady yourself. You came to
this country upon marrying him, with no choice but to trust the person who governed your housing, your immigration status, and your
access to any Indian community here. You were confused, saying he
was such a good man one moment and the next saying you could not
survive another thirty years with him.

Suddenly, you had to move from the only permanent home you'd
ever had in this country, and you could not tell me about it. You had
not wanted to leave, you revealed, but you didn't tell me what pushed
Papa to close his business or move to Canada—changes that appeared
drastic and sudden to me. I do not believe that your threat on your life
was an inexplicable hysteria, or simply due to change, as Papa characterized it to Buaji. I believe you made a desperate choice rooted in
the bleakness of a reality you did not want.

You didn't want Yush or me to see you so anxious, so we waited a
few weeks and planned to see you in Winnipeg over Thanksgiving.
You were looking forward to seeing us, and had asked Buaji not to tell
Papa that Yush and I were coming. You were afraid of what Papa
would do if he found out you had made plans to see us without involving him.

Buaji said she didn't want to keep secrets, so she invited Papa to be
with us, too. Papa declined her invitation.

Winter had settled in the city, draping the flat prairie landscape
with a thick sheet of snow that would last until spring. Yush and I
waited for Fufaji at the airport's curbside parking, jittery in the cold,

excited to see you. When Fufaji picked us up, he said, "I'm afraid I have some bad news."

Hours after you landed in Winnipeg, and hours before Yush and I boarded the plane to visit you, Papa had harmed himself and gone to the ER. He called you from the hospital and demanded that you come home before seeing Yush and me. Buaji remembers the desperation in your voice, as you cried, "But they're almost here, I want to see them." Papa received a brief psychiatric evaluation but declined treatment and went home within twenty-four hours.

Papa needed help, too. But when he used his pain to isolate you from Yush and me, I felt only rage and betrayal.

OUR REUNION WAS NOT a happy one, but I was surprised by its warmth. The closeness I shared with you in childhood returned instantly, as if it had never disappeared. You sat cross-legged on a couch in Buaji's sunroom, with a computer on your lap, and I nestled in next to you, resting my head on your shoulder and hugging you. I didn't want to let you go. I set up a social-media account for you so that I could share some photos. You sent me an adorable test email called "facebook facts," writing: "today i am going to do facebook and see whats out there and if i would like to get involved in wasting time like millions do."

For the first time in years, I felt hopeful because I could see you stumbling back to yourself. You dropped the façade that you had been forced to maintain for so long, and you told me you were proud of me "for being able to stand on my own two feet." I had thought I brought you only shame, but I understood then that you had split yourself into two and buried half in order to survive. That buried part of you, briefly unearthed, likely understood why I had run away from Papa that day just over a year ago. Your words became my North Star. I will always stand on my own two feet, for you.

That night you and I shared a bed, just as we did when I was little and Papa was working. This time I held you as if you were my child. You cried and told me you didn't know what to do. You wanted to stay in Winnipeg for a few months and continue your treatment. But if you stayed, Papa would consider it tantamount to divorce. You didn't believe you were capable of supporting yourself if he left you.

"Buaji and Yush and I will help you," I said. "You can drive. You can work. You are healthy. You are capable," I said.

"You have a choice," I said.

"What choice do I have, Prachi?" you cried.

I didn't know what to say. Neither option was good or easy, but I did not feel like it was my place to tell you that. I had a freedom that you did not have.

Buaji told Yush and me that you had to make the decision for yourself. She told us that if we pressured you to do what we wanted, then we were no better than Papa, denying your agency. I was angered by this advice at first, but later I saw that she was right.

THE NEXT DAY, PAPA called you to say he had bought a plane ticket for you and demanded that you return to Toronto because he needed you. Yush and I couldn't convince you that going back to him terrified us, for both his health and yours. We couldn't convince you that you were not responsible for Papa's choices. We didn't know how to prove to you that we needed you, too.

After only twenty-four hours with you, we drove you to the airport and watched you go back to Papa. I knew then that, just as I had found you, I had lost you again.

The first night in Winnipeg, I'd vented my rage to Yush and Buaji, angry because I believed that Papa was manipulating you through self-harm. Yush had uncharacteristically yelled at me. "Papa is in the hospital, and you shouldn't talk about our father that way," he said, as he stormed out of the room. The next day, after he witnessed Papa twist your love against you in real time, Yush snapped in the opposite direction. He said Papa was dead to him. He insisted that you divorce Papa. You got mad at Yush for pressuring you.

Months after that visit, Yush would send Buaji and Fufaji a handwritten letter to thank them for how they had taken care of you. "I can't stress enough how much of a blessing it is to have the two of you in our lives," he wrote. "It is inspiring really, in terms of what is possible, and is one of the clearest examples of what real love feels like that I have ever felt."

THE NEXT DAY, BUAJI called Papa and again invited him to come to Winnipeg. "Your kids are here, and they want to spend time with their family," she said.

You and Papa flew back to Winnipeg together on Thanksgiving Day. When Papa arrived, Yush refused to greet him. Although I was mad at Papa, too, I was troubled by Yush's whiplash reversal.

Papa sat down with Buaji and Fufaji, and said that he harmed himself because the thought of you seeing his kids without him was too painful. He told them that a part of him had always wondered if he was different from other people. He said that he'd know for sure if everyone he loved told him he needed help. In Papa's words, I recognized the question that he had once presented to Yush and me as a logic puzzle when we were kids. I felt both sad and disturbed when I realized that his question to us had not been hypothetical but an actual navigation tool that he had devised to move through life.

"You're at that place," they said. "You need help. If you continue like this, you're going to lose your family." He teetered on the edge of self-awareness for a few hours.

After Papa spoke to Buaji and Fufaji, he asked to speak to me. I was now in the uncomfortable position of playing intermediary within our family. I was scared of what Papa might say, but Papa saw my stiffness and said, "It's okay, I'm not going to yell." I didn't believe him. I sat before him, tense, rigid, quiet.

"Beta, I know I haven't always been fair to you," he said. The words churned something inside me, something that I had numbed, but the churning stopped when he said, "But I never tried to control you. Everything I did, I did because I wanted the best for you."

AT THE END OF that week in Winnipeg, you went back to Toronto with Papa. From there, you snuck in calls to Buaji. You stole time every few days and begged her, *Don't stop calling me.* Sometimes the conversations were short, like when you called Buaji from the bathroom of a restaurant, desperate to talk. Other times you talked for an hour, hanging up abruptly when Papa came home.

Papa continued to dedicate himself to the illusion of perfection and used you to help him maintain it. In Winnipeg, Papa had said you were both sick and needed help and you should get treatment together. But when you got back to Toronto, it did not take much time for Papa to convince everyone that he was sane and you were not. You told Buaji that Papa picked your psychiatrist for you. She recalls you telling her that he had rejected the first one because the psychiatrist wouldn't allow Papa's involvement. Papa found an older white man to treat you, a man who was willing to let Papa have his say. Unlike the Indian psychiatrist you had seen in Winnipeg, this man did not recommend self-assertiveness or self-esteem classes. I doubt that he had the cultural competency to even begin to understand who you were or what your life had been like. I wonder if he was aware that more than half of women seen in mental-health settings have experienced, or are currently experiencing, abuse from an intimate partner. In sessions, you spoke and this man mostly just listened to your self-censored speech, silently upping your dose of medication, slowly dulling your senses and further undermining your sense of reality.

Then one day that winter, the calls to Buaji stopped. She phoned you repeatedly over the course of several months, but you never answered, and we never found out why.

SLOWLY, YOUR THERAPIST CONVINCED you that you were not an abused woman, you were simply an anxious wife whose biggest problem was having too much time on her hands. I had feared this would happen, and I knew it did when, six years later, I read what both of you had written in a lawsuit defending Papa's upstanding moral character.

Papa's cousin had contested a will that named Papa as the sole beneficiary of her father's estate. The news of the will had surprised Dadaji, who'd encouraged his brother-in-law to write one for years, to no avail. Buaji, Fufaji, and Dadaji wrote affidavits in support of Papa's cousin, offering their perspectives on why the circumstances around the will seemed suspicious to them. In response, Papa collected testimonies from friends and relatives who vouched for his integrity, presenting evidence that reflected no undue influence. They settled the lawsuit with Papa retaining control of his uncle's estate, finding no wrongdoing. But the documents submitted exposed our family's messiness in such plain language that it startled even me.

Through these statements, I learned how you and Papa characterized your weeks recovering in Winnipeg. Papa wrote that you had a "nervous breakdown," which was true enough, but he presented it as some inexplicable craziness that you had brought upon yourself. In your "confused state of mind, at the time, she blamed me for her problems," he wrote. He described you as chronically anxious and himself as your benevolent caretaker: "After many years of medical intervention, my wife realizes that I was simply trying to help her all those years ago when I suggested professional assistance."

You accepted some responsibility for Papa's actions, too, writing, "I was devastated that he would do something like this, and that my actions may have led him to trying to take his life again." You wrote, "My therapist helped me realize that I was not an abused wife and that [my husband] was correct in telling me that I needed professional assistance to manage my anxiety." Even though I already suspected that this was how Papa cast an alternate reality, my stomach dropped when I saw what you had written. I wondered if Papa pressured you to write that or if you now really believed that you were the source of Papa's problems.

For so long, I was embarrassed by how little I was able to recall about you. I was tortured by what I could not remember, left with strong feelings but little dialogue or specific interactions to tack these deep impressions onto. I thought this said something ugly about my love for you. But now I realize that the haziness of my memory was by design. Papa was a storm casting a perpetual fog around you. He did not want us to ever really see each other. Instead, we knew each other by how we anticipated and responded to his actions. We have known each other as small echoes of our own voices.

If I was an outsider reading the conflicting affidavits, I am not sure whose version of the truth I would have believed. The accounts presented such polar-opposite interpretations that it was clear someone was mistaken—but, with everything presented as fact, how could any objective bystander begin to determine who? The familiar childhood feeling of not being able to trust my own senses returned.

By now I had distanced myself from most of the Indian community I'd grown up with, particularly those who viewed Papa as "a saint," as one close relative once called him. I didn't slip away from these relatives and friends because I looked down on them or because I didn't care about my family or my culture, as Papa likely portrayed it. I have wonderful memories of their kindness and love, and it is hard to articulate how much I miss celebrating with them the holidays that rooted me in some sense of cultural identity. But I remained standoffish because everything you and I experienced at home ran counter to how Papa presented himself to the world, and around them, I had to either silence myself and play a role to sustain Papa's performance or risk sounding like a conspiracy theorist to people who had seen nothing but his generosity and kindness. Every time I performed normalcy and denied my reality, I fractured myself; every time I spoke my truth to people who denied it, I fractured myself. Eventually, I had to distance myself to preserve myself.

I understood how scary it was to trust yourself. For me, the hardest part was not dealing with Papa's volatility or verbal onslaught or even the physical violence; it was the way in which our realities were denied and rewritten, how I felt so confused when I spoke the truth. A seemingly benign interaction could snowball into something where my sanity slipped and I couldn't explain what happened or why: When he threw me out of the house over some perceived slight and then complained to friends and family that I was too self-absorbed to ever visit him, their limited interactions with his increasingly withdrawn daughter confirmed the impression that I was cold, heartless, and ungrateful, as he foretold. The more I tried to explain my version of events, the more deranged, bitter, and angry I sounded. The pain of being seen through that lens by people I cared for hurt too much. I knew that they could never see what you and I saw, and so instead of bargaining with them, I let them go.

When I last saw you in Winnipeg, you had been trying to make the same calculations: You were wrestling with whether to perform normalcy and what that might cost you; whether to speak your truth and what that might cost you; trying to determine whom you could trust with each warring part of yourself. I wondered, though, if when you returned to him, you gave up the fight and surrendered to his all-consuming power.

Chapter 21

Remembering

ON THE FIRST MOTHER's Day after you returned to Toronto with Papa, my cousin Dev visited me in New York. He called you to speak to Dadiji, who was staying with you and Papa while she recovered from shoulder surgery. Papa answered the phone. When he heard Dev's voice, the line went dead. Thinking the line had been cut, Dev called back. No response. He called once more.

"Wait, did Mamaji just hang up on me?" he asked, laughing.

"No way," I said. "Why would he do that?"

When I called from my phone, Papa answered. Then you got on the line and scolded me. "Why would you call with him there?" you said. "You know what the situation is."

I did not know what "the situation" was.

But eventually I realized. The flowers that Buaji had sent to Dadiji that day never reached her, either. When Buaji had tried to call Dadiji to wish her a happy Mother's Day, her phone call was cut off, too.

Papa had told extended family and aunties and uncles that Buaji tried to end his marriage and had stolen his kids, turning them against their own father by feeding them vicious lies about him. I think you supported Papa's lies out of fear—but also possibly out of jealousy toward the sister-in-law to whom Papa had always compared you, who now had a closer relationship with me than you did. Those who had been graced by Papa's generosity whispered about how wicked his sister was to break apart a family in this way. Overnight, fiction became fact. Buaji had become the enemy that I once was, her children treated as extensions of her.

Buaji and Fufaji told me that if I needed to limit contact with them in order to save my relationship with Papa, they'd understand. But I said, no. I didn't want to give in to Papa's ultimatums. I wish that Papa could see that my love could not be bought or sold. Nor could my love for either of you be replaced.

Everyone in the extended family seemed so shocked by recent events, but I struggled to understand how no one had seen the depth of our dysfunction until now. Did Papa's actions stun them because he had morphed into someone they didn't recognize? Or had this behavior always lurked below the surface—in which case, why had no one protected you or me?

After I decided that I would not try to find a way forward with Papa, Buaji and Fufaji began giving me answers that helped me make sense of my confusion. They gradually shared with me a history that had been buried. That was when I learned of the different account of your marriage, Buaji's memories of her childhood with Papa, and other past events. When I asked Buaji why she hadn't told me any of this earlier, she said that she wanted to believe that Papa had changed and thought that he had. She'd hoped that he and I might find a way to reconcile our differences. "For a while, you guys just seemed so happy and picture-perfect that I thought he'd mellowed out after having a family," Buaji said to me. "I didn't want to poison you against your father. I wanted you to have your own relationship with him and make up your mind, independent of what my experiences with him have been."

I am terrified of alienating the only people who have loved me without conditions, afraid of pushing them away by expressing my ugly emotions—my anger or my pain or my hurt—the inconvenient emotions which have pushed away everyone else in my life, including you. But omissions about events of the past felt like a betrayal to me. I had felt so alone because I named things that I thought no one else saw, and only now—after you and I had lost each other—was I being told that everything I'd seen had always been there. The past had simply been shoved into boxes and stowed away, out of sight and forgotten, because no one knew what to do with it. Only now, because I refused to forget what I had seen, and only because our family had fallen apart, could no one deny or hide these facts any longer.

There's still so much about the past that I will never know, but when Papa was twelve, Dadaji was so concerned that he approached a well-respected pediatrician in Toronto's Indian community and asked if he should take Papa to a psychiatrist. The doctor said no. "He told me it would hurt your father's career," Dadaji recalled. The doctor believed that a potential diagnosis would deny Papa's ability to get into a good college and succeed, an outcome that would have invalidated Dadaji's decision to leave India.

In a capitalist society, the measure of wellness isn't a person's actual health or happiness but how far one can rise or how much wealth one can accumulate. Somebody seen as "unwell" is unable to produce and to achieve. This was during an era in which many leading psychoanalysts blamed autism and schizophrenia on cold, distant "refrigerator moms," arguing that these conditions resulted from an inability to bond with the mother—a theory that has since been discredited. To seek mental healthcare as an immigrant was to threaten one's security and chance to succeed, to suggest bad parenting, or to imply that one's ethnic culture caused their children's problems. Like you, so much was stacked against Papa, but he had no way of knowing this.

Dadiji and Dadaji handled what they didn't understand the way so many people do: by trying to forget. "But do you think forgetting is really the best thing?" I asked Dadaji.

"What else would be better?" he asked.

"Well, if we forget, and the person doesn't change, we're re-creating the conditions to allow the same thing to happen again," I said.

"I think it's better to leave it as is. Chances are, you will forget it," Dadaji said.

But forgetting, the survival strategy that let Dadiji and Dadaji establish themselves in a new country, also had consequences. I wonder if, in an effort to bend reality to the perfect image they sought to project, my grandparents overlooked your discomfort, deepened your sense of isolation, and further eroded your trust in your own senses in a country where you did not have equal footing to assert yourself. Mummy, did anyone ever tell you that what you saw and felt was real?

I had spent a good portion of my life feeling cheated out of the exceptional family I was told I had. I believed that if I held the same values and followed the rules laid before me, I could make that perfect family materialize. When that didn't happen, and most of the people around me doubled down on that message—to suggest that we were not happy because I was not adhering to the rules closely enough—I felt like I was losing my mind. Now I had learned that the secret of having a happy family was pretending to be perfect. I felt robbed. I didn't want to do that, and I couldn't accept that as the answer. I didn't understand how no one else in our family felt the same level of indignation that I did over living a lie.

Or maybe no one else saw it as a lie. I had once seen abuse as some wicked, inexplicable desire to harm another. But abuse is so often perpetuated under the banner of goodness, disguised in the language of benevolence. Papa believed that he knew best and then took whatever actions he deemed necessary for the greater good, regardless of how they affected us. We had contorted ourselves to achieve because we thought we were building something together as a family: an oasis that would nourish us. I had been so committed to this mission that, if Papa hadn't started to speak of me the same way he had spoken about Buaji, I might not have been willing to consider her recollection of the past when I was younger. Uncovering that history now, though, was like discovering that the original blueprints had never documented a life-sustaining garden; they outlined a monument to one man's greatness. You had dedicated yourself to helping him construct this statue, but I couldn't do it any longer. I threw down my tools and walked away.

WHEN YUSH AND I had visited you in Winnipeg, we joined a session with your psychiatrist there. I noticed that with her—an Indian immigrant woman like you—you did not try so hard to look put-together. She asked us about our home life, attempting to verify what you had told her. In that conversation, she told us about something called borderline personality disorder. I have no idea if you heard her or not or how that term registered with you. I don't remember Yush and me talking about it much, either, because we were dealing with Papa's immediate crisis and your recovery.

I didn't know anything about personality disorders. The American Psychiatric Association's *Diagnostic and Statistical Manual of Mental Disorders* defines a personality disorder as a long-standing, inflexible, and consistent pattern of behavior that appears in adolescence or early adulthood, leads to suffering or impairment, and "deviates markedly from the expectations of the individual's culture." I was wary of that description—not because I thought these illnesses weren't real but because of the level of subjectivity in their determination. Psychiatric diagnoses are not confirmed like broken bones on an X-ray. These diagnoses are dependent upon assessments by a trained professional. As I witnessed a psychiatrist fail to accurately gauge your own source of suffering, I wondered: How did one evaluate a personality disorder in someone raised between two wildly different cultures? And what did that treatment look like in America, where nearly 85 percent of psychiatrists are white, in an institution that continues to view mental health through a Eurocentric perspective?

I would have ignored or put off looking into that label were it not for the fact that your psychiatrist was an Indian immigrant, so I trusted that she wasn't pathologizing Papa or us on the basis of cultural background. When I got back from Winnipeg, as I struggled to make sense of the chaos in our lives and understand why I was losing you and why Papa acted the way that he did, I sought to learn more about this disorder.

At first, I felt an unexpected sense of validation. The books that I read described, with uncanny precision, many aspects of our home life that had seemed inexplicable—Papa's volatility and rage, the rapidity with which I could morph from his beloved daughter to his greatest enemy, the self-harm. I didn't understand at all why Papa acted like this. I guess I still don't, really. But in the books, which described these traits as behaviors of someone who might be living with borderline personality disorder, I developed, maybe for the first time, real sympathy for Papa. The books absolved me, telling me that Papa's behavior was not my fault or yours. They explained how the combination of a person's neurobiology and genetics, adaptive coping mechanisms, and environment could increase the risk of developing the behaviors that had long confused me. Diagnosed patients described living with intense emotional pain. It had never occurred to me that the way Papa acted could be a reflection of his internal state. That thought made me deeply, profoundly sad.

But what I had hoped was an answer soon opened up a series of isolating and humiliating questions. What I couldn't reconcile was how, on one hand, Papa was upheld as the model patriarch of a picture-perfect family. Within the context of the role that America had created for him, Papa excelled beyond expectations. But on the other hand, that same person, when viewed through the lens of Western psychiatry, was potentially living with a serious and untreated mental illness that severely impaired his ability to function and engage with the world. How could both of these things be true? It didn't make sense to me.

I felt trapped in a paradox. Papa's singular obsession with status, his anger and controlling nature, and the conditionality of his relationships could be cast as the far end of the psychic space that Indian men are encouraged to occupy in America—as omniscient providers who lead their families to success, no matter what the cost. Yet, if taken too far, these extreme behaviors indicated a debilitating mental illness, according to Western psychiatry. In asking these questions, I felt dangerously close to pathologizing myself and my cultural identity. It was embarrassing to try to parse Papa's behavior into what stemmed from cultural norms and values versus what indicated a serious mental-health issue, prompting me to wonder to what extent the traits that I had associated with Indian American culture, the rest of America viewed as disordered behavior.

Part of my isolation and confusion resulted from the fact that Papa himself had used the idea of Indian culture to manipulate you and me into behaving how he wanted us to. I was used to making trade-offs, from what I studied in college to how I wore my hair, to fit into his mold of a good Indian daughter. I wondered to what extent your experience assimilating—giving up so much of who you were in order to fit into a new country—primed you to make similar negotiations to keep Papa happy. When you or I failed to perform as expected, Papa believed he was justified in his anger, and each of us accepted that blame because negotiating our identities felt so natural.

Questioning the consequences of these negotiations seemed wrong, too. My cultural identity—often the thing that made me even a little bit special—also felt fragile and poorly defined, so easily threatened by the outside world that anything that challenged any aspect of our tenuous but distinct way of life struck me as a judgment. This isolation exacerbated my struggle: I was not able to separate my true self from coping mechanisms I'd learned to adapt to an environment that did not fully accept me, and then I blamed myself for the limitations of that acceptance.

Anytime I'd attempted to write about my relationship with Papa in a work of fiction or in a script, I got feedback that the father character came across as a caricature. *He goes from 0 to 60 too fast.* I became especially defensive when desi friends, understandably tired of seeing South Asian men portrayed in popular culture as sexist, strict, and controlling, tactfully suggested that I may be perpetuating a stereotype. I wanted to protest, *But this is what actually happened. I'm not a white guy writing this!* I was frustrated that I had to again mute myself because of a trope that had silenced me all my life—after all, white characters are never seen as representative of an entire race or culture. I felt so deflated, but it was true: The behavior I experienced at home went against every impulse I had as a writer, who has a responsibility to build a deep inner life for their characters and illustrate how that shapes their relationship with the world around them.

I had no insight into Papa's emotional life. I still don't. But to me, it was offensive to view Papa's troubling behavior through cultural tropes like "strict Indian dad" or "tiger parent." Such dismissals normalized mistreatment and implied that our dysfunction was an inevitability resulting from our cultural or ethnic identities. The refusal to seek explanations beyond these tropes had severe consequences. At home, you, Yush, and I paid the price.

Another reason it felt so hard to neatly delineate normative and non-normative behavior, though, was that Papa evaded accountability. Dadiji actively encouraged her son. Dadaji rarely challenged Papa. The world discouraged men from seeking help and told women that goodness was self-sacrifice. Social stratification taught people that their color, class, and caste determined their worth. I believed that Papa lived with an invisible illness. But wasn't society a little ill, too, for normalizing the idea that the rules didn't apply to him because of his status? At the end of the day, mental illness or not, Papa treated you and me the way he did because he knew that he could. He felt entitled to do so, and he was right. Nothing stopped him.

All my life, I had wanted to find a reason. I wanted to be able to trace Papa's reactivity and manipulative behavior to some specific brutalizing trauma or maybe point to some inherent brain chemistry, or a set of social norms, hoping that with such an explanation, everything else would suddenly make sense. I had fantasized that, with a clear set of reasons, I could separate which parts of Papa were really him and which parts were that other thing, so that his whiplashed love could feel less painful to me. I had hoped that, by naming whatever ailed him, maybe we could become close again.

But no matter what explanation I sought or what literature I read,

I could not force Papa to change. That realization was painful for me. He would rather watch you destroy yourself to please him, and he would rather risk his relationships with Yush and me, than look within himself. Again and again, you and I jumped over hurdles to earn his love, but seeing us struggle was never enough to compel him to change.

I didn't know what ailed Papa or how to parse what part of him came from what. No one story neatly resolved or fully explained the tension I felt. The biggest thing I learned from reading these books and from watching you go back to him was that Papa would never change for you or for me. He could only change for himself. And I did not know if he could ever do that, because I did not know if he could ever love himself enough to want better for himself. And that thought made me very sad.

RETAINING ANY RELATIONSHIP WITH you now completely depended on Papa. As Papa began to isolate you from anyone who knew the truth—anyone who had supported your independence—I tried to reach out to you in a way that would be safe. I wanted to do something special for your birthday and send a clear message to Papa that I intended to maintain a relationship with him, too. I spent weeks making a photo book in which I shared images of my new life: I included photos of me reporting from the red carpet at Sundance, clips of my headlines that appeared on *The Colbert Report,* and a photo of you and Papa holding me as a baby, with a message saying I loved you both. I sent the book on your birthday. When you received it, you were excited to show it to Papa. "This is awesome," you texted me. You told me you'd call me when Papa got home.

The call never came. When I texted you, you didn't respond. Weeks went by. Nothing. I texted, "I love you," and got nothing back. I texted, "I miss you." Nothing. I didn't hear from you again that year.

I heard from Dadiji and Dadaji that Papa said he didn't want the book in his house. He forced you to get rid of it, so you left it with my grandparents. The story came to me secondhand, as most information about you or Papa now did. But I can try to fill in the blanks. I can imagine you opening the book, excitedly showing Papa. I can imagine him seeing it and becoming irate at this reminder of a daughter who was so distant with him, jealous that it was sent not for his birthday but yours, and screaming at you, breaking things, hitting things for allowing this to enter his home, making you feel inferior and small because he was insecure about his strained relationship with me.

I wonder if he forbade you to talk to me, or if maybe he'd been screening your phone calls all along. Or maybe he didn't have to make an explicit threat, because you knew, you knew, that if you continued to build a relationship with me, he'd get angrier and you'd have to deal with a greater risk: of him harming himself, or harming you, or both. For years I ran through the scenarios in my head constantly, fearing for you and helpless that I could not save you. I dreamed about ways I could force him to set you free. I fantasized about attempting suicide—not going through with it, but like Papa had done, harming myself seriously enough to prove to you that I needed you, too. I thought about showing up at your apartment unannounced and provoking him in public, getting him to hit me so that everyone would see the violence that we saw in private. I considered hunting down the psychiatrist seeing you and trying to expose the truth.

My thoughts scared me. Once, not long after he told us he had been diagnosed with depression, Papa constructed a family tree and indicated how many of his blood relatives had attempted or died by suicide, as proof that we had a genetic predisposition. Papa warned me of this, as if suicide were a cold I would catch sooner or later due to a weakened immune system. He didn't tell me how to stave off the temptation to kill myself should the desire ever arise, just that I should be aware that the desire in my blood must be strong. He treated self-harm as a genetic inevitability, with no awareness of the triggers or patterns that contributed to suicidality, and yet he blamed you and me when he did attempt to take his own life, ignoring his own logic.

I could see that if I continued to accept responsibility for how Papa treated either of us, if I got swept up in his worldview again, what was happening to you was my potential future, too. I would become fearful and forget how to trust myself. I realized that manipulating you into coming back to me would not save you, it would only ensure that all of us drowned together.

I could not do anything to prevent Papa's self-destruction, or yours, no matter how deeply I contemplated these issues or attempted to determine their causes. I could only protect myself and hope you both might find your way. Instead, I had to begin the long, thorny process of letting go of the fantasy that I could have the tight-knit, happy family I had once been told was my cultural birthright. I had to rewrite the story I'd been raised on, the one that said we had fallen apart because of my disobedience, and make peace with the fact that few might ever believe otherwise, but that didn't make my story any less true.

Chapter 22

Home Is a Ghost

No one in our family had died, yet I felt an emotional death. My grief wasn't just about losing my relationship with you. The rickety bridge to my cultural identity had also collapsed. I had mostly participated in Indian culture through family events, like Diwali celebrations or weddings, where I could wear lehengas and speak unsteady Hindi among relatives. As I distanced myself from family, without many friends with whom to create my own traditions, I withdrew from all things Indian. I had once prided myself on being a devoted daughter, but I was ashamed that I could no longer call myself that, either. I must be so profoundly wrong because I couldn't figure out how to hold on to you or Papa and, recently, even Yush.

Months before you and Papa moved to Toronto, Yush had embarked on a new adventure to Boston, where several of his friends from college lived. He told me I should invest in a cryptocurrency called Ethereum. I said I didn't have enough money to invest in anything. He said he didn't, either. He lived off ramen noodles and slept in a walk-in closet. He reserved his actual bedroom for his elaborate computer setup.

As he navigated the cutthroat world of venture capitalism and tech entrepreneurship, Yush told me that these cultures valued blunt ass-holes. He said that women, too, though they claimed to value kindness, seemed to respect only aggressive men who took what they wanted. I attempted to disabuse him of the notion that women preferred jerks or that only tough guys succeeded in the world—or that, even if that were true, why it shouldn't dictate who he became. Yush's criticisms of women felt personal, too: The woman I sought to become did not fit neatly within his paradigm, and it hurt me that he couldn't see that.

As I watched Yush moving in a parallel direction to Papa, I lashed out at him, too, angry that he was changing into someone I didn't like. We repelled each other like magnets meeting at opposite ends. I tried to understand his feelings, but when his views didn't change, I mocked them and silently stewed in my resentments. I began to pull away, avoiding his phone calls and postponing plans to visit him.

Yush had once been so empathetic, vulnerable, and compassionate. But I think, as a way to simplify life and bypass his emotions, he developed a clinical, detached way of being. It was as if he had built a behavioral model of men and women in his head and then engaged with people according to that model. His approach was no longer to feel and respond and grow but rather to understand the expectation that others had of him and to react within those bounds. Yush didn't want to get better. He wanted to be better.

One day, Yush walked through Boston's South Bay to use a Bitcoin ATM. He was so alarmed by the shoddy technology that he contacted the founders of the company and outlined how he planned to hack their machines. They hired him as the company's chief technology officer. He worked for little to no pay, accepting a stake in equity instead. Yush believed in the company's mission, though, and vowed that he'd soon become a millionaire. As Yush leaned into his new, hardened approach, he finally found the elusive success he had long sought.

———

IT HAD BEEN AROUND three years since I quit a lucrative management-consulting job to follow my passion to become a writer. I had been hired to cover pop culture and entertainment at a news website, but mostly I posted a lot of TV clips and paraphrased news that someone else had reported. Only a few months in, I worried I might get fired. I made mistakes—careless ones, like misspelling the names of celebrities in headlines and mixing up city names in the same state. I struggled to keep pace with pitching and writing eight blog posts a day.

But I learned. I asked editors questions when I was confused about best practices. I checked my work more carefully. Slowly, after about a year of consistently strong performance, I started to pitch original reporting. I focused on diversity and racism in the entertainment industry. When a staff writing job opened up at the end of my second year, I made a case for a promotion. I was told that my focus was "too niche" and did not represent the direction in which the site was going.

I didn't know if I could continue to make a living as a journalist. I dipped into my savings every month to survive in New York City. Journalism paid me in prestige, not a living wage. Several of my editorial colleagues had parents who could supplement their meager salaries. Papa had muscled his way into that same world. I had attended a private high school, graduated from college without debt, and racked up extracurriculars instead of working. My choice to walk away from my job, too, was a privilege. But while I grew up with the same comforts as many of my white peers, there remained a barrier between us that prevented my contributions from being seen as valuable as theirs.

The instability of the career that I thought would save me, coupled with the rupture in my relationships with you and Papa and my growing distance with Yush, made me feel alone in the world. Not alone in the way that we are all ultimately alone. Alone in the way that I belonged to no one anymore, that if I fell ill or lost my job and health insurance, I had no support to make it through.

Mummy, I wanted to reach out to you. I wanted, so badly, to hear from you. I sent you emails telling you I love you. But I never heard back, and eventually I stopped trying. Instead, I fell apart in front of friends. I fell apart in front of anyone who seemed kind. I sought out a therapist, a white woman with an office near Central Park whose massive diamond ring split the light into tiny flecks of pink and blue on the wall. I sat in a chair on the far opposite side of the large room, unloading my problems as I looked at the prism of colors. She barely spoke. I wondered what she thought of me as I sat there. I didn't feel any relief, or any better, so after about a year I stopped seeing her.

My loneliness humbled me. It sounds embarrassingly ignorant now, but until I felt the tenuousness of my own safety net, I didn't understand that most don't have access to basic healthcare, savings, or stable familial support. I'd been raised to believe that comfort was the result of hard work or innate intellect, but I was starting to understand that fulfillment of these basic human needs was tied to a person's body, bloodline, and the origins of their birth. Papa's wealth had made me feel entitled to a level of security that no one is owed or guaranteed. I had a simplistic understanding of the world and how it worked because it worked well enough for me, and it was only when it stopped working for me that I began to think about the ways in which it failed to work for others.

SOME TIME THAT SPRING, several months after I visited you in Winnipeg, Fufaji called me. I went into the hallway outside my office, worried that he brought tragic news, as I had come to expect from family phone calls. He said that he and Buaji saw that I was alone and that they hadn't understood the extent of my isolation until that fall, when they realized that Papa hadn't let you talk to me in the year before you had visited Winnipeg. Fufaji wanted me to know that Yush and I could always call them for financial help and emotional support. He promised me that, going forward, he and Buaji would look after us the way they looked after their own kids. I cried.

Fufaji said that they were proud of me and the risks I'd taken in my career and didn't want me to give up on my dreams because of fear of not earning enough. I cried some more. I had always felt slightly ashamed, like I had failed at trying to be normal and happy with a life that most people would have felt lucky to have. I thought I was a disappointment to you both—to Papa especially.

I believed that Fufaji meant what he said about the money, but I didn't want to feel indebted to him, or to anyone, ever again. I wanted to prove that I was capable of taking care of myself. More than anything, I wanted to never have to put up with a controlling workplace, father, or partner, out of financial dependence. I began to think of success not as a job title, wealth, prestige, or social network but as the ability to be myself in the world. To know that, as a woman who had been taught that I needed to serve a man to be complete, I could instead build a life for myself that I loved, and that I could sustain that life by myself. I hoped that, maybe if you saw me live this way, you might choose to come back to me.

ABOUT A YEAR PASSED without any contact between you and me. Then one day Papa called me. I don't remember the conversation; this is based on what I transcribed immediately afterward, while still in shock. I have trouble keeping track of the various periods in which we were or weren't estranged or how often we spoke when Papa sporadically decided to start talking to me again over the next several years. Even when we did speak, we rarely engaged in anything vulnerable.

After I wrote down the simple facts of this conversation, I tried to forget that it ever happened. I didn't know how to deal with the turbulent emotions that surfaced inside me, and instead of acknowledging them, I numbed myself, shoving them far down so that I could continue to move forward.

"Your mom and I have had a rough two years, but we're doing a lot better now and things are calm again," Papa said, according to the notes I transcribed.

I asked him what had changed.

Papa said that you had finally learned how to be "introspective."

You were on the line, but Papa spoke about you as if you were somewhere else.

"When something is bothering her, she's able to verbalize it and it makes more sense," he said. I was floored that Papa could look at the dysfunction of our lives—his self-harm, my strained relationship with him, and Yush's estrangement with him—and think that this entire time the problem stemmed from your communication skills. I registered this as another way in which Papa asserted power over you.

"I'm glad you're doing better. I can tell that you must be because . . . well, this call is happening," I said.

Then Papa told me I should "come home."

What home? I wanted to say. My home didn't exist anymore.

"No matter what, we're family," Papa said. "We'll always share that bond."

I had thought that I could become indifferent or that I could detach from Papa. I no longer expected to get calls on my birthday. I didn't expect to celebrate important milestones together, or see one another on holidays, or go on family vacations ever again. I accepted that our relationship would be like this—a few brief conversations a year. But the truth is, hearing Papa deny my reality and yours still hurt me. The truth is, despite everything, I still loved Papa deeply. And I didn't know where to put that love or what to make of the fact that my understanding of love was to let a man hurt me because he says he cares for me.

Chapter 23

Wanting It All

BY THE TIME YOU and I were back in touch, I had moved to a smaller website that offered better hours and better pay. Around six months into that job, I interviewed for a senior-writer position at Cosmopolitan.com. The role would be an enormous step up in my career: The woman hired would become the face of the brand's political coverage throughout the 2016 election, regularly appearing on TV to discuss women's rights for the most visible women's magazine in the world. I did not believe I had a chance. But after a months-long interview process, the website hired me.

When I was growing up, I saw *Cosmopolitan* as a portal into another dimension. Occasionally, I picked up a copy at a drugstore, and at home I'd sit on my bed and study the world of smooth-skinned, cherry-lipped women who rode around in convertibles and summered in the Hamptons. As a girl, I had longed to be seen the way those women were seen. When the website welcomed me as its star political reporter, I believed that I finally belonged among them.

If Barbie lived in her Dreamhouse, then she worked at the Cosmopolitan.com office, a space manicured to Instagrammable perfection, with cute cat-themed mouse pads, furry pillows, and gold-accented furniture. A bright neon sign in the office's lobby gleamed I WANT IT ALL in capital letters, the motto of the quintessential *Cosmo* girl. In the 1960s, then-editor Helen Gurley Brown marketed the "self-made" woman as effortlessly glamorous, sexually voracious, and endlessly ambitious. Implicit in this influential messaging was that the ideal woman was thin, straight, and white, and she earned her way to empowerment by pleasing men in bed, performing well at work, and buying the products advertised in *Cosmo*'s folds. A woman of color had never held the editor-in-chief role at *Cosmo*. Still, when the website hired me to cover an election that I believed would usher in the nation's first female president, I took it as a sign that the brand, like America, was changing.

The job was more exhilarating than I could have imagined. A few months in, I traveled to Qatar and Jordan with a documentary filmmaker to cover Michelle Obama's first solo trip to the Middle East. I attended fancy galas and interviewed celebrities and leaders who championed abortion rights, fought against sexual assault, and spoke out against pay inequality.

I shared some photos and emails with you, but I did not call you and Papa to tell you much; sharing anything emotional—even positive—felt too scary, and I didn't want to put myself through that pain anymore. Instead, I poured the love that I couldn't give to you and Papa into my work. My reporting earned Cosmpolitan.com an award from its corporate parent, Hearst, and boosted the brand's profile as a political heavyweight. The thrill of my job helped distract me from the pain of losing touch with both of you.

I tried to separate my personal life from my professional life, yet to write about injustice, I had to draw from the well of rage within me every day. And my well was bottomless. As I interviewed more and more sexual-assault survivors, memories I suppressed in my late teens and early twenties resurfaced. I became enraged: Angry at Arthur and other men for what they did to me. Angry that I had become numb to men touching me without my permission. Angry that violence was celebrated as strength, but the ability to endure violence was cast as weakness. Angry that being vocal about my anger made me seem unreasonable. Angry that, because of all of this, trusting myself felt like delusion.

THAT SAME FALL, YUSH called me, sobbing. I had not heard him cry since his suicide attempt. He told me he was pushed out of the company by men he thought of as brothers. The company served thousands of stores across the country, relying on technology that Yush had coded. The company replaced him with the tall white mentee who Yush had personally recruited and trained.

Yush was once again reduced to the boy he had been in our white Pittsburgh neighborhood: a smart brown kid who could help someone with their homework but wasn't wanted for much else. At the height of his professional success, Yush learned that even then he would never really belong.

"I feel like I've been raped," Yush said through his tears.

"Yush, I know this is horrible, but you weren't raped," I said. "Please don't say that."

"No, Prachi," he said, voice cracking. "That's really how it feels. Like they raped me. They took something from me, a part of me," he said. I knew then that I could not share with Yush the memories that had been resurfacing. I let the phrasing go and tried to support him as best as I could.

Ultimately, Yush blamed himself. He continued to tell me that, should an asteroid fall on him tomorrow, it would be his fault, because it would be something he should have been able to prevent. He took responsibility for everything that happened to him—a burden I cannot imagine and an illusion of control that must have been crippling. I worried about how these events might trigger a depressive episode, but I said nothing, afraid that if I pried, he would shut me out just as he was letting me in.

———

A FEW MONTHS AFTER my conversation with Yush, the New York City police department advised women to buddy up in cabs as a response to increased assaults by drivers. The condescending advice enraged me. I funneled my turbulent emotions into an essay that traced the lines between what happened to me at sixteen and a larger paternalistic culture in which survivors are made to feel responsible for the violations of others. I had never written about myself before. I wrote in a voice that was not my own, trying to imitate the anger of white women I admired on the Internet. I mentioned the pepper spray that Yush gave me. I hadn't been able to control my body or even how I responded to the violation in the past, so I wanted to control how I got to talk about and understand it now.

When Yush saw the essay, he was furious. He didn't acknowledge the sexual assault at all. "You make me regret caring for you," he told me over Gchat. "When you use the love that your family has for you to further your agenda of hatefulness towards men, you are a professional victim. You can use that as a quote in one of your articles."

I don't know what to say to you about that moment, Mummy. It felt like a confirmation of everything that Papa had always said about me and that you had tacitly endorsed. That I was too selfish, too emotional, too much, too hard to love. And it destroyed me, because now these words came from the one person in the world who had never made me feel that way growing up. This time, it must be true.

I broke down at my desk and cried. I was so deeply ashamed that I couldn't find a way to hold on to the last person in our family, the only one I had left, the one I had thought I'd have in my corner forever, the one who I had promised to always protect.

Over Gchat, I told Yush that his words really hurt me and that I needed space from him. I blocked him and signed off my email. I left the office and walked in the cold from the Cosmopolitan.com office on 57th Street to my apartment in the East Village. I was finally becoming the woman I had always wanted to be, but I was heartbroken that Yush seemingly hated that woman. I knew, too, that I had crossed into a new identity: I was not trying to learn how to change myself to win back Yush's approval. I wanted to learn how to live with the fact that the person I loved more than anyone could not love the woman I was becoming.

I did not have much faith in therapy. I had seen how therapists failed to catch the severity of Yush's depression and how Papa manipulated therapy to deepen your self-doubt. In my own life, therapy had been a form of witness, a place where I could be honest when I had no other space to speak my truth. But therapy had never been a place where I learned new coping skills, gained insight into my behaviors, challenged myself, or found a sense of peace.

I had always put my faith in people I admired, people whose judgment I trusted above my own. For most of my life, Yush had been one of them. As I saw Yush turn into a person I didn't recognize and didn't like, I needed someone to tell me if they saw what I saw and, if so, why did I feel like I was losing my mind? Was I trapped in a delusion, as Papa appeared to be?

There was a hunger, a want, a rage inside me, but I could not let it out and I did not know how to. I desperately wanted someone to tell me where to situate the dysfunction: Was it in my Indianness? In my Americanness? In my womanness? A combination of these things? Even if I managed to parse any of this—a maddening, anxiety-inducing task that was both futile and impossible—I'd be confronted by circular, ontological questions: What did it even mean to be Indian, or American, or a woman—complex identities that are socially constructed? I felt confused, and then isolated by my confusion, embarrassed by how my questions fed into racist, one-dimensional beliefs, as if I relied on white people to tell me who I was and what was normal.

My sense of culture was so fragile that, for years, I identified with anything that vaguely suggested "Indianness": the ornate paisley-mehndi print that, when added to any graphic design, alluded to South Asia, or the Samarkan font that gestured toward Hindi. When a relative from India visited us and saw that font, he was confused. "What is that supposed to be?" he said, trying to make sense of this strange type that was not satisfying as either English or Hindi. Papa explained to him that it was an English font imitating the Devanagari script.

"But it doesn't look like Hindi," the relative had said. I could tell by his reaction that he was confused. Why did one need an English font that gestured toward Hindi when Hindi . . . already existed? The font was once a useful assimilation tool for a new population of immigrants, but it had become widely used for "namaslay" pendants and advertisements for ubiquitous white-owned yoga studios, alluding to some vague notion of Eastern spirituality.

As a white-bred Indian American girl, I triangulated what it meant to be Indian by Papa's expectations and these limited cultural signposts. When I began to sense how anemic my understanding of my own history was, I became threatened by the way white people appropriated South Asian cultural traditions in part because my relationship with Indian identity felt almost as appropriative. My insecurity over my identity had turned culture into a performance rather than something I inhabited authentically.

I had to find a therapist who would not interpret this ordinary, everyday confusion over identity and culture as self-hatred and who would not further stoke the internal division by treating these conflicts as brokenness. After seeing the effect that an Indian psychiatrist briefly had on you and seeing how a white psychiatrist failed you, I searched for Indian American therapists in New York City. PsychologyToday .com listed only one woman in Manhattan: Reka. On her website, she identified as a feminist and Buddhist. I emailed her, desperately hoping that she could help me.

I did not mention therapy to you or Papa. We now spoke sporadically over the phone, and none of us dared to share any aspect of our lives that felt remotely vulnerable. You always said that you were doing well and that Papa was doing well, and I never believed you, but I never pried. We never discussed the past. We never discussed Buaji's family.

In our family, therapy suggested that someone was potentially suicidal. Therapy felt shameful. I don't know what you believed you were supposed to gain from therapy, but on my intake form, I wrote that I wanted to learn how to be at peace with what I could not control and find a way to be happy.

Just as I began therapy, Donald Trump emerged as a top contender in the Republican Party presidential primary. He was unlike any political candidate I had ever seen. Like many of my peers, I was taken aback by his overt bigotry and his blustery speech. You and Papa could not believe that such a grotesque man could ever become president. Neither could I.

I didn't say this to you, but behind his off-putting display, I recognized something in this man. He presented his feelings in the moment as the definitive truth, no matter how much evidence proved him wrong. He demonized anyone who attempted to expose or correct him. He took advantage of social norms to get what he wanted out of people, leaving them blindsided and confused after he no longer needed them. I did not have formal journalism training, but I had the training of a lifetime of dealing with someone who played with reality in this way.

It was sobering to watch a majority of white America uphold Trump's bullying as the ideal form of masculinity and leadership. I had underestimated both Trump's appeal and the allure of that kind of power to men like Papa. Papa would never be accepted by someone like Trump or his base, but within our home he mimicked the same behavior and reigned as king. When cable news outlets treated Trump as entertainment and journalists failed to hold him accountable, I felt a visceral rage.

In an election stoked by fear of immigrants, many brown women confided to me that they felt safer talking to me because of my identity. As Trump gained popularity, I wanted to use my platform to counter some of the false and dangerous narratives being spread by mostly white commentators on TV. Cosmopolitan.com appeared more progressive by featuring these perspectives, but the site forced me to decline every TV opportunity discussing Trump. I demanded a reason. It was too controversial to weigh in on Trump, I was finally told. I pushed back. *This isn't the Prachi show.* When another Hearst site sent a white male writer to discuss Trump's proposals on a cable-TV panel with a politician who embraced white supremacist views, I understood that what was controversial was not Trump, it was me—a brown woman speaking candidly, moving the political beyond the realm of theoretical and into the personal. *Cosmo*, which had an image to maintain among its white readership, was unwilling to rock the boat with advertisers by letting a brown woman criticize a popular presidential candidate on national television.

About six weeks before the election, I had an opportunity to interview Trump's daughter, Ivanka, over the campaign's paid-family-leave policy. The policy was meager, but because America is the only developed country without federal paid leave, they presented the policy as groundbreaking. Setting up Ivanka as its face enabled the campaign to frame a candidate publicly accused of sexual assault by more than a dozen women as a champion of women's rights.

When my phone call with Ivanka began, she launched into a script, repeating the talking points from an op-ed that she had published in *The Wall Street Journal.* I interrupted her to say that I needed clarity on her policy. She continued with her talking points. I interrupted her again, and then I asked her about details of the policy—specifically, why the policy excluded paternity leave for men. I asked her if her father still felt, as he had said before, that pregnant women were an inconvenience in the workplace.

She said my questions had a lot of "negativity." She insinuated that I was lying about the pregnancy comment. Later, on Twitter, Ivanka criticized the magazine, and then her father, the future president of the United States, told Fox Business News that I was "a non-intelligent reporter," had been "very rude," and "really attacked" Ivanka. Their angry comments motivated a slew of his supporters to harass me online.

An executive at Hearst had cut a portion of my interview where I interrupted Ivanka. I was livid and demanded a reason from my editors. "We don't want it to appear like you are bullying her," they told me. I protested and I pushed back again, further cementing my reputation at work as a difficult woman, as a stubborn woman, as a woman who refused to accept what she's told. After all, Ivanka projected the image of the ideal *Cosmo* Girl, and I did not.

I was the only reporter to poke through Ivanka's polished veneer during the election cycle. The brief interview generated international headlines, brought an extraordinary amount of traffic to the site, and elevated the magazine's reputation as a news outlet. As we celebrated, another editor stopped by my desk and said, "Your family must be so proud!" The polite, innocuous comment took me aback. I didn't know what to say. I mumbled something like, "Oh, I don't know about that."

I think you and Papa were proud of what I had accomplished. I think you both were proud that the world was impressed by my work. But the beliefs of the woman who had produced that work—I worried that woman shamed our family.

Yush reached out to me to say he shared the interview with his friends. His friendly email filled me with hope for reconciliation. I asked him if he wanted to work on our relationship and try to start talking again. He wrote back, "I don't think we can be friends—and at this point I don't want to be. You've dedicated yourself to a political worldview, and one of its founding principles is hatred and disrespect towards people who are very much like me."

His words shattered me all over again.

I told him I liked the woman I was becoming. I told him that even though we didn't share the same views, I promised I wouldn't try to change him anymore. I told him that I would be here when he was ready. I told him that no matter what, I loved him.

Chapter 24

Destroying Illusions

I WORKED NONSTOP IN THE final weeks of the election, publishing a few more pieces that made national headlines. After about a year at work, I was told that I was getting a 2 percent raise. The slight bump, to my knowledge, kept my salary just shy of what my white predecessor had been offered more than two years prior. Pointing to a year of work that had exceeded my employer's expectations, I asked if I could negotiate my raise. I was told no.

I saw that, if I continued on this path, I could become a nationally recognized political reporter. But I felt blocked, denied any cable-TV opportunity that weighed in on Trump. I felt devalued in other ways, too. I had been told when I started that there was no compensation for overtime. But I had discovered that my colleagues received time off in exchange for late shifts, so that week I asked my editor for equitable compensation time going forward.

The week following these discussions, the website editor invited me to a meeting called "2016 media/publicity." I did not know what was on the agenda. I assumed we would plan out post-election coverage or put together a plan for publicity going forward. Instead, the meeting was an ambush.

The website editor told me I should have been thankful for the 2 percent raise I received. She told me that I was not allowed to ask for compensation time or even attempt to negotiate it. She told me that I was lazy, rude, had developed a bad reputation at Hearst, and was sabotaging my career. She told me that when I was working on a deadline, I needed to ask for my editor's permission to eat, and if she said I couldn't, then I was not allowed to eat. When I attempted to seek clarification or to defend myself from her personal attacks, she told me that I should be thankful for the feedback that I received and to say nothing else. "You should be grateful you work here," she said. "It is a privilege to work here, and don't forget that."

At the very moment I started seeing myself as an equal and asked for the same opportunities and rights as my mostly white peers, I was cut down to size, put in my place, reminded that I should be grateful to be allowed among them at all. I saw that I was not valued for my perspectives, only for what I could produce.

I was back in the sunroom, and Papa had just smashed the plate over my head because I refused to accept wrongdoing. I realized that my boss, like Papa, was trying to make me doubt my own senses for objecting to unfair treatment because she didn't see a problem with her conduct. The double standards she upheld were not the problem. I was the problem for pointing them out.

A few years later, I would receive confirmation of what my senses had told me about whose perspectives mattered and whose did not: Multiple employees accused the former head of Hearst's digital magazines of enabling a hostile work environment and sexually harassing employees. In the *New York Times*'s scathing report, Hearst supported the white male executive, who had been promoted despite numerous complaints to HR. A day after the report was published, in the midst of a PR nightmare, he resigned.

MUMMY, I HAD WANTED to think that fame and wealth—conventional notions of success—didn't matter to me anymore. But they did. I didn't get approval from you or Papa or Yush, and the desire to be validated was so deep in me that now I sought it on an even larger stage: the whole world, demanding that everyone look at the very thing that no one in our home could acknowledge—my perspective. But now I could see that, while the world loved what I did, it still didn't love *me*. I didn't know what to do with my ugly desire for validation or the world's ugly response to it.

I burst into Reka's office, crying. I told her the meeting felt racist and I immediately justified and overexplained: It wasn't racist in the way that I had been picked on explicitly for race but racist in a systemic way; I was up against an institution designed to exclude the perspectives of someone like me.

With one of my white therapists, I would not have dared to say the word "racist," knowing that this claim could open me up to a dangerous interrogation that would further erode my shaky sense of trust in myself. I would have described the meeting as it happened, and they would have listened with sympathy and then tried to help me come up with strategies to cope or reframe, all the while eliding the fact that I was operating in an environment that stifled my advancement. I would have more deeply internalized the problem as one of my perspective rather than one of a rigged system, undermining my sense of reality in a space explicitly designed to support it.

Reka stopped me. "Prachi, that was racist," she said, with such absolution that I felt silly for ever having second-guessed myself. The immediate validation of my experience was radical. But in her next sentence, Reka gutted me: "But you shouldn't need me to tell you that in order to know that this was racism. You already know this. I don't want you to be surprised at the racism you experience—you know that the world, that these white institutions, are racist. The question I want you to consider is: How do you accept that reality and not let it take your power from you? How do you stand tall in those moments, when white women speak down to you, without becoming as small as they want you to become?"

All my life, I had wanted to be seen the way the world saw slim

white women, and I had tricked myself into believing that if I followed the same beauty trends they did, I could wield the same power.
Until Reka said those words, it never occurred to me that I could find
that power within myself.

Because the way that Papa undermined my sense of reality was
not so different from the way that white America made me doubt
myself, the notion that I deserved any better—or that better was
even possible—seemed absurd. Vulnerability felt like delusion. When
someone could accept me as I am, as Yush had once done, my outpouring created intimacy and connection. But when I repeatedly
shared my reality with someone incapable of seeing it, like Papa, I
doubted myself and viewed myself as a failure. I did not yet know
how to distinguish between those who could accept me and those who
could not.

I noticed that in Reka's presence, I did not feel the urge to break
myself into parts and neatly arrange them, displaying myself as an
unfinished puzzle, as I instinctively did with the white therapists I had
seen before. Support from a therapist who had navigated her way out
of the same mental labyrinth that currently entrapped me assured me
that up is up and down is down, oriented me when I didn't know how
else to find my way through. If I hadn't seen someone like Reka, who
had wrestled with similar issues, I might not have believed that I could
move through the world any differently.

I had always dismissed the idea of "self-love" as so silly, so white, so
woo-woo and New Age-y. Now I saw that learning how to love myself
was my salvation, a rebellious act of refusing to believe I was what
white institutions or Papa had wanted to reduce me to. To love myself
was to accept myself as I am and to live in a way that honored my
feelings, aligned with my values, and trusted my senses, even when the
outside world wanted me to doubt or shrink myself. Therapy became
a place not for repair but for the formation of a relationship with
someone who helped me see that I am already whole.

THE NIGHT AMERICANS ELECTED Donald Trump president, I stood outside the Javits Center in Midtown Manhattan with a colleague, holding back tears as we interviewed despondent Hillary Clinton supporters passing by in what felt like a funeral procession. The America I knew had died, a painful feeling underscored by the rising awareness that it had never really existed, except in my mind. I had been so invested in wanting a certain idea of America to be true, despite all the evidence that it wasn't.

Next to me, a street vendor hawking NEVER TRUMP pins on one side of the table and NEVER HILLARY shirts on the other hooted and cheered like he was riding a float at Carnival. "Hey, guys, at least now it will be legal to grab pussy!" he yelled to a group of young men who walked past. "America just elected a rapist for president!" They laughed and high-fived one another.

I couldn't continue to work at a place where I'd have to silence myself to appease corporate advertisers or white readership, especially at a political moment that had made the consequences of doing that so devastatingly clear. After Trump's election, I accepted a job covering politics at *Jezebel*. In the interview process, I told an executive there that I wasn't willing to temper my voice to cater to corporations or political figures. He said that's why they wanted to hire me.

Days before my start date, I was in a café when I got a call from an unknown number. It was Nancy's mom. My heart began to race. Either she was calling me because she was planning some elaborate surprise for Nancy or something horrible had happened.

"Nancy was in a car accident," she said. I began shaking. Before I could ask if Nancy was okay, she continued. "She was airlifted to a hospital but died in the operating room."

I shrieked and then stumbled, nearly falling to the floor and dropping my tea. I began to cry, but then I remembered that I was talking to a mother whose child had died. I tried to steady my voice and ask her about the funeral and what I could do to help. The next week, instead of going to a new office, I watched my friend get lowered into the ground in a casket.

My grief over Nancy's death felt selfish. I suppose that all grief is, in a way. Nancy was vibrant and complicated, like anyone. But in her death, I could not hold her as a full person anymore. I could only fixate on what I had lost: a confidante and witness. A key piece of my past and a source of joy and fulfillment for my future had inexplicably vanished. I mourned her, but, really, I mourned the loss of what could no longer be, of all the gifts from her that I would never receive. I decided that to honor her life, I would try to be more present in my relationships, including with Yush. I wanted to extend to him the sort of witness that Nancy had once so graciously offered me.

I called Yush. We had not spoken in about a year. I wanted him to hear about Nancy's death from me. I told him that I wanted to talk about our issues but that I needed a little bit more time. Yush told me that he lived in San Francisco now. Nancy had been completing a PhD at UC Berkeley. He had just sent her a message inviting her to a party at his new apartment and was wondering why he hadn't heard back.

"It really makes you appreciate how short life is," Yush said. "Thanks for telling me."

THAT SUMMER, DADIJI WAS admitted to the ICU. She stayed there for one week and then remained in the hospital for another six. Fufaji, Buaji, Chachaji, a few of my cousins, and I each took extended shifts visiting Dadiji at the hospital.

Dadaji and Dadiji lived in a small suburb outside Toronto. They kept their tiny apartment hot, at eighty degrees, even in the summer. Dadaji filled his days by napping and watching Hindi soap operas at a volume so high that I could not focus on anything else while I was there. On the days he felt strong enough to stand, I took Dadaji to the hospital to see Dadiji. When he got tired—usually after about fifteen minutes—I drove him home, and then while Dadaji napped, I went back to the hospital and sat with Dadiji.

Buaji told me that I had just missed Yush by a few days. I was surprised to hear this. She said that Yush had taken a red-eye flight from San Francisco to stay with you and Papa in Toronto. I was surprised by that fact, too. Over the past six months, Yush and Papa had rebuilt a relationship through regular phone calls. Yush had told Buaji that Papa appeared to be more honest and introspective. He must have forgiven Papa and become close to him again—close enough to stay with you both in the new condo.

Over the past few months, Yush and I had mustered a shaky though regular email correspondence. He had described to me his new company. He told me that he was preparing for the Singularity, the moment when artificial intelligence became smarter than humanity and could no longer be controlled. His writing was split between two personas—someone who loved me and someone who hated me. I worried about him, but the expression of concern felt like an act of hostility. Instead, I said I hoped that he was happy.

He wrote that he wasn't.

On his unannounced visit to Toronto, Yush had stopped by the hospital and sat with Dadiji for about an hour. Long after Yush left, as Buaji, her daughter Priya, and I took shifts sitting with Dadiji, she crooned to all of us that she was so lucky to have a grandson who would fly across the continent to visit his grandmother. We hid our irritation.

Yush had also stopped by to see Dadaji. Dadaji said that Yush talked mostly about robotics, remaining in the safe territory of work, not engaging in any of the questions about his life, which Dadaji was more interested in.

Then Dadaji brought out an essay I had written about his life: "How Dadaji Became a Feminist." Yush yelled at Dadaji for calling himself a feminist, saying, "Is this true? How dare you!" He stormed out of the apartment. He came back, apologized for yelling, then left. I could not imagine my brother raising his voice at our grandfather. Yush was even more troubled than I had thought.

———

I TOLD YOU BOTH that I was coming. I told you that I planned to stay with Dadaji. I told you both that I would be happy to see you, if you'd meet me at Dadaji's place. Though you and Papa lived only forty minutes from Dadiji and Dadaji, Papa would not come with you to see me. Later that week, Papa dropped by Dadaji's apartment and yelled at him for not having cut off contact with Buaji.

Dadaji had initially wanted to live with Papa after retirement, in accordance with Indian custom. But he had changed his mind after a visit to Papa's condo, when, in a fit of rage, Papa lifted a chair over my frail octogenarian grandfather. "We had some jovial conversation," Dadaji told me. "I said something and he didn't like it. I don't even know what."

"And he stood there with a chair in his hand, the chair over my head. I still remember the thought in my head: My God, if he hits me, he will never be able to excuse himself. I just kept quiet."

Papa did stop himself, but Dadaji had nightmares over that moment for years. "I was scared to live with him after that. I talked to my family doctor. She heard the story and said you cannot live with him. This is in his nature. It will come out again."

Papa continued to tell Dadaji and Dadiji that he would cut them out of his life if they didn't discontinue all relations with Buaji. When Dadiji was in the hospital, he asserted his power: Papa was the point of contact for her medical care. On my second visit, even as Dadaji and I sat at her bedside, we could not see her medical examination results, and Papa did not respond to Dadaji's calls. Dadaji and I tried to explain to Dadiji why she should tell the doctor to talk to Buaji instead, but it was useless. Eventually, we gave up. Buaji thought that Dadiji was missing Papa, and this was her way of trying to keep him involved in her life. Thankfully, Fufaji had connections at the hospital. He was able to find out the doctor's treatment plan for Dadiji and kept the rest of us informed. I don't know if you knew about these incidents or not.

For all of Papa and Yush's anger at how unreasonable the women in their lives were, it was these very women who had organized care and shown up for my aging grandparents. "I would have fallen apart without my granddaughters," Dadaji said to me. It was heartbreaking to hear him say, "Thank you, Prachi," so many times. I was surprised by how much strength Dadiji and Dadaji drew from us, and I was surprised by how unburdened I felt offering it to them. I reassured him, many times, that we were going to continue to be there for them. "We love you, Dadaji. You are not a burden. You will not have to do this alone." For the second time in my life, I saw Dadaji cry.

A FEW WEEKS LATER, Yush and I reconnected through a phone call. We agreed to maintain some boundaries. We wanted a relationship in whatever limited form both of us could handle. Yush told me that he was in Italy, working remotely on a new start-up company. He mentioned that he was dating someone named Chelsea.

"Is she your girlfriend?" I asked.

"No," he said, with some hesitation. "I wouldn't call her that. She's just someone I'm seeing, you know, and it's totally cool if she sees other people, too."

"Well, is she seeing other people?" I asked.

"No."

"Are you?"

"No."

"How long have you been . . . sort of seeing her?" I said, trying not to laugh.

"A year," he said. "But it's not that serious," he added.

"Right."

It was obvious to me that Yush was in love with this woman. But he was too afraid to admit that he did not have control over the feelings that he held for her.

After the call, I sent Yush a message on Facebook reminding him to call Dadiji on her birthday at the end of the month. I asked him if he wanted to set up another time to talk soon.

I never heard back.

Chapter 25

Welcome You to the Prachi-Prach

ONE SUNNY MORNING IN November, three months after my last phone call with Yush, Papa called me. I was about to run some errands. I ignored his call.

Papa didn't call often. When he did, I usually let it go to voicemail. I needed time to calm myself and plan out carefully what I'd say to him. I had to consider what I'd reveal about my life versus what I would not share, what topics might lead to a fight and what felt safe, and I had to make the call when I felt I could remain calm throughout, no matter what he said.

This time, though, he followed up with a text in all capital letters: EMERGENCY. CALL BACK NOW!!!

My mind cycled through the other times I'd received a call that urgent: Yush's suicide note; your threat to jump out of a speeding car; Papa downing a bottle of pills.

Standing in the bedroom, my hands trembled as I called Papa back.

"Beta, I have terrible news," Papa said.

I fell to the ground before my brain grasped the words that came next. When I imagine that moment now, I am not in my own body; I am watching someone else collapse.

"Yush is dead."

I was the second person in our family to know. You were still at the dentist's office. Papa sounded irritated with you for not being home or answering your phone, as if you should have anticipated your son's death and planned your day accordingly.

I crawled from the floor and onto the bed. I asked Papa if I could help call the other family members, including Buaji. Papa got angry at the suggestion. Had this been a routine phone call, one that I had prepared for, I would have remembered to not mention the name of the sister he hated. But in my rawness, I was caught off guard, and my aunt's name carelessly tumbled out of my mouth.

"I have to tell her," I heard myself say.

"Fine," he said. "Call her."

Papa asked me if I would join you both in Italy, where Yush had lived for the last few months, to bring Yush's body back. Instinctively, I said yes. But hours later, as I sat on the couch, immobilized by shock and devastation, I became enraged. I thought about walking around a city I did not know with parents who had barely spoken to me in the past six years, haunted by the ghost of a brother who was, as you would later tell me, "waiting for you to rejoin the family."

I texted Reka to request an emergency therapy session. As I cried, I told her I was going to go to Italy. Had I not been in such a vulnerable state, Reka might have gently asked me to rethink my decision. But in my wrenching anguish, as I was drowning in front of her, Reka yanked me back above the surface. "Prachi," she said, "I want you to really think about why you're going. I want you to reconsider." She asked me things like: What did I need right now? What support would I have there? What were my reasons for going? It was an alien line of questioning: so much "me," so much "I." There was not supposed to be an "I" when thinking about our family. Besides, what kind of daughter demanded space from her parents at a time like this?

I imagined how that week in Italy might go. I saw myself turning into whatever Papa expected me to be. The unbearable, wrenching pain of losing Yush would become somehow even worse as I'd numb my feelings to exist however Papa demanded.

I called Papa back and said I could not go. To my surprise, he didn't yell or ask for an explanation. He accepted my wishes. My guilt worsened. I momentarily questioned myself. I didn't tell him that I had decided to go stay with Buaji, the sister he despised, for the week. I didn't know how to explain that I didn't do it to hurt either of you. I did it because I needed to feel safe. I just wanted to feel supported by someone, too. But in a family where there is no "I," there is no "self" that requires protection. I can imagine your voice: *Prachi, I didn't have anyone to support me when I came here, and I put up with it.* I don't know what to say back. I wish you hadn't put up with it. I wish you had demanded more—for both your sake and mine.

THAT WEEK, AS YOU and Papa sorted through Yush's belongings in Italy, I did almost nothing to help you. I was useless. I thought I might be able to write Yush's obituary, but I couldn't do that, either. I was ashamed that I didn't know the facts of his life well enough to write it. Worse, I feared that Yush wouldn't have wanted me to write it.

I tried to handle other small things for the funeral, like picking the casket. Papa asked me for suggestions for the pallbearers. When he rattled off a list that included a former high school teacher and Ambika Aunty's son, I said, "Dev and Nikhil should be on the list," confused by the omission. The names of Buaji's sons had tumbled out of my mouth before I had time to think about his reaction.

"This is what Mom and I want," Papa said as his voice rose. "Don't question us. You don't understand."

He always spoke for you, and you always backed him up. I hated that I could never tell whether you complied because you truly agreed or because you were too scared to disagree. What really terrified me, though, was that both of those things could be true at the same time. I could no longer tell where you ended and where he began.

I asked him to consider what our cousins meant to Yush. Papa screamed at me, "Yush didn't love Buaji! He never loved her!"

I hung up on him, shaking and sobbing. I realized then that this funeral was not truly for Yush. It was a pageant for Papa's pain. The familiar sensation of numbness, the armor I wore to shield myself as a girl, returned.

THE FUNERAL WAS IN Toronto, where you, Dadiji, and Dadaji all lived now. On the eve of the service, their seven remaining grand-children kept Dadiji and Dadaji company as they struggled to under-stand how two immigrants raised in colonial India had outlived their healthy twenty-nine-year-old American grandson. The apartment filled up with the people who felt Yush's death as an irreparable tear in the universe. We ate chicken biryani and drank boxed wine and told stories about the dumbest genius, the smartest idiot, we had ever known.

One of my cousins told us about the time Yush needed to rent a car to attend a wedding, but he realized that he had locked his license inside an electronic safe. He couldn't retrieve the license, though, be-cause the safe's battery had died, and he had amazingly also locked the physical key inside the safe—to keep the key safe, you see. It was late at night, hours before he needed to hit the road, and he had to break into the safe—a task no mechanic would likely help him with. He finally called up a friend who had a workshop, and the friend used an angle grinder to cut into the safe to get out Yush's license. He made it to the wedding on time.

But even among people I loved, I was agitated. I wanted to hold you and be held by you. I didn't know if I was a sister anymore. I wanted to know I was still a daughter and for you to know that you were still a mother. I wanted to tell you this with my body, by falling into yours and laying my head on your lap, your golden bangles clinking together as your hands stroked my head gently like I was your little girl again. I had not seen you or Papa in four years, since that painful Thanksgiving in Winnipeg. But because of Papa's hatred of Buaji, you and Papa did not come to Dadiji and Dadaji's apartment to be with us.

I didn't see you until the next morning, the day of Yush's funeral. It was the first time I'd ever stepped into the condo that Papa had bought. I recognized much of the furniture from my childhood home. I noticed Yush's belongings set up around the apartment. I didn't see any trace of me in this alternate universe.

As Papa sat with relatives in the living room, I pulled you into your bedroom. I sat on your bed. You gave me your old silk peacock-blue salwar suit to wear to what would be my first Hindu funeral service. You told me that you were planning on dedicating yourself to taking college classes so that you could "one day earn Papa's respect." You said you were a bad communicator and needed to improve your skills so Papa could understand you better. It devastated me to hear this, but I held my tongue. I did not say that a man who forces you to prove your worth is a man incapable of seeing it.

It's a strange thing to miss someone who is right there. When I talk to you is when I miss you the most, because I am confronted by what I cannot have. It was then that I realized that, even in the wake of Yush's death, I could never tell you the things I wanted to say. It was then that I realized you needed to believe in Papa's worldview in order to survive and to justify the tragedy that had consumed all of us.

Papa came into the room and asked if he could speak to me. In the narrow space of the hallway, crushed by the death that had turned me into his only remaining child, we shared a rare moment of vulnerability.

"I wanted to know if you're open to having a relationship—a real one," he said softly. "It will take time, but maybe we can start by email."

I had longed to hear these words from Papa for years, an awareness that the issues between us were complex and could not be resolved with just a hug. Through the darkness of grief, the possibility of a reconciliation also opened up a sliver of something else within me: hope. Yush's death, a black hole that had sucked us all in, would surely cause inward reflection and prompt a journey of healing.

"Of course," I said. "I would like that very much."

"Good," he said. "I'll send you the email that helped me and Yush start talking again." I nodded awkwardly, a gesture reaching for a day when we could genuinely embrace.

In your kitchen, Ambika Aunty came up to me. "Can you do something for me?" she asked. Before I could respond, she said, "I need you to keep your Buaji away from your parents at the funeral."

I was shocked and enraged by the insensitivity of her request. Today, even today, when I would have to look at my brother's costumed corpse and release him into a fire, I could not simply grieve. I could not fall apart. I could not submit to my wrenching anguish and my unbearable rage. I had to perform and behave in the ways expected of me.

Summoning all of my strength, I said no.

THE FUNERAL HALL WAS palatial but cold, with polished stone floors. In the hallway, before the doors to the service opened, I grappled with where to stand and with whom to talk. On one end of the hallway stood you and Papa. You barely spoke to me. On the other, Buaji and Fufaji and my cousins; I wanted to cling to them. But I felt a sense of duty to be beside you and Papa and, beneath that, rage that even at a time like this, I had to play Papa's game of chess.

You and Papa requested an open casket. I had told Papa that I didn't want to remember Yush that way. Papa said this was what you both wanted. I avoided the room until we had to enter.

Before the service, the pandit invited close family into the room for a prayer—my grandparents, cousins, aunts, uncles, and us. I searched for Buaji and Fufaji and their children. I needed their strength to get me through what I was about to face. But at the doorway, a staff member blocked Buaji's family from entering. Papa had forbidden them from participating in Yush's funeral. They were forced to enter with the rest of the public and sit in the back of the hall, apart from close family and friends, among people who didn't even know Yush. The cruelty of the act shocked me. In a culture of log kya kahenge, Papa had declared: *Let them talk. Let them know how evil she is.*

When I walked into that lifeless chamber, forced to lay my eyes upon Yush's body, I fell over. I sobbed at my feet until one of my cousins lifted me up and held my hand as she walked me forward. Soft devotional bhajans played in the background. Yush was dressed in an ivory kurta pajama. I kept thinking that he should have been wearing his signature white T-shirt, jeans, and Brooks sneakers, with ambient trip-hop playing in the background. Nothing about the service reflected his personality.

I had never felt so tremendously alone before. During the service, the room filled with friends, relatives, and people from your new life—people who did not know Yush. People who did not really know you or Papa, either. They introduced themselves to me as they left the funeral. Buaji's family, castaways, sat several rows behind me. I spent the service in shock, standing in front of dozens of people, most of whom I barely knew, pouring ghee over Yush's body as I choked back sobs and tried to control the mucus dripping out of my nose. The pandit compared Yush's life to borrowing a great book from the library, telling us that it was time to return the book. I cursed at him under my breath. I tried to hold your hand and I put my arm around you, but your hand was limp, and your body did not push back into mine. I did not blame you. I had abandoned you, so how could you trust me to support you now?

At first, I declined to speak at the service. I didn't know what to say or whether I had the right to speak about a man who had barely spoken to me in the last years of his life.

Papa took the podium first. He emphasized Yush's brilliance in his speech, telling the story about how Yush learned to paddle a canoe when he was eleven or so. "Yush, it's acceleration control, not velocity control," Papa had said on the river. Yush then immediately corrected the canoe's trajectory. Papa smiled as he told the story, but I cringed. Yush had always hated that story. He thought it was nerdy and self-aggrandizing.

As Papa spoke, I searched my email for the silly, funny, dumb poem that Yush had written for my thirtieth birthday. We were estranged at the time, but he sent it anyway. I remember how it made me laugh and feel loved, giving me hope that we would find a way back to each other, regardless of our differences.

After Papa walked away, I changed my mind. I went to the podium, and I read the poem out loud from my phone:

welcome you to the prachi-prach
prach-prachi prach prach prach.
you want to prach with the prachi-prach?
prach-prachi prach prach prach.

we can try to prach with prachi-prach
prach-prachi prach prach prach.

but how and why does the prachi-prach?
prach-prachi prach prach prach.
do two need to prach the prachi-prach?
to each prach-pracher prachi own?

you dare to prach at the prachi-prach?
prach-prachi prach prach prach.
prachi veni prachi vici prachi khaleesi.
[*Flight of the Valkyries* begins playing]
prach-prachi prach prach prach.

you prach-prachi will prach too
prach prachi will prach-prachi prach,
all will prach when the prachi prach
prach-prachi will prach prach on you.

feel the pulse of the prachi-prach
feet march too, to the prachi-prach

prachi prachi prach prach prach
prachi praCHI PRACH PRACH PRACH

As I read it, people laughed, catching a glimpse of the boy who I loved and remembered. A glimpse of the boy who did not have to succeed to know he mattered to me. A glimpse of the boy who was searching so hard for love—and searching for a way to return.

Chapter 26

Five Foot Ten

WHEN PAPA HAD CALLED to tell me that Yush died, my first question was, "Was it suicide?"

"No," he said.

After a long pause: "But he did something very stupid."

Hours before Yush died, Papa had been on the phone with him. Yush was coughing. Papa had suspected something was very wrong. "Go to the ER," he told Yush. You and Papa watched a movie with one of your neighbors that evening, and after the funeral, she told me that you had said you didn't sleep that night. You, too, knew that Yush was in trouble.

Papa told me Yush died from a pulmonary embolism. I thought the "stupid thing" Yush did was ignoring Papa about going to the hospital. But I didn't understand why coughing was severe enough to warrant an ER visit, and Papa didn't explain.

Moments after hanging up with Papa, I called Buaji and told her how Yush had died. She was confused. Pulmonary embolisms are rare in young people. Statistically, he was among those least likely to suffer a pulmonary embolism. In the United States, they are even less common among Asian Americans than among white people. Yush was a lifelong long-distance runner. He was healthy and active. Despite the statistics, that is what ended his life.

Then Papa's brother, my Chachaji, called me. He said something about a procedure. "What procedure?" I asked him.

"Oh, you should talk to your dad about that," he said.

I called Papa back to ask what was going on. Papa didn't want to tell me. I begged him. "Please, Papa," I said. "He's my brother. I need to know."

Yush had lied to me about why he'd traveled to Italy. He was not there to work on his new start-up. Papa revealed that Yush went to Italy to get limb-lengthening surgery: a lengthy and risky surgical procedure that involves sawing through one's bones, drilling nails and screws into the breakage points, and in the months afterward slowly, painfully, pulling the broken legs apart by a few millimeters every day, to add a few inches of height. Yush, who was five foot seven, desperately wanted to be taller. He had lost his life in an attempt to be five ten, an inch taller than the average American man.

You and Papa had kept the surgery a secret from me. On the morning of Yush's funeral, you told me that over the past few months you both had flown to Italy and helped set him up in a tiny, temporary apartment. Papa flew back to Canada to return to work, but you stayed. You cooked and cleaned for Yush, helpless as he downed shots of liquor to dull the intense pain of clicking his broken legs further apart every day. In that dark room, you listened as he screamed out in pain and skyped for hours every day with his girlfriend, Chelsea, a pretty white woman I met for the first time at his funeral.

A few days before the service, Papa had called me from Italy as I walked aimlessly through a Canadian department store with Buaji's youngest son. You had just met with Yush's surgeon, Dr. Jean-Marc Guichet, who told you that none of his patients had ever died, as if this was supposed to offer you some sort of relief.

Papa had an idea: He wanted me to write an exposé on Dr. Guichet and surgeons who preyed on the insecurities of men like Yush. "You can make a real difference," he said on the phone. You cried in the background, and I held back tears, trying to modulate my voice as I walked through racks of discount jackets.

"With your platform, you can expose what's really going on," Papa said.

I promised you both that I would think about it. But I didn't know how to tell you that I disagreed. I was angry at Dr. Guichet, too, but I was more disturbed by whatever thought process had led Yush to pursue a cosmetic procedure that could cause permanent nerve damage, chronic pain, and even death. Yush had added risk on top of risk by pursuing the surgery in isolation in a foreign country, where he didn't speak the language or have any support. This was not a symptom of Yush's forgetfulness or eccentricity. It was a planned, major, deliberate life choice, reflective of deep longing.

Over the next several months, I began to piece together what Yush's life looked like during our estrangement. I talked to his girlfriend, Chelsea. I emailed Dr. Guichet. I even spoke to Papa once. At first I assumed that Papa had paid for the surgery, which baffled me. But Papa told me that Yush had given you both an ultimatum: *If you don't support me through this, I will cut you out of the process.*

I couldn't figure out exactly how much Yush paid in total, but I knew that between the procedure, the apartment, medical care, and the tickets to and from Italy, he'd easily spent upward of a hundred thousand dollars.

How could Yush afford something that expensive?

You and I had always worried about Yush's financial stability. For the past seven years, he'd worked at corporate jobs only when he ran out of money, living meagerly as he funded his own tech ventures in the meantime.

Yush's vision of success surpassed financial gain. He wanted to change the world. In the months before his death, he had been engineering a system of blocks that could form the skeleton for any structure, inanimate or living, and take on its behavioral properties. The implications for its use, according to his vision, were vast: He built a skeleton of a manta ray that looked and moved like the animal. There were other potential uses, too. "He wanted to be able to build homes for the floodplains in India, for people who, if the flood destroyed the homes, would be able to pick up the pieces and build a new home out of it," Papa told me.

To Yush, money was a resource to achieve grander ambitions, but it was not the goal itself. This had been apparent in his lifestyle: Most of his wardrobe consisted of free shirts from college-recruitment fairs and 5K races. I remember Buaji asking Yush what he wanted as a college graduation present. He told her: "A laundry basket."

After he started working at Intel, he called me to ask me if he should buy a mattress—not for himself, but because you and Papa were coming to visit for the first time. "Where do you sleep?" I'd asked, incredulous.

"In a sleeping bag on the floor," he responded.

So, you, like me, must have been shocked to learn that he had recently become a millionaire—not through any of his start-up ventures but by investing in cryptocurrency.

Before most of the world had ever heard of Ethereum, Yush had written a white paper on why the cryptocurrency was going to skyrocket. I assumed that he had no money to invest. But he had struck up a deal with friends at college who worked at places like SpaceX and Facebook, offering to invest their wealth for a significant percentage of their profits. I do not know how much money Yush made, but one of his friends estimated that between her investment and their friends', tens of thousands of dollars turned into millions by the time of his death. Yush's commission must have been in the seven figure-range.

The paper trail Yush left suggests that his wealth was significant. He bankrolled at least fifty thousand dollars per month on running his new start-up, his former business partner told me. On a whim, Yush transferred ten thousand dollars in cryptocurrency to a former Carnegie Mellon administrator who was recovering from an illness and had lost her job. He paid for Chelsea, who lived in Connecticut, to fly

to his spacious apartment in downtown San Francisco. To my knowledge, he had no other source of income or savings.

Learning about Yush's massive amount of wealth, and the cutting-
edge technology he was using it to build, further confused me. If all
of this was true, he had far exceeded the success we'd both been raised
to achieve. Why gamble with his health for such an invasive cosmetic
procedure?

THREE DAYS AFTER THE funeral, Papa emailed me to reconnect. He
forwarded an exchange between him and Yush from just over a year
before Yush's death, writing, "This was the e-mail that started my
reconciliation with Yush." I was aware that Yush and Papa had started
talking at least six months before this email exchange took place. But
Papa wanted me to read this email specifically, as a way to rebuild our
own, separate relationship with each other.

The email exchange was short. I scrolled to the bottom. Yush had
sent Papa a link to a website called Illimitable Men. I clicked the link.
"Destroy your delusions," the site's subhead read. "Actualise your potential. Cultivate your masculinity." Below, there was an image of a
gavel resting on the Bill of Rights and the text: "The Red Pill Consti-
tution."

I don't know if you knew anything about the Red Pill community
or not, Mummy. But as a woman who made her living writing about
feminism on the Internet, I was already familiar with the rhetoric.
The term "Red Pill" referred to a choice Morpheus presents to computer hacker Neo in *The Matrix:* The blue pill keeps Neo plugged into
the illusory world, and the red pill reveals the reality that machines
control us. The truth that Red Pillers believed, according to the website: Women are "Machiavellian by nature," and feminism is an ex-
tremist, hateful "female supremacy movement." These men called
me a "curry whore" on Internet forums, sent my colleagues rape and
death threats, and shared tips about how to pressure women into

sleeping with them. Opening the link was a surreal, unnerving experience. I was familiar with this virulent rhetoric, but receiving it from Papa—and seeing that it had bonded him and Yush—shook me to my core.

"The point about women causing emotional abuse caught my attention," Papa had written back to Yush. He wrote that Buaji "has been emotionally bullying me all my life," an insight that he said he received from his therapist. I again worried about the effects of the therapy he, and you, received. "If you have the inclination, we can talk more about it."

I was stunned. Papa's message to me was clear: Any ensuing relationship between us could only be predicated upon the basis that I agreed that Buaji was abusive and that women are inherently manipulative.

I was now sure that, even after Yush's death, my acceptance back into our family would remain as conditional as it had always been. So long as Papa blamed Buaji for the problems that existed within our family, I would not be able to have an honest relationship with him.

I did not reply to Papa's email. I wonder what he told you when I didn't respond to his reprisal: *Prachi doesn't care about us.* Or maybe: *Prachi turned her back on the family.* Or maybe he didn't say anything to you at all. I don't know.

I HAD LONG DISMISSED Red Pillers as vile and pathetic, but my quest to try to understand Yush's motivations for his surgery compelled me to look deeper. "If you are weak, depressed, small, poor, uneducated, unconfident, or anything else that prevents you from being powerful, nobody will care about whether you live or die," the website read.

These men were clearly not much kinder to one another than they were to women like me. But behind the extreme and harsh language, I saw an element of truth in their observations about height and masculinity. Numerous studies show a link between height and workplace success, and in Western cultures, many straight women prefer dating tall men. Though in recent years I had dated men Yush's height or shorter, I had been guilty of perpetuating that same bias when I was younger. And though I barely stand above five feet, my height had never limited my dating prospects.

Moreover, Western culture has a long history of trying to emasculate Asian American men—particularly East Asians—going back to the 1800s, when Chinese men emigrating to the United States during the gold rush were viewed by white people as an economic and racial threat. Anti-miscegenation laws, formed in the 1660s to bar marriages between white people and enslaved Black people, expanded in the late 1800s to include the small but growing population of Asian Americans in an effort to preserve whiteness. These laws remained on the books until 1967, the same year Dadiji and Dadaji moved to Canada.

Yush and I grew up absorbing these messages in movies and television: Indian men are nerdy and clumsy with women, like Raj in *The Big Bang Theory*, or thickly accented human punch lines, like Apu on *The Simpsons*. On the dating site OkCupid, among straight men, Asians have the fewest responses—a statistic that Yush often cited to me. He created an algorithm programmed to respond "Yes" to any woman who viewed his profile—his solution to improving his odds on the dating site. Society had sent Yush the message that to be short and Asian was to be less masculine, and I had underestimated the impact of this message and the severity of that pain.

The Red Pill offered a tempting solution to take back the kind of power that Yush likely felt had been stolen from him. According to the website, "All racial barriers are overcome by power, for money is power. If you're a 5'0" Asian . . . a big bank balance and confident attitude will offset that."

I don't know what role the Red Pill ideology played in Yush's decision to pursue the procedure, if any, Mummy, but I could see how these ideas validated Yush's insecurities and appealed to his binary approach to problem-solving. The guidelines fed an addictive need for external validation, predicated on internalized feelings of unworthiness and perpetuated by a pressure to conform to impossible societal expectations of the idealized man. For men who are forced to disconnect from their emotional needs and then further alienated by society's narrow conception of masculinity, the belief that success solves all problems offers a sense of power. It was easier to believe that people would automatically respect someone tall and rich than to accept that no one can ultimately control how others see them. But in this bleak outlook, men turned themselves into products, treating women as a hive mind of consumers. Intimate emotional connection became a myth, condemning all interactions to be transactional. It was a deeply cynical, isolating worldview that reinforced itself, pushing away anyone capable of or interested in authentic connection.

Yush had long treated emotional problems like mechanical ones, searching for a step-by-step fix to interpersonal issues in dating and conflicts with friends. I think that, rather than facing his emotions and unearthing the pain that he'd buried and compartmentalized, he used his wealth to turn his body into "another project" to solve, as he had told Chelsea.

Though Yush could have pursued the surgery in America, he traveled to Italy because he believed that Dr. Guichet was one of the best surgeons in the field. He met with Dr. Guichet in person in Italy, where they reviewed the statistics on patient outcomes together. In an email exchange that Chelsea forwarded to me, Yush explained his reasons for wanting the procedure: "It's definitely an unconventional decision," he wrote, "but I think I'm being level-headed here." She and Papa tried to talk Yush out of the surgery, but Yush refused to reconsider.

"There's a huge social stigma in our culture against body modification. Basically, if you change yourself through what sounds like 'extreme' measures to change yourself or whatever, it comes off like you're just really insecure," Yush wrote in the email. "In the future, it's probably going to be totally normal for people to get body modifications like cybernetic implants and stuff. At that time, getting longer legs is going to seem like a pretty mundane thing to do. I just don't hold the same stigmas that other people do on how I should behave." But in his pontificating, Yush was talking around the emotions of the issue: What problem did he think being five foot ten would solve?

Yush had complained to many friends that his height was an impediment in both attracting women and being taken seriously by investors. But because the surgery's risks include long-term damage to nerves, limitation of joint motion, chronic pain, and, in rare cases, pulmonary embolisms, reputable surgeons screen for patients who may have body dysmorphic disorder, a form of obsessive–compulsive disorder, which cannot be fixed by surgery. Guichet's website acknowledged that patients like Yush, who pursue limb-lengthening for purely cosmetic reasons, "are really asking the surgeon for a solution to their psychological issue or insecurity," and "This means that we have to carefully evaluate and coach the patient psychiatrically to ensure their informed decision will have the best possible results." While Dr. Guichet described to me via email his general precautions before performing the surgery, including a psychological evaluation, I do not know what his mental-health screening entailed. I do know, however, that Yush passed the evaluation.

I believe that being taller may have boosted Yush's confidence. He may even have enjoyed more success in attracting women and investors. But I wonder how long that newfound confidence or happiness would have lasted, especially if Yush experienced disrespect or rejection again—an issue that should have, in his mind, been resolved through his added height. And I wonder how he would have responded to that slight the next time. Would he have been able to soothe himself and move forward? Or, lacking those emotional skills, would the pain intensify precisely because of what he had put himself through to prevent this very thing from happening again? And what mechanical fix would he have pursued to resolve *that* mounting feeling of helplessness and resentment?

———

As CHILDREN, YUSH AND I were united in a world of white by our otherness, expecting each other to be in lockstep as we bonded over a shared sense of alienation. As a teenager who felt invisible, I had once used a parallel set of rules to try to gain power and a sense of belonging. I followed the steps to become what I thought would make me an ideal woman. The rules had worked—to a point. I acquired what I believed to be the perfect man, the perfect job, and the image of the perfect daughter. But the things that were supposed to make me feel good didn't make me that much happier in the long run. They only further impressed upon me the need to hide my true self in order to be accepted. And then I was rejected anyway.

The Red Pill rants left out the most important part: In the end, even if every step is achieved, it will never be enough. Yush was trying to belong to a club that would never accept him. He clung to a hierarchy, climbing to the top, but the whole point of a hierarchy is that the people at the bottom will be forced back to the bottom.

I believe more intensely than ever that rigid gender roles harm men, too, and the effects can be deadly. But as a woman, and as the defiant sister who had challenged the natural order of our patriarchal family, though I was the closest to Yush, I had also become the person least likely to reach him. The ultimate, tragic irony was this: It was Yush—a boy—who had first shown me what true love and compassion looked like.

I will never fully know or understand Yush's motivations for the surgery, Mummy. But I believe that the logical explanations Yush presented to you and Papa couched a deep, unresolved pain from boyhood. The child who was raised to believe that hard work and intellect could overcome any problem took a chilling, clinical approach to solving a deeply emotional one: He believed he was not respected by white America's elite. His extraordinary success hadn't eased his pain. Instead, success gave his pain more power over him.

Chapter 27

The Truth

I WENT THROUGH THE SCENARIOS again and again, wondering what could have prevented Yush from making the decision that he did and what would have helped him resolve his insecurities and face his internal pain. I needed to understand how Yush had changed, and why, and what any of us could have done differently to save him. I knew that the answers to these questions could not bring Yush back to life, but maybe there was a lesson here that could help heal us. The best way to honor Yush's legacy, to me, was to learn from the pain that had taken his brief life.

When I approached Papa to ask him about who Yush had become, he told me to read Yush's essay. "What essay?" I asked.

"Yush wrote an anonymous essay about our family in a book," Papa said. "If you really want to know the truth, read the essay. Then we can talk."

This is the hardest part to write to you, Mummy. I have been delaying it and, to be honest, the words are almost as impossible to write as they are to speak. Words usually come to me on the page more readily than in speech, but in this case, that is not so. It is like the words are lodged deep inside me in cavities and I have to search for them and then excavate them, one by one. I might not be able to get them all out. As I write to you, I am gripping the pen so tightly that my hand is cramping, just as it did when I was a girl.

You loved Yush, but like me, I am not sure you liked the man he became, either. After his death, when the secret of Italy was finally revealed to me, you told me that he was mean to you. You nursed him to health, but he treated you like a servant. When you spoke of this, it reminded me of Papa. I was so sad to hear this, especially since your last memories of your son were not ones of joy but of more pain. I was surprised, though, when you told me that you had scolded him. You told him it was not okay for him to treat you like that. I was proud of you for standing up for yourself. You said that he felt bad. After that, he was more appreciative.

PAPA HAD LEFT A copy of the book, a men's rights anthology, with Dadiji and Dadaji. He had told them to make sure to share it with Buaji. She had read Yush's essay, but I didn't want to, and I certainly did not want to hear Papa's analysis. Eventually, though, I had to know if the essay held any answers about Yush's death or about how Yush had changed.

In the essay, published posthumously, Yush had disavowed Buaji, criticized you, and empathized with Papa's pain. Yush wrote that he used to feel bad for you when you cried, but now he saw the toll that your marriage had taken on his father as the sole provider and a short brown man rejected and emasculated by white America. He lamented a society that valued the emotional pain of women over the burden men had to provide for them. He complained that women were inferior in logical ability and that women in abusive relationships were not held accountable for their decision to stay, while the societal pressures upon the allegedly abusive men were overlooked and ignored. Yush wrote that he planned to "sever ties" with me and our extended family over our views.

Yush was dead. I could not argue with him, I could not debate with him, I could not help him. I was disturbed by what Yush had written, alarmed that Papa was unable to see how deeply troubled Yush was, and enraged that he was so eager to share something that threatened to permanently warp my memory of my brother. I wondered whether Papa made you read this essay, too. I can only imagine how awful it made you feel.

As I read the essay, I thought back to the loving handwritten letter that Yush had sent to Buaji after that traumatic autumn in Winnipeg, just four years prior. There was a line in it that haunts me still: Yush wrote that he was angry with Papa, but it was "hard to hate him more than I hate myself, because I have so much of him in me."

Had Yush lived, I am not sure I would have gotten him back. It is very likely that the boy I lost to anger and resentment would have never returned to me. But I am sure, beyond a doubt, that the boy I loved did not have to become the man he became and, further still that it was our family's turmoil and the pressure placed upon him to be exceptional that set Yush so far adrift.

If I was the image of failure, then Yush was the image of perfection. In a household where affection was doled out as reward and with-drawn as punishment—where care was dispensed by how successful one appeared to be and what image one projected into the world—Yush learned he must be exceptional to be worthy of love. Yush was forgetful and eccentric, but I don't remember him ever making any mistakes or miscalculations when it came to achieving, and because he was naturally brilliant, his performance was operatic. But I wonder if he lived with a constant fear, a low hum underscoring everything, a nagging suspicion that if he just stopped or decided to step back, his life would fall apart and the people who said they loved him would no longer be there for him. All around him, he saw evidence of this: Papa leaving you stranded on the street for misreading a map; you and

Papa cutting me off for talking back; Papa throwing me out of the house when I failed to say what he wanted to hear.

Whenever Papa turned on me and you followed suit, Yush was put into the position of peacemaker. The youngest person in the family took on the responsibility of keeping his family together. It only further instilled this pressure to always be perfect, to never mess up, because now three other people relied on him to get along and to function. Yush had to always remain calm and detached in the volatile situations of our household. In crises, he had to lead us all to resolution. What an unfair burden.

At home, Yush and I had both absorbed a casual sexism that was reinforced by the world outside. But, of course, as a woman, this affected me differently than Yush. The double standards that I eventually felt as constraints, Yush experienced as power. As the war between you and Papa intensified, Yush saw himself in Papa's struggles, and I saw myself in yours. But I reduced you to helpless victim and demonized Papa as a monster because I could not face the pain of realizing that some part of you chose to stay with a man who mistreated you. I think Yush eventually saw Papa as the victim and you as weak because he could not face the pain of realizing that the father who cared for him also psychologically tormented his mother. Each of us yelled at the other for vilifying the parent we empathized with so deeply. We had difficulty accepting the "both/and" of the situation: that you have both been victimized and you have agency; that Papa both loves you and hurts you in profound ways.

I think that when you went back to Papa despite how he'd treated you, Yush's emotions ate up his insides like acid. To make sense of your decision, one that defied the 1–0 binary of how people are supposed to behave, Yush concluded that women cry abuse for sympathy, because if they were truly abused, they would leave; that they complain but ultimately stay because of the material comforts they enjoy and rely on from a man. I think that he could not separate your personhood from the role you played, because he could not separate his own personhood from the role he felt pressured to play. He strove to meet the expectations of those who relied on him and mistook this performance as his identity.

Then I—the person who had always been there for Yush, the person who had always supported him—withdrew from him, too. I think that Papa's anger toward his own sister baited Yush's rising resentment toward me, rage uniting estranged father and son as they became even more isolated from everyone else who cared about them.

I have been afraid of asking you what you think, about whether you believe that they are justified in their anger toward the women in their lives.

WE HAD EACH BEEN raised to believe that every unknown could be resolved through willpower and intellect, a message reinforced by America's rigid conception of who we are supposed to be. The truth is, society doesn't raise people to aspire to be kind or compassionate or happy. It pressures adults to achieve and accomplish. It teaches people that what matters more than their character or how they treat others or how they feel about themselves is how much money they can hoard, who they know, how famous they can get, and how much power they wield over others. Emotions have no basis in this framework. They are a nuisance, a hindrance, a distraction, a weakness.

I wonder, then, if success became a reminder to Yush that even when he followed the rules, even when he achieved, he was still somehow less-than and he was still not happy. I think that when he achieved such success, he sank deeper into feelings of self-hatred, and assuming that more success would relieve him of this pain, he sought to attain more. He drank poison, believing it was medicine. I wonder if you ever sensed, as I did, that this obsession with achievement had led us astray—or if, like Yush, you drank the poison, trusting it to be the cure.

As an Indian American boy, Yush learned to carve out a path to belonging that was similar to Papa's, acquiring power and respect by learning the rules of masculinity and compensating for the racialized feminization of Asianness by projecting toughness and stoicism. But I watched this oppressive idea of manliness constrain Yush like a strait-jacket. What Yush saw as parallels between him and Papa, I saw as pressures upon men whom the world reduced in similar ways. They were both brilliant in the way capitalism rewards, but as people, they were hardly alike. Yet how do you distinguish between your true self and a persona when you've spent your life becoming what others expect you to be?

I HAD ORIGINALLY BELIEVED that the pain of Yush's death would compel Papa to reach out to the people who loved him the most. I thought that the weight of our love for Yush would be stronger than our resentments toward one another. But now I understand that coming together in shared grief is a choice, not an inevitability. Unless we choose to face it, grief folds us inward and pushes us deep into our own pockets of suffering, intensifying our pain and further isolating us from those we love. There is no hack, no quick fix, no step-by-step solution to navigate grief. We only have ourselves, and one another, to make it through.

Papa had referred to Yush's essay as "the truth" about our family. I have doubted so much about myself. I have doubted who I am. I have doubted my own perceptions of reality. I have doubted that I am worthy of love. I have doubted my right for agency and the right to control my own body and my right to feel pleasure. But one of the only things in life I have never doubted, Mummy, is this: The love Yush and I shared was real, and it is the memory of Yush's love that guides me still. There is nothing that anyone else can ever say or do that will make me question that love now.

Chapter 28

When the Earth Splits Open

In THE YEAR AFTER Yush's death, I didn't know how to be a person. I was nothing but a body, and sometimes I wasn't even that. I was a collection of disparate parts, connected but unable to work in unison. I was a head, detached and floating in the sky, foggy and unable to think or speak for hours. Or I was my legs, moving against the ground but seeing only Yush in strangers around me. Other times I was just eyeballs, watching text and images roll in front of me but unable to process their meanings in my mind.

When Papa invited me to celebrate his birthday with him a few months after Yush's funeral, I didn't know what to say. A part of me wanted so badly to come together to remember Yush with you and Papa. But when I played out the fantasy of togetherness in my mind, I imagined Papa parading me around as his prized daughter among people I did not know, only because I was the child who lived. I could see that at the very moment when I'd begin to believe the performance was real, when I'd feel vulnerable and let my guard down and reveal myself, everything would turn, and the rage of my childhood would rush into the present. And even though I had been cast out so many times and survived, if he did it again now, now that Yush was gone, now that I felt so tremendously alone, now that I had shoddily patched up a bottomless crater that could never be filled, I feared that I wouldn't be able to pick up and move forward.

I made up an excuse and said I could not go. Papa didn't get angry. We both understood what it meant. He let me drift away. I was thankful for that, at least.

We saw each other only two more times after Yush's death—once for Dadiji's funeral, and once when Papa planned a trip to visit another relative not long after. You and Papa came to New York. As I walked with you through Prospect Park, I felt my grief and shame braided together as one. When I stood with you two, I had to face that this was our family now. Yush was never coming back to us.

A year later, you called me and told me you wanted a closer relationship with me. I cried, "Of course. I want that, too."

"But I don't want to live in the past," you said over the phone. "I can't go back to that dark place. I want to move forward."

"I want to move forward, too, Mummy. But I am a writer. I have to write about my life, too, to make peace with the past."

As briefly as the door between us opened, it shut again.

"Okay," you said. "Never mind."

It was the last time we ever dared reveal ourselves to each other.

When I hung up the phone, I sobbed—deep, snotty belly sobs—for all that I wanted to tell you but did not know how to say, for all that we wanted from each other but did not know how to give or receive. When we spoke on the phone, I felt a boulder in my throat, blocking my speech. But as I wrote in my journal, a river of feelings flowed around it, an entire valley of thoughts and memories emerged, hidden from you by a mountain of rocks. I did not know how to speak to you, but I realized that maybe I could write to you.

In college, I wrote a short story for a fiction class in which I tried to imagine our relationship from your perspective. The main character—a hardworking, smart, ambitious college student on break from Yale—wasn't me but how I wanted others to see me: successful but aloof and oblivious of my immigrant mother's sacrifices. But it is the description of her mother, the character inspired by you, that embarrasses me more now: a quiet, melancholy woman who wafted through the home, looking longingly at photos of her family in India while her husband worked long hours and her daughter was away at college. I had smoothed out the rough edges of our relationship with the good-immigrant narrative, imagining you as a helpless woman who sat back as life happened around her.

The hollow woman in my story was nothing like you. I gave you the short story for your birthday that year. When Papa read it, he said it was very good. I wanted to hear your reaction. You hesitated, quiet, and then when I pressed you, you said, "I don't really relate to it," or something to that effect. My heart sank. You didn't elaborate, and, assuming you didn't appreciate my gift, I didn't ask you to. At the time I believed that I understood you because I could predict your reactions to many situations. But I realize now that being able to foresee what you might say or do meant only that I understood what role you were supposed to play: Woman as mother. Woman as wife. Woman as Indian immigrant. Woman as daughter-in-law. In turn, you sensed that your acceptance was based on your ability to play these roles. These assumptions bonded us to each other.

I wish now that I had seen your feedback over my short story not as an ending to the conversation but as an opening for me to begin to learn who you were. It was losing contact with you years later that made me want to know you. I finally have the curiosity to ask you all the questions that my assumptions about you once answered for me. I now understand that this type of unrestrained, nonjudgmental curiosity is the key to intimacy. But, like all learning, it began with surrender, with admitting that I do not truly know you.

For years, you felt my anger, my desire for you to rise up and fight and leave him. I believed—I still believe—that you are capable of so much. You navigated a new country and culture without any emotional support and endured so much hardship. Maybe there is no part of you that can forgive me for writing this, for broadcasting what you feel should be kept private, and for taking away your power to reveal what is yours when so much has already been taken away from you. But maybe there is also a part of you waiting to be seen, a part of you that has been buried, a part of you that hopes someone pieced it all together. I want you to know: I see what you have lost. I want you to know that you have not lost me.

But by insisting that you fight when you had chosen not to, I was, in a way, no better than the father I criticized. I was telling you that your choice had no value, that it wasn't good enough for me. You must have felt my judgment, my lack of acceptance over who you are or what you have chosen for yourself. I had failed to see how, from your perspective, Papa and I were two sides of the same coin: He sought to mold you into some image of who he needed you to be for him. And I, too, refused to accept you as you are, not willing to listen when you made your desires clear to me. Instead, both of us held your own wishes against you, sending you the message that you were not good enough as is. That you should be something different. I am sorry that, for so long, I behaved this way.

FOR YEARS I DID not understand how so much suffering was possible in a family who had prioritized success. After Yush died, I realized that this was precisely the source of our suffering: that we never understood ourselves, or one another, beyond our capacity to meet these expectations.

In my grief, I felt suspended in air, floating without family or cultural history to tether me to the ground. In my desperation, and upon my therapist's encouragement, I turned to my history and the culture that I had distanced myself from when I'd distanced myself from Papa. I had struggled to see a place for me within the same culture that Papa used to enable and justify his behavior. But part of rising from the ashes of grief was learning how to reclaim my identity.

To my surprise, I discovered a rich history that placed me within a deep and ancient context. I had related to Indian culture through the dominant Hindu narrative of the *Ramayana,* which equates Sita's measure as a wife with her ability to sacrifice herself over and over again for Rama. But when I revisited even that version of the story, I realized that Sita was not the submissive waif I had always assumed her to be. She had agency. After Rama imposed yet another brutal trial upon her, she said no to him. Instead, she chose to leave her husband and children behind and return to Mother Earth. The earth split open and swallowed her back.

I learned that, like culture itself, the *Ramayana* has never been a static story. It is a diverse tradition, where, for centuries, people from different cultures, castes, and religions across South and Southeast Asia crafted their own versions to address social issues and pass on their values. I was especially inspired by the fourteenth-century text, the *Adbhuta Ramayana,* in which Sita manifests the ferocious Kali, the Destroyer of Illusions, to save Rama from death. She slays the demons who attacked Rama and plays with their severed heads as thousands of female deities spring forth from her skin. Rama, humbled by her awesome power, bows down to his wife and becomes Sita's devotee. There are seemingly infinite Sitas and Ramas and ideas on how people can exist, but many of these versions have been overlooked or ignored in the mainstream because they don't support what people in power want us to realize about who we are and who we can be in this world. They don't want us to know that we can write our own stories. They don't want us to know that we are infinite.

This world of scholarship, once unknown to me, introduced me to stories about my cultural history that were so different from the ones upon which I had been raised. When I saw that this ancient past could hold my present-day experiences, too, I wondered why I had not encountered myself in my own history before and why it had been so hard for me to piece together. From the tension of this inquiry, I began to articulate my story.

The truth was available to me, had I searched for it, but how does one seek answers without knowing what questions to ask? My history had been rendered unimportant, completely erased, and then replaced with stories of my inferiority. Though from time to time I experienced a fuzzy dissonance, a nagging feeling of something-isn't-right-here, underscored by shame, the story that I was caught up in—that everyone around me also recited and reenacted—was so powerful, so omnipresent, that the right questions could not arise until and unless something happened that forced me to punch a hole in the wall of that story and be shocked to find that something else existed on the other side.

I HAD THOUGHT OF love as a taut chain with a tight clasp that carried our weight as we clutched one another, no matter what dragged any of us down. I had believed that when I love someone, I should hold on regardless of what else I have to give up in order to keep them. The more one gives up, the greater the love, I thought. To love someone well was to perform perfection for them, and to be loved well was for them to perform perfection for me. But that is not true love. That is self-abandonment masquerading as love.

Now I understand that intimacy can form only when I accept someone as they are, not as who they can be for me. I cannot summon you and Papa back into my life in the form that I would like you each to take. I can only acknowledge that what I so deeply wanted is not reflected in what I know to be true. And this is another hard truth: That even though I did not get what I wanted, I am still okay. And being okay despite not having your closeness does not mean I never needed either of you, or that I do not love you both, or that I do not long for you two still. I know that you both love me with your entirety, as I do you. I know that letting go of my fantasy of togetherness does not mean that I do not want the best for you and Papa or hope that each of you finds your way back to me. I still want all of that. But I no longer live in the space where I tell myself that if I silence or shrink myself, I can one day have that ideal relationship with you both.

I told myself that I wrote this for you. I fantasized that you would read this, and I thought that if I could share my real self, maybe you would recognize my shape through the darkness and embrace me.

But now I see that I wrote this for me. I wrote what I needed to face that I had avoided looking at for so long. I wrote this to understand what stands in the way of sharing love with the people I long to share it with the most.

I had once thought that I came from a line of Gods, and I had punished myself for failing to be Godlike. But we were not Gods, and I was not the avatar for our family's unraveling. I was just another product of inherited trauma, unresolved grief, and reactive survival mechanisms, like everyone else who came before me. We were mortals who felt ashamed when we failed to appear omnipotent. Now I see that my job was to release my ancestors from this burden, to allow those who come next the freedom to be ordinary.

For a long time, I felt ashamed of who I was. I didn't know what it meant to be me, only that to be me was to be wrong. I was rejected for speaking my truth, because it was not what anyone wanted to hear. I was rejected for who I am, because I did not portray an image that people wanted to see. I thought people could see an ugliness in me that I had to work hard to hide until I appeared flawless to them. But when I finally achieved what I thought was such perfection, I learned that, even then, I did not belong.

Now I feel grateful for that rejection, because rejection forced me to learn to find value in myself, value that I had jockeyed to receive from others. I learned that I am not defined by how others perceive me. I learned that the limits of their acceptance are not a symptom of my failings. I am grateful, because not only did I survive, but I expanded. I grew in infinite directions. I learned that I am not done growing. I am just beginning.

Acknowledgments

I n 2017, while deep in grief, I set out to write about that which obsessed me, that which I could not understand: who Yush had become, and why I had lost him. I was fortunate to have worked at *Jezebel* at the time, among colleagues who offered unwavering grace and support through an immensely dark period. My former editors, Julianne Escobedo Shepherd and Stassa Edwards, encouraged me to reach deeper in my writing than I had ever done before, helping me shape the piece over the next two years. I was terrified of publishing the essay, "Stories About My Brother." I didn't know if anyone would care—or why they would care—about my grief over losing a complicated person that they'd never meet. I braced myself for backlash, judgment, and criticism.

Instead, I received an outpouring of support. To every person who left a comment, wrote me an email, shared my story, or told me in person what the essay meant to them: This book would not exist without your support. When I realized how many people struggle with similar issues in shame and isolation because they think they are alone, I knew that I needed to tell my full story. Thank you for giving me the courage to do so.

My agent, Anna Sproul-Latimer, believed in my vision even when

I could barely articulate it, and helped me unearth emotional truths through the proposal-writing process and beyond. I found a mentor and friend in my talented book editor, Madhulika Sikka, who has built a career championing writers of color, and whose trust and support enabled me to write with deep vulnerability and honesty. Thank you to Aubrey Martinson and Matthew Martin and the incredible team at Crown Publishing for your wisdom and attention to detail. I am grateful to the South Asian Journalists Association for their support, to Santul Nerkar for assistance with fact-checking, and to Stassa for her careful eye.

Thank you, also, to everyone who spoke to me for this book and trusted me with your memories and experiences, and the friends who counseled me along the way.

The perspectives of this book have been shaped profoundly by years of conversations with my therapist, Reka Prasad, and by the scholarship of countless writers and academics, some of whom are cited in the book. The following works, in particular, helped me articulate my own story: bell hooks's *All About Love;* Vijay Prashad's *The Karma of Brown Folk;* Margaret Abraham's *Speaking the Unspeakable;* David L. Eng and Shinhee Han's *Racial Melancholia, Racial Dissociation;* Sara Ahmed's *Living a Feminist Life;* Rafia Zakaria's *Against White Feminism;* and Gayatri Chakravorty Spivak's *Can the Subaltern Speak?.*

I have relied on so many to carry me through this journey: Apphia Maxima for your uncanny ability to tell me what I need to hear, including the hard truths; Leah, Rashi, and Kabu, who love me at my silliest; Marin Cogan, who has been at my side for everything—both the darkness and the light; Elody Gyekis for offering me space to fall apart during a grueling year; Cory Tamler for offering such thoughtful feedback. There are so many others who have supported me, and I am forever grateful to have had their care.

Words will always feel inadequate in expressing my love and gratitude for the family members who have encouraged me to tell my full truth. You have made my small world feel large again.

Sources

Abraham, Margaret. *Speaking the Unspeakable: Marital Violence Among South Asian Immigrants in the United States.* Rutgers University Press, April 2000.

American Psychiatric Association. *Diagnostic and Statistical Manual of Mental Disorders, 5th ed.* American Psychiatric Publishing, 2013.

American Psychological Association. (2022). Demographics of the U.S. Psychology Workforce (interactive data tool). Retrieved September 21, 2022, from https://www.apa.org/workforce/data-tools/demographics.

Brown, Ashley. "'Least Desirable'? How Racial Discrimination Plays Out in Online Dating." NPR Morning Edition, January 9, 2018.

Chakravorty, Sanjoy, Devesh Kapur, and Nirvikar Singh. *The Other One Percent: Indians in America.* Oxford University Press, November 2016.

Chand, Tara. *The Problem of Hindustani.* Allahabad: Indian Periodicals Ltd., 1944.

Cilluffo, Anthony, and Rakesh Kochhar. "Income Inequality in the U.S. Is Rising Most Rapidly Among Asians." Pew Research Center, July 12, 2018.

Cohmer, Sean. "Early Infantile Autism and the Refrigerator Mother Theory (1943–1970)." *The Embryo Project Encyclopedia*, August 19, 2014, ISSN: 1940–5030. http://embryo.asu.edu/handle/10776/8149.

Dirks, Gerald E. "Immigration Policy in Canada." *The Canadian Encyclopedia.*

Historica Canada. Article published February 7, 2006; Last Edited October 23, 2020.

Durvasula, Ramani, Dr. Personal interview, July 27, 2020.

Eng, David L., and Shinhee Han. *Racial Melancholia, Racial Dissociation: On the Social and Psychic Lives of Asian Americans.* Duke University Press, February 2019.

Friedel, Robert O. *Borderline Personality Disorder Demystified: An Essential Guide for Understanding and Living with BPD.* Da Capo Lifelong Books, February 2018.

"Indians in the U.S. Fact Sheet." Pew Research Center. Accessed November 29, 2022. https://www.pewresearch.org/social-trends/fact-sheet/asian -americans-indians-in-the-u-s/

Islam, Farah, Dr. Personal interview. June 18, 2020.

Kisch, Jeremy, E. Victor Leino, and Morton M. Silverman (2005). Aspects of suicidal behavior, depression and treatment in college students: Results from the spring 2000 National College Health Assessment Survey. *Suicide and Life-Threatening Behavior,* 35, 3–13.

Klatsky, Arthur L., Mary Anne Armstrong, and Jacqueline Poggi. Risk of pulmonary embolism and/or deep venous thrombosis in Asian-Americans. *The American Journal of Cardiology.* 2000 Jun 1;85(11):1334–7. doi: 10.1016/s0002 -9149(00)00766-9. PMID: 10831950.

Lee, Erika. *The Making of Asian America: A History.* Simon & Schuster, August 2016.

Littler, Jo. *Against Meritocracy: Culture, Power, and Myths of Mobility.* Routledge, August 2017.

Marche, Stephen. "Swallowing the Red Pill: A Journey to the Heart of Modern Misogyny." *The Guardian,* April 2016.

National Center on Domestic Violence, Trauma, and Mental Health. "Prevalence of Intimate Partner Violence and Other Lifetime Trauma Among Women Seen in Mental Health Settings," May 2011.

National Center for Health Statistics. Anthropometric Reference Data for Children and Adults: United States, 2015–2018, tables 4, 6, 10, 12, 19, 20 https://www.cdc.gov/nchs/data/series/sr_03/sr03-046-508.pdf

Prashad, Vijay. *The Karma of Brown Folk.* University of Minnesota Press, March 2001.

Richman, Paula. *Many Ramayanas: The Diversity of a Narrative Tradition in South Asia.* University of California Press, August 1991.

Richwine, Jason. "Indian Americans: The New Model Minority." *Forbes,* 2009.

Robertson, Katie, and Ben Smith. "Hearst Employees Say Magazine Boss Led Toxic Culture." *The New York Times,* July 23, 2020.

Schick, Andreas, and Richard H. Steckel. "Height, Human Capital, and Earnings: The Contributions of Cognitive and Noncognitive Ability." *Journal of Human Capital* 9, no. 1 (2015): 94–115. https://doi.org/10.1086/679675.

Seligson, Hannah. "The Queen of Spin." Columbia Journalism Review, Fall 2017.

Sohoni, Deenesh. "Unsuitable Suitors: Anti-Miscegenation Laws, Naturalization Laws, and the Construction of Asian Identities." *Law & Society Review* 41, no. 3 (2007): 587–618. http://www.jstor.org/stable/4623396.

Spivak, Gayatri Chakravorty. "Can the Subaltern Speak?" *Marxism and the Interpretation of Culture,* eds. Nelson, Cary, and Lawrence Grossberg. Urbana: University of Illinois Press, 1988.

Statistics Canada. Toronto (census, metropolitan area), Ontario and Ontario (province), table. Census Profile, 2016 Census. Statistics Canada Catalogue, no. 98-316-X2016001. Ottawa, released November 29, 2017, from https://www12.statcan.gc.ca/census-recensement/2016/dp-pd/prof/index.cfm?Lang=E (accessed October 18, 2022).

"Success Story of One Minority Group in the U.S.," *U.S. News & World Report,* December 26, 1966.

Topsfield, Andrew. "The Indian Game of Snakes and Ladders." *Artibus Asiae,* 46, 3, 1985.

Vanita, Ruth. "The Sita Who Smiles: Wife as Goddess in the Adbhut Ramayana." *Manushi,* no. 148.

Wu, Ellen. *The Color of Success: Asian Americans and the Origins of the Model Minority.* Princeton University Press, December 2015.

Yancey, George, and Michael O. Emerson. "Does Height Matter? An Examination of Height Preferences in Romantic Coupling." Journal of Family Issues. Vol. 37, Issue 1, January 2014. https://journals.sagepub.com/doi/10.1177/0192513X13519256.

Zakaria, Rafia. *Against White Feminism: Notes on Disruption.* W. W. Norton & Company, August 2021.

ABOUT THE AUTHOR

PRACHI GUPTA is an award-winning journalist and a former senior reporter at *Jezebel*. She won a Writers Guild Award for her investigative essay "Stories About My Brother," and her writing has appeared in *The Best American Magazine Writing of 2021*. She has published bylines in *Marie Claire*, *The Atlantic*, *The Washington Post Magazine*, *Salon*, *Elle*, and elsewhere. She lives in New York City.

ABOUT THE TYPE

This book was set in Baskerville, a typeface designed by John Baskerville (1706–75), an amateur printer and typefounder, and cut for him by John Handy in 1750. The type became popular again when the Lanston Monotype Corporation of London revived the classic roman face in 1923. The Mergenthaler Linotype Company in England and the United States cut a version of Baskerville in 1931, making it one of the most widely used typefaces today.